## Einstein on Thinking

"I very rarely think in words at all. A thought comes, and I may try to express it in words afterwards" (Wertheimer, 1959, p. 213).

"Conventional words or other signs have to be sought for laboriously only in a secondary stage, when the associative play [of images and feelings] already referred to is sufficiently established and can be reproduced at will" (Hadamard, 1945, p. 143).

"I have no doubt that our thinking goes on for the most part without the use of symbols, and, furthermore, largely unconsciously" (Schilpp, 1949, pp. 8-9).

"The words of the language, as they are written or spoken, do not seem to play any role in my mechanism of thought. The psychical entities which seem to serve as elements in thought are certain signs and more or less clear images which can be 'voluntarily' reproduced and combined.... The above mentioned elements are, in my case, of visual and some of a muscular type" (Hadamard, 1945, pp. 142-3).

**Pre-publication praise**

"It's rare to see someone tackle such a mind feast of thought with such an easy and engaging style. It's also rare to see someone with the ability to both appreciate and express the groundbreaking original thought of others, which Ken Bausch demonstrated in his classic *The Emerging Consensus in Social Systems Theory,* go on to join them on the high plateau for originality."
                -David Loye PhD, author
                publisher Benjamin Franklin Press.

"Ken Bausch has written a remarkable book. This book takes its reader on a journey into the realms of transcendent consciousness. Bausch finds an underlying order in chaos, one that can be experienced through one's "body's wisdom." One might say that Bausch has his head in the air, but his feet on the ground. His readers will not be disappointed and will find themselves transformed in the process of reading *Body Wisdom.*"
                -Stanley Krippner, Executive Faculty
                Saybrook University

"Ken Bausch takes us on an adventure in which we come to understand ourselves, each other, our world, and our universe from a bodily perspective. When we understand the dialogue between body and ego, we can leap over our frightening personal limits. Then we can debate the most relevant issues of "growing up" as humans and as humanity. We discover emergent and enjoyable mysteries, and find ourselves on the threshold of consciously deciding which way to go, which faith to put in practice, and which mission we are to pursue. In this faith and mission, we decide which content of the big dynamism that we all possess needs to be achieved... Would you dare to come with us...?"
                -Reynaldo Trevino-Cisneros
                Advisor Mexican Public Policies Office
                Vicente Fox Administration

# BODY WISDOM

# Interplay of Body and Ego

by

Kenneth C Bausch

*Ongoing Emergence*
PRESS

Riverdale, GA 30274

Body Wisdom
Interplay of Body and Ego

© Copyright 2010, Kenneth C Bausch

    Bausch, Kenneth C.
    Body Wisdom, Interplay of Body and Ego
    p. cm.
    Includes bibliographical references and index
    ISBN 978-0-9845266-0-4
    1. Psychology 2. Philosophy 3. Body/Mind/Spirit

Library of Congress Control Number 2010904619

All rights reserved. No part of this publication may be reproduced, stored in a retrieval system, or transmitted in any form or by any electronic or mechanical means, or by photocopying, microfilming, recording or otherwise without written permission from the publisher.

Cover Design by Ward Flynn

*Ongoing Emergence*
            Press
Riverdale, GA 30274

For permissions, contact the author.

Ken Bausch
ken@globalagoras.org

# Dedication

This book is dedicated to all those thinkers
secure in Body's unspoken unity with the Universe,
whose imaginations soar above
the contradictions of language
and strive to express our personal and collective
not-two/not-one unity.

## Acknowledgements

Thanks to all the wonderful people
who have shaped my life and thought. Particular thanks to
Thomas Flanagan, David Loye, Stanley Krippner,
Reynaldo Trevino and Stephen Rosen
who read the manuscript,
and made invaluable contributions.
Very special thanks to Marie Kane,
my anchor and inspiration

# Prologue

by

Dr. Thomas Flanagan

If you think of philosophy as an impenetrable soup of ideas, then take heart. Dr. Bausch provides a memorable tour as he swings through the jungle canopy of both familiar and exotic philosophers. With sure hands, he carries us from philosophical vine to philosophical vine on a voyage that brings us to a new understanding of self, along with emergent ways of thinking and seeing ourselves. The new understanding is not so radical that it hasn't been sensed and voiced by others. However, the voyage has never been reasoned so broadly or so profoundly. It is the author's personal reflection of a trail discovered while dealing with the crisis of living a good life in an imperfect world. It is a voyage that requires a seasoned philosophical guide, and in *Body Wisdom*, Dr. Bausch marks the trail with philosopher stones to assure us that there is solid ground below.

*Body Wisdom* is a voyage that takes us to a specific destination: it takes us to a rediscovery of a holistic view of the experience of self. Recognizing our current analytical fragmentation of self into body, mind and spirit, Dr. Bausch mends us into a being where body, mind and spirit fold back upon themselves and re-anneal into a complete being. His voyage reminds us of profound truths discovered through simple actions. Borrowing from one of his examples, when folding your hands together behind your head, one hand seeks the other, and when they meet, the sensing hand becomes the sensed hand. The simple act repeated so often could sink below the horizon of self awareness, but Dr. Bausch prompts us to realize that this reunion of the dual roles of sensor and sensed object within each single hand triggers a feeling of fulfillment of purpose. The body makes and finds its comforts by discovering, affirming and creating connections.

Stepping more deeply into the philosophical jungle, our understanding of our presence in the world is analogous to reaching out with our mind's hand and, upon finding the matching touch of the flesh of the world, folding back upon itself ... with either a contented sigh or affirmative grunt that echoes softly or loudly through the fibers of our bodies. The "folding back" theme appears once again as Dr. Bausch links his voyage to Chaos Theory, strange attractors, and the emergence of order within disorder. We hear familiar echoes of regenerated wholeness when we consider the use of "talking therapy" to affect a physiological impact of spoken words upon the body and provide physical relief in concert with a sense of meaning and wholeness.

In essence, Dr. Bausch's vision of self is nothing less than an earthy way of intuitive knowing. It is an animated amalgam of spirit, mind and body vibrating in a world that is equally animated. The role of the body is discovered as a part of our cognitive self -- experiencing the world through its obvious and its subtle senses, and translating those experiences into the metaphors upon which our language and essential understandings are constructed. The boundary of the cognitive self is transcended, and, through this discovered transcendence, new horizons arise.

The view along the voyage shifts, and in the overgrowth Freud's shadow hovers over the unconscious mind. In this terrain there also are recurrent encounters with Nietzsche as he argues for the virtue of well placed words of heresy. Merleau-Ponty swings in to remind us to heed the "*flesh*" of the universe. Joseph Lyons stops by to help us cross some tricky landscapes with a framework, and Heidegger brings us some food for thought. In the thick mist, John Wellwood arms us with the warning that "*thought can only grasp and remember what has form.*" A host of denizens of the jungles of philosophy -- some familiar and some exotic -- arise to help or challenge us on our passage.

*Body Wisdom* is not a simplistic book. It is not a quick jump to a punch line. The voyage presents an array of differing perspectives. However the art that Dr. Bausch applies allows us to see the differences not as petty philosophical turf wars but as complementary snapshots of a complex understanding of self. From the very start, Dr. Bausch cautions us to fasten our seat belts with the admonition *"When Descartes inaugurated our Western mode of critical thinking, by means of the systematic doubt, he fixed the center of our consciousness in our rational minds by his famous dictum, "I think, therefore I am." He thereby enforced an ex-centric (off-center) position upon us. He put us in thrall to a strange idea: that the center of the world around us, which we everywhere perceive to be physical, is an immaterial entity (the mind) which we never perceive."* Dr. Bausch kindly and carefully decodes this text throughout the trip.

In Chapter 12, he gives a check list and pauses to allow us to inspect our backpacks as we reach our destination by taking in the view of the remaining three chapters. Through this final span, Dr. Bausch introduces us to a technology of "heart vision." It is a lens crafted to see the unseen. Through this practical exercise of *Body Wisdom*, travelers will come to experientially discover the wisdom of the body. Like the traveler before the Sphinx, we are asked three questions: Do the statements feel right (endo)? Do the statements work (meso)? Do the statements fit with accepted facts and theories (ecto)? When we recognize that we are saying yes, yes, yes, then we have reached Dr. Bausch's destination.

Readers who are familiar with Zen Buddhism will find harmonic threads within *Body Wisdom*'s message of oneness. The inseparability of mind, body and spirit may cause concerns for spiritualists who seek immortality. How can a soul outlive a body if it is not separable? The answer may lie in part with the expansive notion of oneness. Dr. Bausch places the human mind-body-spirit as a transcendent sensory object within a living world. The connections in this world are not connections between distinct parts, but rather are simply perceived this way much as an electron can be richly perceived as a particle or a wave -- but can never be concurrently perceived as both. The living human within the living world is only abstractly separable.

Yet the perception becomes a living reality and human existence is mobilized by the unfulfilled desire to recapture pre-birth unity. Accounts from those who have recovered from near death states arguably support the view that unity does exist after life. Dr. Bausch's case that spirituality is intimately associated with *Body Wisdom* is compelling.

I encourage you to take this voyage with Dr. Bausch. Part of its magic is due to the author's admission "*I sought to identify with other people's lives in order to feel alive.*" Through a kaleidoscope of animated voices, *Body Wisdom* applies its psychology, logic and spirituality to confront you with new ways of thinking. Some of the new ideas will bend or break some preconceptions. And at times the trip can feel mildly heretical as the bushwhacking hews away at some sacred hedgerows that hide the horizon. In the end, you will reach a new beginning. The experience will give you the permission you may have long needed to believe what you feel.

-Thomas R. Flanagan PhD, MBA
Author of *The Talking Point*

## Interplay of Body and Ego

Body is wiser than Ego.
Ego is cleverer than Body.
When Ego catches Body's tune, a song happens.
When Ego catches Body's intuition, magic happens.
An idea is born.

Our bodies are one with the universe and privy to its unspoken secrets. They are the unconscious source of our intuition. When we focus with our hearts on troubling questions, our unconscious comes through for us. Open questions posed to the unconscious act as the strange attractors of chaos theory. They enable the creative speech of discovery

# # #

*To comment on the statements in this book,*
*To challenge them,*
*Or just to enter into conversation,*
*Go to our blog*
*www.bodywisdombook.com*

# TABLE OF CONTENTS

Introduction ---------------------------------------------------- 1

Part One: THE HUMAN CONDITION
1. The Living Body -------------------------------------15
   a. Descartes' Dream
   b. Completing the Copernican Revolution
2. The Prophets ----------------------------------------- 31
   a. Nietzsche the Prophet
   b. The Legacy of Merleau-Ponty
   c. The Body Is the Mind
   d. The Freudian Unconscious
3. Individuation ---------------------------------------- 53
   a. First Impressions of Myself in the World
   b. Scientific Analogies of Creation
4. Transcendence and Dynamism ---------------------- 65
   a. Big Mind, Little Mind, Beginner's Mind
   b. Alternating Current: Change Is Constant
   c. The Sun Within: Implosion at Our Core
5. Am I God? --------------------------------------------- 73

Part Two: APPROACHES TO THE WORLD, OURSELVES, AND THIS STUDY
6. How we See the World and Ourselves ------------- 79
   a. Three Perspectives
   b. I-Feeling and Boundaries Part One
7. Methods of Study ---------------------------------- 85
   a. Phenomenology
   b. Methodology Part One
   c. Interviews with Three Me's
8. Ecto, Meso, and Endo Modes------- ---------------- 100
   a. Thinking
   b. Learning
   c. Remembering

Part Three: THE DEEP STRUCTURES OF EXPERIENCE
- 9. The Big Historical Picture ------------------------- 119
- 10. Depth Communication ---------------------------- 125
   - a. The Subjects
   - b. The Language of the Unconscious
   - c. Interpersonal Depth Communication
   - d. The Necessity of Separation
- 11. Chaos and Ego ----------------------------------- 133
   - a. Chaotic Faith
   - b. The Ego as a Strange Attractor
   - c. I-Feelings and Boundaries Part 2
- 12. Theses ------------------------------------------ 149

Part Four: HEARTSCAPES
- 13. Heart Knowing ---------------------------------- 159
   - a. The Heart
   - b. Empathy
   - c. Visions, Hallucinations, and Dreams
   - d. Methodology Part 2
- 14. Language --------------------------------------- 181
   - a. Perception and Language
   - b. Creativity and Language
   - c. The Reality of Language
- 15. Time and Space --------------------------------- 193
   - a. Time
   - b. Space
- 16. The Imaginal Realm ----------------------------- 203
   - a. The Creations of Imagination
   - b. Objective Reality
   - c. Religious Myths
- 17. Death ------------------------------------------ 221
- The Dance of Life---------------------------------- 225
- The How of Heart Vision---------------------------- 229
- Have Your Say! ------------------------------------ 233
- Bibliography -------------------------------------- 237
- Index --------------------------------------------- 241

# INTRODUCTION

Many years ago, I discarded alluring religious and metaphysical explanations of creativity and transcendence. In accord with Occam's razor, I sought explanations that worked with a minimum of presuppositions. In opposition to a major tenet of Cartesian and positivist science, I did not accept an ultimate separation of body from mind, nor of matter from spirit. I was not a dualist in those senses; I was a kind of hybrid monist. I was not a strict materialist monist who would deny spirituality. I was not an idealist monist who would hold that material things are mere creations of the mind. I felt, instead, that the physical world was creative of the spiritual.

I was bolstered in this belief by a number of great thinkers and traditions that seemed to share this point of view:

- A distant acquaintance with Hindu (Vedanta) philosophy
- The thoughts of Heraclitus and Spinoza
- The dialectics of Hegel and Marx
- The evolutionary thought of Henri Bergson and Teilhard de Chardin.

As I began to seriously probe into the sources of creativity and transcendence in the realms of psychology and philosophy, I ran into the thoughts of the thinkers presented in this book, each of whom have their own way of describing how the ineffable comes to be expressed. These thinkers derive from various traditions and use different terminologies to expand upon the simple question of "How does a simple idea come to expression?"

Any modest contributions made in this book should be credited to the giants upon whose ideas it was built. A partial list of those giants follows: Friedrich Nietzsche, Maurice Merleau-Ponty, Martin Heidegger, Sigmund Freud, Carl Jung, Jacques Lacan, Joseph Lyons, W.R. Bion, Heinz Kohut, Michael Eigen, Mary Watkins, and George Lakoff. I have simply pulled together their thoughts, collated theses from their works, and added corollaries consistent with those theses.

This book is written on several levels. In part, it addresses my 6-year-old's curiosity about his body. Some of it addresses my 12-year old's curiosity about life and death. Another part is addressed to the insufferable college kid who wants to be smarter than his teachers. The bulk of it, however, is offered to my 70-year old who still insists on understanding how everything is put together.

**Body Talk to Me as a 6-Year Old**

The body is smart. It knows how to survive. When you were born it turned you to your mother so she could feed and cuddle you. It showed you how to be like her, to learn from her and to become a separate individual, to become her child and not just her baby. It taught you how to talk.

The body talks in a different way than you and I do. Often it talks and we don't even hear it. When you eat your body swallows; it makes that food into you. That food becomes part of your muscle and bones. Then it gets rid of what you can't use. The body is smart. It knows better than we do how to do all this stuff.

Sometimes the body talks to us by having feelings. You know how you feel when it's time to eat? Those feelings are your body talking to you.

You can listen to your body and learn a lot. You can know when you're hungry and when you're sleepy. You can learn who is nice to you and who is not so nice. You can know what feels right and what feels wrong. You can learn to do what feels like the right thing.

Your body is you. It is that part of you that secretly knows everything about you. If you pay attention it will tell you what you want to know.

You have a mind, too, don't you? Sure you do. You're smart. You know all kinds of things. You know what two plus two is? Yeah, four. You know what color your jeans are? Yeah, blue. You know lots of things.

Your body helped you create your mind so you could understand things and talk about them. Pretty smart of the body, eh? Your mind is not as smart as your body, but your body-created mind gives your body its voice. Neat, eh?

As you grow older you will listen to your body and do all sorts of neat things.

## Body Talk to Me as a 12-year Old

People die. So do animals and plants. Still the world of dying is a world of becoming. Alfalfa dies so it can become a cow. The cow dies so it can become you. You will die to make room in the world for your grandchildren. Nations die too—as the Soviet Union did when it became several nations. Cultures and fads come and go too. Scientists tell us that this whole world we live in is constantly both dying and being reborn. The world's dying and becoming joins our own in a dance of life. That dance creates a field like a magnet's only much, much bigger—and smaller. The atom has its own field with electrons, protons, neutrons, quarks, and gluons all behaving as they ought to. The solar system moves in the field of the sun. All the galaxies, nebulae, and black holes influence one another and create a field of the universe.

All these fields are sensitive to every little thing that goes on in them. In the field of the earth's weather, for instance, meteorologists talk about the butterfly effect. It seems that accurate long-range weather forecasting is impossible because even if we knew this moment's weather exactly (we don't and never will) and knew all the factors involved, we could never predict when a butterfly in Hong Kong might flap its wings and so completely mess up our forecast. True.

This very sensitive and complicated field of the universe is like a big living body. In the old days we called it Mother Earth. In the really old days people worshipped the universe as the great Mother Goddess. We have lots of statues from about 20,000 years ago of her. Those ancient people were pretty smart because the universe is the source of our life. Your own mother and the Mother Goddess worked together to bring you into the world. All of this is part of the universe's master plan.

The universe is smart, too, but unconscious-smart like your own body is. You know how sometimes you know something, but don't know how you know? Your body knows what's going on and you are picking up its signals. Your body and the universe are like that. They react to everything; they know and communicate in that sense; but they don't tell us straight up how they do it. By paying close and sustained attention, scientists have come up with plausible explanations of how it happens.

In a way, we are like Mother Earth's inventive dummy. We sit on her knee as bodies and get a sense of what is going on, but we have to put those inklings into words. Of course, it's not quite that simple, but, that's basically the way it is.

Freud is the man who really started us talking about the body's unconscious knowledge. He also pointed out to us the way that we become separate, conscious people. You know we get born out of our mothers' bellies; and, in the first days, weeks, and months, we stay real close to our mothers, suckling at their breasts and cuddling in their arms.

During this time our bodies in their unconscious wisdom are learning a lot about being human from our mothers. In particular, they begin to be able to see themselves as mirrored in the nurturing, cuddling, and smiling of our mothers. They identify with their image in that mirror. They begin to become fully us at that time. For a long time we need our mothers in order to maintain our self-image, but eventually we wean ourselves. When we start making use of language we finally make our image independent of our mothers'; that image is what we call our ego. Our ego is conscious; it is a separate individual; it can talk. It is us.

Okay, maybe it isn't all of us. It isn't the wise unconscious body that created it. It is the conscious us, but it is not the unconscious us. Confusing, eh?

Confusing, yes, but very dynamic. On the one hand, the universe now has another bright kid who can understand his world and say out loud what it's all about. In this way, you help the world become alive and human. You help create the universe that created you. Neat. Over the centuries, people have created great civilizations and cultures in this way. What our grandparents did made the universe smarter and better. Because of them the universe made us smarter and better when we were born. We'll do the same thing for our grandchildren.

On the other hand, there are now two "me's," the conscious one and the unconscious one. The conscious me, the ego, generally wants to go out and achieve, to become somebody. The unconscious me, the body, craves intimacy and security. The ego looks for life "out there;" while the body seeks life back in its unity with mother and universe. Our emotions drive us both ways. In your teen age years you are already learning that. You have a lifetime to sort out those emotions and get them into balance. The goal of life is to be both free and intimate, both individual and responsible. When you've done that you'll be a star, Mrs. Universe's pride and joy.

Mom and dad will be proud of you, too.

**Body Talk to Me as a College Graduate**

Michael Eigen in his *Psychotic Styles* (1986) constructs a debate between Freud and his pupil, Federn. For Freud I-feeling begins with a primitive body ego, called the Id that has a drive toward pleasure and away from pain. Only later is a mental ego, or Ego properly so-called, formed. For Freud awareness develops in the body and spreads outward.

Federn believed that I-feeling was originally universal and that it shrank over time to become our limited practical everyday ego. He says,

> Primordial I-feeling drenches the entire cosmos. Everything is invested or imbued with I-feeling. Original I-feeling is infinite... [then] the everywhereness of I- feeling comes up against the hard facts of life....[then] a smaller I, more successful in material terms, becomes dominant. But a nostalgia for boundlessness lingers....We live through the tension of our larger and smaller I (in Eigen, pp. 144-145).

Eigen concludes the comparison by saying, "I-feeling spreads through earth and heaven. For Freud it comes from the body, for Federn it moves toward the body. Where is its point of origin? We grow and fade in the mystery of doubleness" (p. 147).

Sometime after reading the above, I read Lacan's interpretation of Freud and was struck with the realization that there is no Freud/Federn disagreement here. Freud saw the unconscious as possessing a knowledge, logic, and language of its own. In the development of the infant, the body (the unconscious) comes to identify with its image thus creating the ego. The unconscious after the creation of the ego remains as the original subject which Lacan dubs the Other. Thus the body (as

Other, as Unconscious) has the universal aspects that play so prominently in Federn's description.

This book makes clear the Subject-structure that we refer to when we use the term, "I." It describes the nature of Ego and Other and their relationship with language. It describes the three corresponding operating modes that we engage in as Subjects: ecto, meso, and endo. It sketches the importance of both ego and language. It describes how the unconscious speaks to our consciousness and how our "unconsciouses" communicate with each other. It sketches aspects of the vast unconscious, pre-personal wisdom of the body. It lays out the geography of our vast imaginal realm. Finally it speculates on the eternal fate of an ego that is created by imagination, inhabits an imaginal and symbolic realm, and gives the unconscious its longed-for individual definition.

**Body Talk to Me as a 70 -Year Old**

Nietzsche was the prophet who created the first rumble. Before him the Church, Kant, and Hegel had God in His heaven and everything in its place on earth. Nietzsche, a driven iconoclast, appeared as a wolf in the wilderness proclaiming: "God is dead." The hallowed edifice of staid philosophical rectitude felt a first tremor.

Nietzsche was an intense—and loud—truth seeker. He lived on the edge where chaos meets rationality. At this wild frontier, he met his two guiding spirits, Heraclitus and Dionysus. Heraclitus taught him that life was conflict and becoming. Dionysus showed him, by way of Greek tragedy, how the struggle of opposing powers enhances life and leads to a final reconciliation. Dionysus initiated him to a "will to life," a "saying Yes to life even in its strangest and hardest problems." With this Yes, a man immerses himself in the struggle where he reaches "his heights, when lightning strikes him" (quoted by Pfeffer, 1972, pp. 49-50). It is in this ecstasy that man meets Apollo and merges Apollonian individuality with Dionysian primal unity.

Nietzsche worshipped Dionysus who represents, as Plutarch observed, the "whole wet element" in nature—blood, semen, sap, wine, and all the life-giving juices. Dionysus is a synthesis of both chaos and form, of orgiastic impulses and visionary states—at one with the life of nature and its eternal cycle of birth and death, of destruction and creation.

Nietzsche was a public and controversial figure in the late nineteenth century—and even more so in the twentieth. He was claimed by both sides in the Nazi debacle. He still shakes people up.

Freud rivaled Nietzsche in his intense devotion to truth and his recognition of the centrality of body/chaos, which he called simply, the unconscious. He envisioned the unconscious first becoming conscious as it created the ego, thus creating a rift at our center and setting the battleground of the opposing drives Eros and Thanatos (Love and Death). Freud found the center of life not in a God out there, or in our self-conceited minds, but in the Dionysian world of the unconscious. The temple of reason quaked and the tabernacle was burgled. The psychoanalytic establishment eventually tamed Freud, however, and transformed him into a benign healer of sick minds.

Jacques Lacan, a Gallic iconoclast, insisted on reading Freud in the original and reading him originally. He re-trumpeted the message that the unconscious is the center and that our egos are ex-centric to reality. He explicated how the ego is created through language and how the rift thus created in us is what makes us human. Because of this insight he was able to truthfully state, "I think where I am not, and therefore I am where I do not think." Lacan crafted that aphorism as a terrorist might craft a bomb. It emphasizes the revolutionary character of Freud's "unconscious mind." It did not create much cultural havoc, however, because the rational minds of the West had just wrought World War II. Physically and mentally Europe was rubble.

Lacan stayed in France during the war. Martin Heidegger stayed in Germany. Heidegger enshrined his devotion to Nietzsche in a four-volume opus about him. He took up Nietzsche's themes, especially his love of the pre-Socratic philosophers who considered the world as body-subjects and did not separate mind from the body. Especially he loved Heraclitus with his ideas of experiencing the conflict, becoming, and being both in and of the river. He described man as being-in-the-world and being-unto-death thus echoing in his own way the insights of Freud and Lacan.

Maurice Merleau-Ponty spent the war in France. He was not as theatrical as the others we have been discussing, but he was just as iconoclastic. In addition, he was a combination of intense truth seeker and systematic research scientist in the phenomenology of knowledge. He established that the body perceives, the body creates the mind, and that soul is a body-created higher integration of human-bodily striving. He found Being underneath us, the creative force from below. He showed in painstaking detail how the body folds back on itself becoming both object and subject. He then proceeded to describe how each of our higher functions is built upon its predecessors. He also demonstrated that Being and body are transcendent in their essence.

Heinz Kohut left Germany to avoid the war and came to live in the United States. He became dissatisfied with the standard psychoanalytic interpretation of Freud while still recognizing its power. Rather than delving deeper into Freud's thought, as did Lacan, he analyzed what was going on in his own practice and developed a self-psychology, which is complementary to the standard ego-psychology. Self for him is the dominant sense that we have of ourselves, our predominant I-feeling. This I-feeling is developed in early childhood by the kind of mirroring that developed the ego in Freud's conception. Kohut recognizes that we have various senses of ourselves at different times. He also stresses the necessity of a certain stability of our self-sense if we are to escape serious pathologies.

Zen Buddhism had nothing to do with WWII, but it has everything to do with the thought of Nietzsche, Freud, Lacan, Heidegger, and Merleau-Ponty. Its concepts of big mind, little mind, and beginner's mind parallel Nietzsche's ideas of Nature, Reason, and Will to Power. Freud matches them with the unconscious, the ego, and the sustained tension between Eros and Thanatos. Lacan follows Freud. Heidegger lays a typically Zen emphasis on Big Mind with both of his celebrated hyphenations: Being-in-the-world and beings-unto-death. Merleau-Ponty venerated the same trinity by saying that the body (a ray of Being) creates the mind and is a unity with it. Kohut looking at psychological growth from an empathic viewpoint recognized several selves at work; his necessary dominant self seems to be beginner's mind.

Chaos theory cannot be blamed for WWII as it was not created until the 1970's. Still it picks up the threads of intuition floating in the work of all the people we have been discussing and creates the science of chaos. The same science, which is employed in electronics, telecommunication, weather forecasting, agent-centered modeling, and countless other areas, works marvelously in philosophy and psychology. When it is combined with the science of linguistics it lays open many secrets of knowledge and creativity. The chaotic, fractal, and holistic sciences are the recognizable waves of the future to explain our world, our bodies, and our minds.

Our bodies are the holographic image-reality of Being itself (chapter three). As such they are self-transcending beings (Nietzsche, chapter two and Merleau-Ponty, chapter two) that identify with their imagos as they are mirrored back to them by our mothering objects. With the advent of language, they separate those imagos from the mirrors provided by our mothers and create our egos (Lacan chapter three). In this event, we become fully human: the very eyes, ears, brain, and mouth of Being itself; that is, conscious, language-using, self-transcending makers of meaning who "stamp Becoming with the character of Being" (Nietzsche). But this event also ruptures our unconscious (animal) identity with universal being. Henceforward, we live in the ambiguous human situation where we are not two/not one with the universe. That is, we live in a tension between the One and the Many. In this tension, we ache for our lost, wordless intimacy with nature, but, at the same time, we strive to become separate individuals. Freud expressed this truth by saying that we are driven by the opposing drives of Eros and Thanatos.

Our human world, as a result, is a world of bodily creation (Merleau-Ponty), becoming (Nietzsche), being-unto-death (Heidegger), creative contradiction, creative imagination, and symbolization (Lacan). It is a beautiful world built on the principles of chaos theory. In this cultural world the strange attractors of attention, imagination, and symbolism, function as substitutes for the non-linear equations of physical chaos theory.

According to Lacan's analysis, the three dominant elements creative of our human reality are the unconscious, the ego, and language. Corresponding to these are three modes of relating to the world: endo, meso, and ecto; which are shown to be different ways of thinking, learning, remembering, communicating, and acting (Lyons, chapter six).

The proper standpoint for gaining perspective on psychological matters exists within the body, the heart, and the unconscious, which ideas are shown to be basically the same (chapters one, six, and nine).

Freud declared this when he called his emphasis on unconscious knowledge "a new Copernican revolution" on the grounds that the unconscious pushes man as ego out of his position as imagined center of the universe. The preferred thinking mode for human science is the endo, empathic one. The method of choice is phenomenology.

Viewing human reality from the heart, with endo vision, and operating with the phenomenological method, it is easy to see and formulate the essential nature of: I-feelings, boundaries, ego, the unconscious, the self, self-estrangement, and psychological strange attractors. In so doing we gain perspective for understanding visions, hallucinations, dreams, perception, imagination, religion, God, objective reality, the real world, and death.

This book is a result of long private conversations with the writings of the luminaries who have pioneered its concepts and opened up new ways of understanding our lives. It introduces and explains their ideas, but not in a dispassionate way. At all times, it strives to integrate their ideas into a coherent worldview that makes sense to me. It apologizes to Nietzsche, Freud, and the others who might strongly disagree with my interpretation of their ideas. It gratefully recognizes their genius, but as pioneering thought, not as scripture. It tries to create a comprehensive topography for integrating our vast knowledge of our human predicament.

The essential greatness of their thought, it seems to me, is their daring to stake out points of view that are outside ordinary ego-consciousness, that dare to ask the question: How does consciousness come to be? Their questioning leads us beyond naive realism. It breaks down our mythical assumptions and lays the foundation for a new comprehensive mythology.

The methodology used in this book is a refinement of the common sense used by every writer when faced with overwhelming complexity: (1) immerse yourself in the material (endo), (2) try to make sense out of it by sorting again and again (meso), and (3) devise frameworks to encompass and show the structure of the material (ecto). The refinements are supplied by the disciplines of phenomenology and human science. Some of the evidence supplied is philosophical, some experiential, some clinical, and some experimental. The more formal arguments are strategically placed in the book in separate chapters.

The book has four sections. The first, The Human Constitution, situates us as bodies in a chaotically beautiful not two/not one universe. The second, Approaches to the World, identifies three basic viewpoints for viewing life and reality. The third examines The Deep Structures of Experience. The fourth, Heartscapes, describes heart-knowing and the structures of ordinary and esoteric experiences.

I have been trying to write this book for years. In the process I have completed two unpublished books and have rambled far afield in a third. My childhood experiences drove me to make sense of my world. My philosophical and theological training honed my perceptions. Social activism, spiritual seeking, life's nitty-gritty, avid reading, and psychological training have broadened my horizons. Still my viewpoint did not crystallize until the last few years. At age 74 I think I've got the knack of it.

This book is needed because it was not yet written. Parts of it have been well-addressed, from somewhat different perspectives, in terms of physics-religion, biology-religion, personal and transpersonal realities, psychology and befriending the inner child. This work has been accomplished by excellent thinkers and writers. Nevertheless the cultural paradigms of an immaterial mind and its comprehension of the material world by the sole method of empirical science remain entrenched in our consciousness. Heidegger and others have broken the intellectual grip of these conceptions, but not their emotional spell.

This book offers a synoptic rendering of the accounts of great thinkers on the origins of our thinking. It promises to free our emotional selves from the classical but hoary conceptions of Greek and religious metaphysics. It intends to relieve our cultural anomie by introducing pivotal ideas that define who we are in the world and how we function.

Debate like this is long overdue. Every society needs a coherent, living philosophy or religion in order to thrive. We hold on to old conceptions because there are no new ones that seem desirable. Yet we long for a quantum leap into the present. This book intends to assist in taking that leap.

# PART ONE

# THE HUMAN CONSTITUTION

**Part One situates us as living bodies
in a chaotically beautiful world.**

Chapter 1 traces a growing realization of the body's wisdom in Western thought that is paradoxically evident in the thought of Descartes. This appreciation of our bodies creates a kind of Copernican revolution in our thinking, in which our egos are no longer fundamentally detached from the world.

Chapter 2 details the pivotal thought of Nietzsche and Merleau-Ponty. They lay the groundwork for defending the statement, "The body is the mind." Their thought also meshes well with Freud's unconscious (body) knowledge and its manifestation in language.

Chapter 3 outlines my own personal journey toward individuation, emphasizing the role of language. It also explains my paradoxical relationship to the world. It descrtibes three analogies drawn from current science: the hologram, strange attractors, and the Mandlebrot set.

Chapter 4 expands the description of our relationship with the world through the Eastern ideas of "not one/not two" and the role of heart thinking. It also relates our paradoxical relationship back to the chaotic state of our quantum base, which enables the dynamism of the universe and our human civilization.

Chapter 5 speculates on our likely divinity as creators of our own worlds.

# CHAPTER ONE

## The Living Body

In this book, the body is not seen as merely a mass of tissue, blood, organs, and neural networks. It is seen as our base of interaction with the world. In the words of Chris Aanstoos, "Through the body, we embody a network of lived relations with other people and the world" (1991, p.94). Our bodies burst with creative ingenuity. Our "every perception is a...coition [an intercourse], so to speak, of our body with things" (Merleau-Ponty, 1962, quoted ibid. p. 95).

In one sense, our bodies (the unconscious) know everything about us: our transcendence as well as our animal, vital, and material roots. In another sense they know nothing. They know everything in an indistinct way. They need their minds in order to know things in an explicit, verbal sense.

This concept of the body is different from that employed in Western science since the time of Descartes, which conceives a dichotomy between the material object (*res extensa*) and the thinking subject (*res cogitans*). In a Cartesian universe, our bodies are seen as just material stuff, organized to be sure and even marvelous, but ignorant matter nonetheless. By seeing our bodies as living creative communicators we uncover ways that the body is wise that are not accounted for in Cartesian-bound intelligence.

A long and glorious history of Western thought leads us to this anomaly. The beginning lies, perhaps, with the ancient Egyptians, who recognized transcendence after death and created an underworld to house the spirits of their ancestors. The idea of a transcendent spiritual body, separable from the physical body, became intellectual currency. The same idea, of course, was expressed in the burial mounds by Paleolithic peoples. With these mounds they wanted to show that their friend and family member really had/has an existence beyond the mere living body.

Zoroaster (c. 600 BC) elaborated on these ideas as they had been developed in Persia. He described warring kingdoms battling in human affairs: A realm of light ruled by God and an abyss of darkness ruled by the Devil. Throughout the Mid East and Greece these ideas became common. Plato continued the process in his exaltation of the mind and his low regard for the body.

A conception of human beings as spirits and/or minds encumbered by bodies became dominant in our subconscious culture. We came to conceive of ourselves as layer cakes with the body on the bottom, the mind in the middle, and soul (or spirit) on the top. This conception was sharply defined by Descartes. It is, paradoxically, the conceptual underpinning of the objective viewpoint espoused by materialistic science.

In the new millennium, we can face afresh the questions answered by our Egyptian and Paleolithic ancestors 4000 years ago. We can see what they saw, recognize their insights, applaud their accomplishments, and be grateful for their legacy. At the same time, we can discover the critical flaw of their thinking, which was their splitting up of our body/mind unity into separate parts.

The philosophic analysis of this flaw was led by Nietzsche who exalted the body and ridiculed both the Platonic world of ideas and the Christian heaven. Heidegger subsequently redefined human beings as beings-in-the-world, that is, as not being separate from their embodied situation. At about the same time, Merleau-Ponty painstakingly showed how our bodies perceive the world and consequently develop our mental and spiritual consciousness.

Freud and his interpreter, Lacan, described the imaginal and linguistic origin of our mental egos. They exposed the unconscious as having thought with its own logic and language. They gave an account of the creative conflict between our conscious egos and our unconscious bodies. They demonstrated the centrality of the unconscious.

These insights of our psychology and philosophy were, of course, unavailable to the great thinkers who developed our civilization. Since their tradition had divided our bodies from our minds and souls, they were then free to choose sides, to idealize the mind and to despise the body.

Manichaeism, with roots in the Zoroastrian religion, did just that. It equated spirit with goodness and matter with evil. St. Augustine, the North African bishop who died in 430 AD, was one of its believers. He later renounced it, but was not cured of all of its ideas. All of Western civilization was infected through him with an endemic intellectual and cultural virus. Its effects are seen in the Catholic religious vows of poverty, chastity, and obedience. This virus shapes our puritanical attitudes toward sexuality and perverts our science into devaluing our bodies.

In this lengthy historical process, we have hidden from ourselves the wisdom and creativity of the body. We have hidden them in a shadow realm called the unconscious. Into this shadow realm we have banished all sorts of sexual, bodily, earthy, and "feminine" notions. The Greeks called this realm Hades and celebrated Dionysus as its ruler. Left unattended and stuffed with our repressed fantasies, this realm exists beyond the bounds of our intellectual comprehension and threatens us as the devil's own kingdom. Freud called it "another scene" (eon wanderer Schultz) (Freud, Letter 83), or simply, "the unconscious." Jung explored aspects of the unconscious not touched by Freud and (among other things) opened the way for our understanding of mythology.

For centuries our society has had an aversion to the body, especially in its irrational and sexual aspects. We have been enamored of light, clarity, reason, goodness, and mastery of the world. We have banished mystical, dark, moist, and untamed inclinations to our unconscious depths. Jung named these exiled parts of "the Shadow."

Michael Eigen (1986) writing from a clinical background discusses what we are calling the body-mind-spirit wedding cake by invoking the metaphor of upright posture. In this metaphor, vision and speech are given premium value because they are above other physical functions (eating, breathing, copulating, evacuating, walking, and so on), which go on below in our upright posture. A hierarchical universe emerges in which heaven above and earth below assume paramount importance. For millennia, "lower" was viewed as animal; while "higher" was human or divine. He says,

> Today, we seem to have broken through our image of ourselves as upright. We identify with the streaming, spineless life of a universe we cannot see with the naked eye, an abundance that changes form or direction as fast as we try to observe it. We know [that]...our bodies are that life and feel that our visible forms are somehow secondary to the swarming imperceptible sea of energy that makes us up. We let go of the once-formidable upright father image, the dying patriarchy, and see

through the idea of authority in general. Writers emphasize how present-oriented, episodic, and fragmented our experience is. We no longer simply gain identity from well-defined social roles and institutions (p. 239).

In spite of these kinds of breakthroughs in understanding and valuing the wisdom of our bodies, we everyday fail to treat our bodies with respect. This disrespect resembles our disdain for our environment in that we obsess at being in control of our world. Our concern with dominating the world brings with it environmental destruction. Our censoring of unsettling occurrences and feelings in an effort to maintain images of ourselves inevitably brings personal degradation upon us.

Robert Bly (1988) poetically describes the degrading process. He says that we stuff feminine, animal, and vital feelings into our "unconscious bag" because they are unsettling. In this process, we weigh ourselves down and sap our vitality because we carry this "bag" on our shoulders constantly. In time, our Shadows turn out to have more gravity than our eviscerated selves. As a result, we turn immobile and lifeless.

As children, we created the Shadow when we sorted out those things that our parents found offensive and hid them in our bag. As we grew we hid more things in it: the taboos of the classroom, things judged to be uncool by our peers, and all manner of socially incorrect inclinations. Bly says, "We spend our life until we're twenty deciding what parts of ourselves to put into the bag, and we spend the rest of our lives trying to get them out again" (p.18).

The United States is over 200 years old, not 20. But we're still in our early adult stage. We have just begun to examine the contents of our bag. Feminine things, black things, sexual and bodily things are jumping out at us. Even though this chaotic vitality seems to threaten anarchy, it is really healthy. By recognizing it, accepting and integrating it, we become mature and whole. We may lose our nerve at times and retreat to old white, chauvinist, priggish, orthodox barricades. But we have begun the process of growing up.

A counter-current in our society moves some of us to intensify traditional values and further repress the Shadow. When we do this, we do not integrate the repressed Shadow into our lives, and we become loose cannons with awful potential for violence. Seventy years ago, the repressed Shadow erupted into Nazism. It erupts now in ethnic cleansing, terrorism, rampant street and executive crime, contempt for our environment and for each other. It saps our national will while it creates seemingly insurmountable challenges for our survival.

How did our Shadow get so repressed? For centuries we have pursued our myth of scientific progress and tried to eliminate the dark side of life. We have affirmed the mind and denied the body. We have rationalized (mechanized) ourselves and squeezed out our unconscious vitality. This process continues in the behavioral and psychoanalytic traditions where the main concern is to control the rat in the laboratory and the rat-nature of the unconscious. In our society, "A steadfast project to achieve control over the rat undergirds both traditions of scientific psychology" (Aanstoos, 1991, p. 8).

The origins of this worldview go way back. Some philosophers find Descartes (d.1650) at fault for separating body and mind with his dictum, "I think, therefore I am." Robert Bly points to the disappearance of the wild man of the forest (c.1100 AD) from western mythology. Some theologians blame St. Augustine (d.430) who incorporated Manichaean ideas about the evil of matter and sex into Christianity. Other theologians give credit to St. Paul (c.60 AD) and his advocacy of celibacy and chauvinism to women. Friedrich Nietzsche blamed Socrates (d.399 BC) and his humorless pursuit of logical clarity for our culture's decline into rationalism. Riane Eisler (1987) blames the militant patriarchy which overran the mother-centered culture of Old Europe (c.1500 BC).

In olden days, the myths of the Great Mother and the Wild Man gave our ancestors access to their dark, vital, sexual core, and helped them integrate the Shadow into their lives. Traditional tribal elders used the mythical Wild Man to initiate boys into the mysteries of their masculine power and to provide mentors for them. Older women used the myth of the Great Mother, as maiden, mother, and crone to show girls the mysterious depths of female experience. Today the Wild Man is banished and slandered as if he were the devil. Womanhood, too, has lost much of its mystery. The old myths provided our ancestors access to dark channels of knowing and holistic ways of living that elude us today.

In this regard, Robert Bly (1990) writes,

> When we look into the past, holding the Wild Man telescope to our eyes, many fuzzy images come into focus, among them

> John the Baptist, the wild man who baptized Christ, and Mary Magdalen. Mary Magdalen carries some of the feeling of light hidden in darkness, which we associate also with Sophia. Both Sophia and Dionysus contain in their legends the secret of a sun that does not shine from the sun down, but rather a sun deep in earth which shines up toward us (p.242).

The body's wisdom began reentering our discourse through the pioneering work of Nietzsche, Freud, Jung, and Merleau-Ponty. Today Afro-American and feminine issues are demanding respect. Mysticism, both East and West, is alive and well. The body is making a big comeback. Ecology has us thinking holistically again. Scientists and philosophers are reintegrating the worlds of reversibility (abstract science) and irreversibility (cosmic and biological historicity). We are uncovering, via Alice Miller, John Bradshaw, and Oprah, our civilization's horrible underbelly of abuse, incest, psychosis, and murder.

We repress our Shadow because we are scared of it. We let it out of its bag because we yearn for its vitality. As we let more Shadow out of the bag, we integrate it into our egos and, in so doing, become heavier, more real, and more whole. It is because we are getting heavier that this book is possible. This book is simple recognition that we are about ready to accept the vitality and wisdom of our bodies.

**Descartes' Dream**

Rene Descartes was ten years old in 1606 when he entered *l'ecole* to study logic, ethics, metaphysics, literature, history, science, and mathematics. A great deal of this education consisted in memorizing what the Greeks and Romans had to say. Young Rene was not impressed. When he was eighteen, he declared that his schooling was a farce because he had only learned his own ignorance and the limitations of the way knowledge was gathered and validated.

At that time, he abandoned his classical education to study law. He quickly became disenchanted with law. "As soon as he attained his degree, he declared law to be as intellectually bankrupt as the rest of Western knowledge, and set off for Paris, where he met notable success—as a gambler" (Harman, 1984, p. 73).

For all that, he did not lose his intellectual curiosity. He felt an urgent need to understand his world in a way that his teachers and Aristotle did not. At the ripe age of 20 he retired, dropped out of sight, and began to think. His methodology was unorthodox: he spent half of his day in bed, ruminating. "It has been said that Descartes later invented analytic geometry while watching a fly crawl on the ceiling" (Harman, p. 74). Two years later when a friend tracked him down, he left his retreat and returned to normal society, for a while. Soon, he volunteered for the army and found himself fighting in the Thirty Years War. While wintering with the army at Ulm, he continued thinking while lying on his cot.

He was stewing over his life. What would he do with it? He amused himself with abstruse mathematical problems and came up with novel solutions, like analytic geometry, just to pass the time. But he was really agitated over his education. Why wasn't there some discipline in what all these smart men said? How could one tell who was right and who was wrong? Wasn't there some way to tie all this knowledge stuff together? He had to know.

> The night of November 10, 1619, found Descartes in an overheated room, virtually feverish with "enthusiasm." That night he dreamed three dreams, sleep images of such staggering import that he took care to write out detailed descriptions...
>
> In the first dream episode, he experienced strong winds blowing him away from a church building toward a group of people who didn't appear to be affected by the gale. After this image, Descartes awoke and prayed for protection against the bad effects of the dream.
>
> Falling asleep again, he was then filled with terror by a burst of noise like a bolt of lightning, and dreaming that he was awake, saw a shower of sparks fill his room.
>
> In the third and final dream of the series, Descartes saw himself holding a dictionary and some papers, one of which contained a poem beginning with the words "What path shall I follow in life?" An unknown man handed him a fragment of verse—the words "Est et Non" caught the dreamer's mind's eye.
>
> At the end of the third dream came an even more extraordinary state of consciousness—a dream within a dream. Descartes dreamed he awoke to the fact that the shower of

sparks in his room was in reality a dream, and then he dreamed that he interpreted the previous dream!

In the dreamed interpretation, Descartes explained to himself that the dictionary represented the future unity of science—"all the various sciences grouped together"; the sheaf of poems symbolized the linkage of philosophy and wisdom; "Est et Non" signified "Truth and Falsity in human attainment and in secular sciences" (Harman, p. 75).

Descartes had discovered his life's work. He was emboldened by his dreams to proceed with his great ambition, to boldly search for the truth with a method of his own devising. He took his dreams to mean that he was the person who was going to reform and unify the sciences. He stated that the dream was the most decisive event in his life. In his diary of that day he proclaimed that,

He had constructed a universally applicable tool for finding truth, and had answered his dissatisfaction with the previous history of Western thought by building the foundations of "an admirable science" which could proceed beyond the boundaries of existing methods of inquiry (Harman, p. 76).

Descartes turned directly from his dream to beginning his work, *Discourse on Method*, which he originally titled: "Project of a Universal Science Destined to Raise Our Nature to Its Highest Degree of Perfection."

With this work, Descartes achieved a major breakthrough in the evolution of human thought, a paradigm shift, a new standpoint to think from. Thinkers before him had thought logically and well, but they had not given systematic consideration to their premises. In all fields, except mathematics (and logic), they began their arguments with statements that were justified by vague appeals to common sense, or by citing all-knowing authorities such as Scripture or Aristotle. Descartes changed all that.

He extended the method of mathematics to all of life, demanding critical doubt at every stage of a step-by-step logical process whose goal was to uncover the secrets of nature. In his time and place he thought a heretofore *unthought* thought. He had four simple rules:

1. Never to accept anything for true which I do not clearly know to be such.

2. Divide each of the difficulties under examination into as many parts as possible.
3. Begin with the simplest and easiest and then work step by step to the more complex.
4. Make enumerations so complete and reviews so general that I might be assured that nothing is omitted (cf. Descartes, On Method, 1952, p.47).

He had created a new outlook on the world and a new method to understand it. The twenty-three year old soldier, aristocrat, malcontent, dreamer with a fever for truth, had started the scientific revolution. From his indomitable curiosity, his dream, and his explanation of it, sprang the grandeur of Western science and technology.

Descartes' paradigm has two parts: a method (systematic doubt) and a standpoint (that of the detached observer). He arrived at his standpoint when he wracked his mind for some statement to get his project off the ground, some statement that he could not doubt, a bootstrap to pull on to lift himself to solid ground. He found it in his thinking. While he was thinking, (he reasoned) he had no doubt that he was doing the thinking. Thus his immortal dictum: *Cogito ergo sum* (I think, therefore, I am). He had severed the thinker from the body and from the world, but no one at that time noticed the beheading.

We have all drawn the usual depiction of the Cartesian man; that is a thinker with minimal connection with his body. We have drawn the stick man. The stick man is all head and practically no body. It is an extreme picture of what Kohut calls the upright man. It is also a classic depiction of ecto consciousness.

The power of a good paradigm (rigorous method and singleness of viewpoint) is proclaimed by the fantastic success of the natural sciences. The Cartesian method and viewpoint transformed the world. Not only did they unlock nature's secrets, they also gave us power over our environment.

At the time of Descartes, people lived in a world that was mostly natural and only minimally cultural. That is, most things, like hills, trees, animals, and families, just were; they were not the object of scientific scrutiny and manipulation. During the course of the scientific revolution, the balance shifted as we progressively impressed our concepts on nature and endeavored to bring it under our control. Today, we live in a world that is almost totally seen in terms of science and technology and only minimally in naturalistic terms, thanks to Descartes. We really don't want to go back.

Still, there is that troubling beheading to think about. Did Descartes accidentally disown the very thinking that produced his method? As a result, does science do the same? Good psychology today tells us that if we are going to think productively about our thinking, we cannot do so as thinkers antiseptically separated from our bodies. Our thoughts originate in our bodies.

We do not, however, have to give in to muddy thinking. All we have to do is adopt a heart-centered standpoint instead of an abstract mind one, being clear about what that involves, and apply rigorous thought to our new situation. In other words, we have to maintain rigor, but move into a new paradigm.

The new paradigm includes Descartes' as a special case. The situation is similar to the way Einstein's theory of relativity affirms Newton's theory of gravitation while at the same time placing it in a larger context. In this way, the beheaded head of science will regain recognition of the body that sustains it, and was never really lost—just forgotten.

The history of Western philosophy and science since Descartes shows the power of its method and its eventual limitations. Philosophy and science joined ranks and started their monumental quest to discover "objective truth." There were a few poets/philosophers/prophets like Blake, Thoreau, and Nietzsche, all of whom protested the march of science, but to no avail. Science was so awesome. For three centuries, wonder after wonder was discovered; life became better and better. Descartes' dream of "a universal science destined to raise our nature to its highest degree of perfection" seemed to be a reality. Science and technology marched on and on.

Then, one by one the ranks broke. Husserl broke with Hegel, Descartes, and the whole Platonic tradition by simply pointing out that all our knowing is "intentional" knowing; that is, we always know things and are involved with them. Therefore, we never have a detached objective viewpoint; we cannot be detached observers; and we cannot see reality "objectively." Merleau-Ponty proceeded to show that all our thinking and culture develop from the body.

Physicists came to realize that they could not observe sub-atomic reality objectively—which truth was stated in Heisenberg's Uncertainty

Principle. They observed that quanta were particles when you were looking for particles, but waves when you looked for waves. With the proof of Bell's theorem they were forced to admit that particles communicate over immense distances at a speed greater even than the speed of light.

Then Godel proved that every mathematics (and logic) is based on unproven assumptions. Saussure showed that language and reality are separated by a bar of signification: words never directly signify objects, but only locate them in a web of signification. Freud uncovered the unconscious mind that is central to our being.

Today scientists are bereft of the Cartesian objectivity that had been their guiding ideology. Their brightest officers and theoreticians are no longer true believers. Still the troops march on. They continue to find marvels, but they have the nagging suspicion that they are forgetting something.

The leading free-thinkers who shape our soundest science begin by targeting the fundamentals of our most popular myths. Rather than pursuing the simple realism espoused by Descartes, they tackle the question of consciousness itself—"I think, therefore I am," is not enough. They ponder the question of identity. "Yes, we think, but who are we? And why and how have we come to this state of awareness?"

We might wonder: What would have followed if Descartes had found his certainty in his body; if he had declared "I feel, therefore I am?" He could have reasoned that he could not doubt that he had feelings. He hurt when he bumped into things; had pleasure upon hearing a song; feared in dark and unknown places; and was exhilarated in discovering his life's work. How would Western civilization have developed had it been based upon the pivotal sentence, "I feel, therefore I am."

This line of thought leads naturally to a re-evaluation of our myths and folkways with which we have come to identify, and which support our self image. It is unsettling, but full of promise. In honoring and understanding our bodies, we rob our intellectual Shadow of much of its menace. With this lightening of our unconscious bag, we gain freedom to be ourselves and a better appreciation of what it means to be human.

## Completing the Copernican Revolution

Up to the time of Copernicus (1473-1543), scientists knew very precisely where stars and planets would be in the heavens, even though they believed that the earth was the center of the universe. Using the system of Ptolemy (c.90-168 AD) they devised intricate systems of cycles and epicycles that did the job. They were good scientists. Yet they were not able to make dramatic progress in astronomy because their conceptual system was off center. They did not have the right point of view.

When Copernicus considered the possibility that the sun, and not the earth, was the center of our planetary system and showed its plausibility, he started the revolution named after him. Physical science had found a center and a new point of view. All of a sudden the way was open to amazing discoveries. Physical science had discovered a viewpoint and then a method supplied by Descartes (1596-1650) that sustain it until this day.

The human sciences have not fared so well. When Descartes inaugurated our Western mode of critical thinking, by means of the systematic doubt, he fixed the center of our consciousness in our rational minds by his famous dictum, "I think, therefore I am." He thereby enforced an ex-centric (off-center) position upon us. He put us in thrall to a strange idea: that the center of the world around us, which we everywhere perceive to be physical, is an immaterial entity (the mind) which we never perceive.

When the scientists of our human condition accept this point of view they make Descartes their Ptolemy. Using his point of view, they see themselves as separate from the universe, from plants, from animals, even from their own bodies. They view all these things objectively thereby devitalizing them and making them prey to callous manipulation. Our environment, other people, and even our own bodies suffer as they are used and then discarded.

The mind is the most abstract thing about us, yet we make it our center. We do so in an apparent effort to separate ourselves from the rest of creation and so make ourselves special. In doing this, we repress the rest of us. That repressed reality lives in our shadowy unconscious where it is ungratified and mad as hell. It is no wonder that we feel uncomfortable with dark, moist, slippery, slimy reality.

We have scorned our bodies and the earth's vital forces and hell hath no fury like theirs.

We go even further. We project this abstract mind of ours onto the universe and create a God in our abstract image who rules over heaven and earth. We are beginning to realize that this is insolence.

Physical bodies are the stuff of the universe. Its center has to be the physical that we experience, not the immaterial that we postulate. The center of our personal universe is demonstrably our whole physical presence, poetically called the "heart," and not an immaterial presence called mind.

Social scientists, psychologists, and philosophers do function in this ex-centric universe devised by Descartes. They are good scientists. But they would function much better in a new Copernican universe centered on our heart, our sun within, our unconscious.

One hundred years ago Nietzsche saw the tyranny of rationalism as an obscene absurdity. He advocated intuition and art as bodily ways to comprehend our lives. Heidegger furthered this new Copernican revolution fifty years ago when he demolished the Cartesian viewpoint by highlighting the content of our experience and showing that it is relational. Merleau-Ponty pushed the investigation to new depths of body awareness. Werner Heisenberg, the physicist, with his indeterminacy principle, showed that the body-relational nature of our observations applies to even our most sophisticated "objective" observations. It is time to complete the revolution by fixing the center of our human universe in our bodies.

All of the above, of course, is not news. Freud himself proclaimed the completion of the Copernican revolution in 1900. In the words of Jacques Lacan (1977), "It was in fact the so-called Copernican revolution to which Freud himself compared his discovery [the unconscious], emphasizing that it was once again a question of the place man assigns to himself at the centre of the universe." (p. 165). The unconscious expresses itself preeminently through the body. Unconscious wisdom is body wisdom. As Lacan has so dramatically shown, the conscious ego is radically ex-centric to our unconscious centers. Therefore, the center of the unconscious is somewhere other than our ego-center.

The center of the unconscious is the center of the universe itself. It is in our unconscious being that we embody our paradoxical unity with the universe. This quirky unity is expressed in various ways. Hegel expressed it as a fundamental identity of the particular and the universal (Lacan, p. 80). In Zen, the phrase that describes this situation is: "Not two/not one." Xenophanes in ancient Greece said, "It is the whole that sees, the whole that thinks, the whole that hears" (Wheelwright, 1966, p.32). Heraclitus envisioned a Logos that functions as One in Many (Muller and Richardson, p. 186). Lacan states, "Psychoanalysis may accompany the patient to the ecstatic limit of the 'Thou art that'" (p. 7) [which is the Hindu statement of unity in diversity]. David Bohm, the physicist, describes the complexity of universal movement as an "implicate order" whose every part resonates with its totality. Merleau-Ponty says that vision "is a mirror or concentration of the universe" (1964a, p. 166).

We are not autonomous individuals. We cannot be. There is a basic ambivalence, gap, dehiscence, at our core of being. (Dehiscence is a biological term for the splitting of the seedpod that releases its seeds.) The unconscious speaks to us through our bodies from a place radically distinct from our ego-center. Most of us, however, still operate on the premise that ego awareness is all there is. Lacan, the phenomenologists, and the existentialists are trying to point out the error of that naiveté. This book joins their chorus. It locates wisdom in the body. It describes the body's language and what it tells us.

Charles Darwin's *Origin of Species* (1859) and *Descent of Man* (1871) revolutionized the way we look at our world and ourselves. We now see ourselves as evolved except for a strange omission. For whatever reason, we insist on seeing our thinking as radically discontinuous with that of other animals. The exceptions to this august isolationism are the researchers working in the area of animal intelligence. Yet their findings have made only superficial incursions into our accustomed feeling of superiority to and radical difference from animals.

Stimulus/response psychology, of course, tries with some success to show that both animals and humans behave in similar ways and share a rudimentary form of trial and error (meso) learning. Researchers in primate and dolphin intelligence are able to show a degree of abstract (ecto) intelligence in their animals. The work being done on primate language, on dolphin language, and on the language of bees, clues us in that animals do have the ability to communicate in abstract ways.

Still, no serious research that I am aware of deals with the predominant mode of animal (and human) intelligence: the immersion (endo) mode of empathy and intuition. The overlap in animal and human intuition has not been systematically explored.

Simply put, our physical consciousnesses can merge. Dogs can sense my sense of fear, anger, or friendliness in this way. Mothers know the needs of their babies. Babies incorporate the personality structures of their mothers. Young robins learn to fly and build nests by incorporating the wisdom of their parents. Boys learn ideals by identifying with their fathers.

For the chimpanzee and the human babies, stimulus/response (meso) learning is secondary to immersion (endo) learning. Abstract (ecto) communication and learning come much later, but they are on a continuum with the earlier endo and meso modes. The straining of chimpanzees for vocabulary, which is promoted by both stimulus/response conditioning and deep empathy, points to this continuity. All thinking is bodily thinking in its origin.

Our bodies are where we are not one/not two with the universe. They are the confluence of the evanescent and the everlasting, the implosion of the one and the many, an alternating current of contradictions, our personalized energy fields. They are our key to understanding ourselves as both discrete and continuous. They are our passage to higher consciousness.

In the next chapter we will review some of the insights of Friedrich Nietzsche, Merleau-Ponty, and Freud.

# CHAPTER TWO

# The Prophets

**Nietzsche the Prophet**

This book is written in homage to Friedrich Nietzsche who saw and proclaimed that our logical rationalistic approach to life was fundamentally flawed. With Heraclitus as his mentor, he located Becoming, symbolized as the River, as the essence of reality. He honored our bodies as the instruments that join us to the onrushing stream of life and allow us to take a stand in it.

For millennia we had split ourselves into a psychic layer cake of body-mind-spirit. This split helped us develop philosophy, science, and our ideas of spirituality. It was an icon of our consciousness, a religious triptych devoutly honored by theist and atheist alike. By the end of the 19th century, thinking people began to question this Platonic-Christian worldview. At that time, Nietzsche recognized the obvious and stated it in dramatic language, "God is dead."

The trouble with the Platonic conception is that it postulates a metaphysical realm that is totally separate from the world of living things. This realm is supposed to be more real than our experience. From this postulated realm, it decrees how things are and how we are to behave. We do not really believe in that realm anymore nor can we believe in the God that inhabits it. Thus, "God is dead."

Nietzsche realized that this was not an easy to digest. He commented sardonically, "The time has come when we have to pay for having been Christians for two thousand years. We lose the support which gave meaning to our lives." (Unpublished notes quoted from Pfeffer, pp.78-79). He realized that we would not easily part with a myth system that has sustained us for so long. He said it this way, "God is dead; but as is the way with human beings, there will perhaps be thousands of years yet in which his shadow will be seen in caves" (Nietzsche, 1974, p. 167).

We continue to see God in our caves and situate ourselves in a subconscious layer-cake world because those old ideas have a grip on our imagination. The cogency of new ideas is no match for the entrenched power of old imagination. In any contest with mind, imagination always wins.

Nietzsche's ideas of will to power, eternal return of the same, justification, and the higher man are powerful. They do not, however, grab our imagination and control our lives in the manner of the culturally inculcated layer cake. That is not to say that his ideas have not caught our attention. The ideas of will to power and the superior man (*ubermensch*-superman) inspire moviegoers all over the world to idolize Sylvester Stallone and Arnold Schwartzenegger—an incomplete idea of *ubermensch*, but a compelling one.

Still, an overall imaginative picture to rival the layer cake has not yet made its appearance. Perhaps this is the way it should be. Nietzsche predicted that the age of nihilism (the absence of culturally-accepted values) would last 200 years. By his calculations we should grope in the dark for another 100 years. Be that as it may, the general shape of our new imaginative conception of ourselves is beginning to take form. Simply put: *The body is the mind.* Nietzsche himself inaugurated this conception by his emphasis on intuition and also on the connection that our bodies give us to the onrushing stream of life.

Since Nietzsche's time, Einstein has demonstrated the convertibility of matter and energy. Quantum physics has shown how chaotically alive our universe is. Time and space have been collapsed into spacetime. It has been shown by the proof of Bell's theorem that local causality does not hold true in an objective universe as understood by quantum theory; in other words the universe seems to talk to itself over great distances at a communication speed faster than light. Biology has discovered that our whole body is encoded into our every cell by DNA and RNA. The hologram has been invented. The laws of chaos have been codified in chaos theory.

In addition, our world has become much more intuitive and body conscious. Out of necessity we have had to jump into situations that we did not understand and make the best of them. Often we succeeded. We are gaining our confidence. As both men and women we are becoming *ubermenschen*—in a more accurate sense: as people who take responsibility for their lives.

The workings of our unconscious minds have become part of our practical worldview through the pioneering work of Freud and Jung. Phenomenologists have made it their project to describe our pre-reflective experience. They describe our perceptions, dreams, etc. as they are received and before we categorize them or fit them into our conventional reality systems. Clinical psychology supplies us with ever more compelling descriptions of what actually goes on inside ourselves. More underlying structures of experience are coming into focus through the efforts of psychologists such as the English object-relations school and Heinz Kohut. A whole panorama of basic insights into the psychotic experience has been organized and deepened by authors like Michael Eigen.

In the United States, at least, the body has made a big comeback. We respect our bodily selves more. We pamper them; we exercise them; we feed them right; we listen to their messages. We have learned to feel again.

Today there is a burgeoning interest in the mind/body connection. It produces dozens of books, tapes, and workshops every year. The interest is broad and vigorous. The emphasis in holistic medicine is the maintaining of balance between body, mind and spirit. Meditative and Eastern perspectives emphasize the value of stilling the body and mind so that they can heal themselves. Imaginative approaches demonstrate the value of imaging ourselves as healthy. In particular, they show the importance of imaging our immune cells as active and effective. Deepak Chopra (1990) calls this quantum healing. Body therapists report on memories locked in our musculature and fascia. The breakthrough work of Joseph Lyons (1987) demonstrates the body's knowing styles.

Non-linear (chaotic, body-style) thinking is the rage for deciphering how the brain operates and for constructing artificial intelligence. Exotic physical and biological processes like solitons, far-from-equilibrium chaos, dissipative structures, bifurcation points, iteration, fields, and non- linear objects point to an understanding of us and our world as co-evolving systems caught in an ancient and creative tension.

Recent research, pioneered by that of Candace Pert, demonstrates that our minds are present all over our bodies. Our muscles, immune cells, and other parts of our bodies communicate directly with our brains by means of neuro-peptides. Our mind is present not only in our brains but throughout our bodies. Our bodies do our thinking.

Merleau-Ponty describes the basic mechanisms of this, but in a non-biological manner.

These advances in body appreciation are still on the periphery of science. They are rather recent and have barely begun to be assimilated into the mainstream. Often they are not even acknowledged because they fail to fit into prevailing theories. Their emphasis is often practical and clinical. As theory they are holistic and non-conforming to conventional theory. They do not fit politely into steady scientific evolution; they demand revolution.

Nietzsche laid the groundwork for the revolution. Over one hundred years ago, he observed that God was dead in his nineteenth-century world. The old psychic layer cake of body-mind-soul-God was irrelevant in a society like his which no longer took seriously the Platonic and biblical world views.

In *The Will to Power*, Nietzsche glorified the body as superior to the soul. It is in "the human body,"

> that the most distant and most recent past of all organic development again becomes living and corporeal, through which over and beyond which a tremendous inaudible stream seems to flow: the body is a more astonishing phenomenon than the old "soul"! (1968, p. 347).

In his view of society, churches are enemies of human freedom. He scorned those who retreated to the old verities. He called them "optimists" who thought that by wishing it they made God live again. He saw himself and his fellow philosophers and scientists as pessimists, people who saw the world as it is.

Given pessimism, the recognition that the old world order was fatally flawed and unacceptable, he set out to discover what could be done. He had little patience with weak pessimism which tried to escape the suffering by transcending it, and thereby abandoned the struggle of life. He advocated *strong pessimism*, the impulse to overcome, to engage the nihilism of the situation and make a stand. He dedicated his life to this strong pessimism. This quest was his "one thought," as Heidegger aptly describes it. In his final formulation, this thought is expressed as "will to power."

Heidegger (1987) expresses Nietzsche's thinking as follows: "Will to power means: empowering to the excelling of one's own essence.

Empowering brings excelling—Becoming—to a stand and to permanence" (p.156). Nietzsche saw us as bodies in the raging stream who consciously immerse ourselves so that we can feel the developing situation and state what is going on for ourselves and our world. Our statements, then, embody the onrushing energy of reality, making it permanent and real in an individual sense that it never had before. This is not done only by our statements in words but also in the very lives we live as we are immersed in the swift-flowing river.

We manifest Becoming as the nature of reality in everything we authentically say or do, that is, we affirm life and growth. That is what it is all about. That is the will to power.

The will to power is not the urge to be an aggressor over our human, animal, plant, and inorganic relatives, an obvious truth that the Nazis overlooked. And so it seems at times do we. It is, instead, an active taking control of our lives from the inside as we activate the Becoming that enlivens us. This taking control requires us to assume nothing as certain and go with the flow of life so that we can sense by intuition what is going on. Finally, it requires us to embody that intuition in our activity and in language.

Nihilism for Nietzsche meant facing life with no unquestioned presuppositions, but not anarchy. He distinguished between weak nihilism and classic nihilism. He called weak nihilism "the decline of the power of the spirit" (Unpublished Notes quoted from Pfeffer, 1972 p. 83), which is based on passivity, resignation, and resentment. Classic nihilism is something else.

> "Classic [or] active nihilism" is to Nietzsche "a phenomenon of strength and of the heightened power of the spirit." Here weak nihilism is overcome. The strong, heroic individual not only recognizes the artificial and deceptive character of traditional values, but has the strength to free himself from the need for these deceptions. He accepts and affirms life as it truly is and, thereby, achieves a revaluation of values. In this "God is dead" world, man himself is responsible for creating his own values and grounding them in his own existence. In its heroic and affirmative spirit strong nihilism is, to Nietzsche, the foundation for a new philosophy of the future. (Pfeffer, pp. 86-87).

Nietzsche, then, had no desire to wallow in nihilism; he wanted to overcome nihilism by establishing values and a philosophy that came from within the human experience of living. Such a philosophy would never claim the status of dogma, but it would claim fidelity to lived experience.

What follows in this book is philosophy of the classical nihilist variety. It is what I have been able to intuit from years of chaotic immersion in life. This is not its first formulation, but it is the best so far, the first that is worth publishing. I think I have now found the center of my circle as it is described by Heidegger (1987), "A thinker's thinking must in advance make a leap into the whole for each step it takes and collect itself in the center of a circle" (p. 12). For me, this center is the body, symbolized as the heart, and sometimes called the unconscious. From this center, many things become clear. They are what this book is about.

Next, we will examine some of the thoughts of Maurice Merleau-Ponty (1908-1961). He was the outstanding systematic philosopher of the dynamism, creativity, and wisdom of the body.

**The Legacy of Merleau-Ponty**

The philosopher who probed the body-mind-spirit relationship to its depths was Maurice Merleau-Ponty. He was an original and avid student of Edmund Husserl, the founder of phenomenology. He was a contemporary of Martin Heidegger, a friend of Jacques Lacan, and a collaborator of Jean Paul Sartre. His lifelong quest was to uncover the processes we use when we perceive things and the kinds of relationships that we have with our world. He found the key to this understanding in the body. He said, "For contemporary psychology and psychopathology the body is no longer merely an object in the world, it is our point of view on the world" (1964a, p. 4). In other words, we see and feel the world with our eyes and senses—with our bodies. Why, he wondered, do we imagine that our disembodied minds grasp the essences of things?

Our bodies are paradoxes. We often think of them as if they were objects like other objects, say cats and dogs that we experience. There is a limited truth in this conception, one which biology and medicine have exploited. At other times, we think of them as ourselves as when

I say, after cutting my finger, that I hurt myself. There is truth in this conception also and its truth is the original, pre-reflective truth we learned as we were growing up. In the one sense I say I have a body; in the other, I am a body.

Already with this paradox we find ourselves in the realm of seeming contradiction. If we are a body then it is us and is a conscious subject that faces the world. If we have a body then it is an object, something that is known by a subject. Our bodies therefore are both subjects and objects. Herein lies the logical problem. Subjects are sensing beings. Objects are sensed, or sensible, things. By logic, therefore, we are either sensing subjects or sensible objects. The terms "sensing objects" and "sensible subjects" are oxymorons because these conjunctions of adjective and noun are self-contradictory. Yet that is precisely what we are. We as our bodies are sensing objects and sensible subjects. We are oxymorons.

What are we to do with this? Are we to deny our manifest experience so that we can have uncontaminated, logically clear statements divorced from reality? Or do we face our contradictory reality squarely and try to deal with it in all its logical messiness? Merleau-Ponty opted for the second alternative. He said,

> The accusation of contradiction is not decisive; if the acknowledged contradiction appears as the very condition of consciousness....There is a vain form of contradiction which consists in affirming two theses which exclude one another at the same time and under the same aspect. And there are [other] philosophies which show contradictions present at the very heart of time and of all relationships. (1964a p.19)

Our bodies, then, are contradictions when we try to think about them philosophically. These contradictions, of course, are not puzzles to us in our normal living because they are what we are and what we are used to. The mental puzzle, however, is by no means trivial. How we resolve it affects our outlook on everything else we might consider or observe.

Merleau-Ponty stated this paradox from a slightly different perspective when he said,

> The enigma is that my body simultaneously sees and is seen. That which looks at all things can also look at itself and

> recognize, in what it sees, the "other side" of its power of looking. It sees itself seeing; it touches itself touching; it is visible and sensitive for itself. (1964a p. 62)

Traditional philosophy "solved" this problem by positing a knowing spiritual mind and giving no consideration to the position that the body itself knows. Philosophers, up until the last century, tried to work out the confusion that this "solution" generated. Merleau-Ponty abandoned that "solution". He accepted, instead, his pre- reflective observation: The body knows.

The body is a special kind of thing. It is not just an object, something separate from us, yet it is made of the same "stuff" as everything else. Merleau-Ponty terms this stuff the "flesh" of the universe. My personal "flesh" is, of course, corporeal or carnal, yet it is not inert, insensitive, or unintelligent. On the contrary, it is alive and alert. Somehow our flesh manages to have an outside and an inside. The stuff that we are somehow splits open and folds back on itself recognizing itself. We notice this sometimes when we reach for something with our right hand and somehow touch that right hand with our left. The right hand, at that moment, stops feeling the object (say a book) and becomes the object felt.

In many respects this development of awareness of our bodies resembles the development of the human embryo. We continue folding back on ourselves and eventually develop both the physical organs of perception and perception itself. Merleau-Ponty says,

> Our body is a being of two leaves, from one side a thing among things and otherwise what sees them and touches them; we say, because it is evident, that it unites these two properties within itself, and its double belongingness to the order of the "object" and to the order of the "subject" reveals to us quite unexpected relations between the two orders. It cannot be by incomprehensible accident that the body has this double reference; it teaches us that each calls for the other. For if the body is a thing among things, it is so in a stronger and deeper sense than they (1968 p.137).

Our body is able to turn back upon itself, to detach itself from itself and from other things. Thereby our body gets the distance it needs to make perception possible.

This distance does not remove our body from the world. Instead, it provides both a detached viewpoint on the world and a certain thickness that allows us to position things in space. In fact, it creates our experience of space (cf. chapter 15). Once our body has developed an ego it can relate to the world in two ways. It can relate as a thing among similar things (as body), and also as a somewhat detached observer (as ego) which has awareness of both itself and the things around it.

In the terms of systems and field theory, the body is a field of awareness integrated in an ever-broadening relational field in which it is both co-created and co-creator. The field of the world produces my body in its image. My body expands and develops that image; and, then, with the leap of language that creates the ego, it simultaneously transcends and fulfills the relational field from which it sprang. The original field (the world) is self-transcending; my body advances this self-transcendence by creating the ego. My body and ego together further transcend (explicate, make individual, creatively develop) the world by their symbolic acts. Aanstoos (1991) states the essence of that transcendence when he says, "The body is a movement of the heart, reaching out to touch, to embrace—as ecstasy" (p. 95). In reaching out this way, I create the world while I am simultaneously being created by it.

David Michael Levin summarizes this dialectical process as follows:

> In his *Phenomenology of Perception*, Merleau-Ponty contends that "I find in myself, through reflection, along with the perceiving subject, a prepersonal subject given to itself" (1962, p. 352)... This "prepersonal subject" is centeredness, or an axis, that is constituted more or less without explicit awareness in and by the ... motility-body, as it inhabits its local environment. Our personal life, our life, that is, as ego-logical subjects, comes into existence from out of a prepersonal existence, an anonymous and generalized corporeal existence. ...This prepersonal sense of being ... continues as a subsidiary awareness carried by the body—even though, eventually, the body is shaped and formed (socially produced) in conformity with the kind of body-image that befits the social existence, the social conditions, of an ego.
> 
> However ... we never entirely leave behind our affective prepersonal existence, and indeed can always at any moment

subside into its archaic modality of experiencing, returning to the matrix of subject-object experience. ...The prepersonal dimension of our embodied experience is without an egological subject, an explicitly conscious ego-center, or center of agency. Even when there is some subject-object differentiation in the interactions, the boundaries remain more or less fluid, open, and immediate: exceedingly responsive to circumstantial changes. There is no relatively fixed identity, no tenacious clinging to explicitly established boundaries, roles, and patterns of experiencing (Levin, 1988, p. 295).

Merleau-Ponty described how our experiencing of other people enriches our lives: "For the first time, the seeing that I am is for me really visible; for the first time I appear to myself completely turned inside out under my own eyes" (1968, p.143). This experience of seeing myself for the first time in the seeing of another person is the primary component of what developmental psychology terms "mirroring." This experience lives on in our future life and enriches it, especially in the experience of love. Merleau-Ponty continued,

For the first time, through the other body, I see that, in its coupling with the flesh of the world, the body contributes more than it receives, adding to the world that I see the treasure necessary for what the other body sees. For the first time, the body no longer couples itself up with the world, it clasps another body,...fascinated by the unique occupation of the floating in Being with another life, of making itself the outside of its inside and the inside of its outside. And henceforth movement, touch, vision applying themselves to the other and to themselves, return toward their source and, in the patient and silent labor of desire, begin the paradox of expression (1968, 143-44).

At this point we might imagine our Neanderthal forbears existing on the frontier of a mute world, trying to communicate. Merleau-Ponty puts himself into such a world

where, in the presence of other seers, my visible is confirmed as an exemplar of a universal visibility, [then] we reach a second or figurative meaning of vision which will be the *intuitus mentis* or idea, a sublimation of the flesh, which will be mind or thought. [Then he explains that] thought is a relationship with oneself and with the world as well as a relationship with the other; hence it is established in the three dimensions at the same time. And it must be brought to bear in the "infrastructure of vision" (1968, 145).

Merleau-Ponty also points out that an idea has no separate reality from the words that express it. Speaking of ideas as immaterial, spiritual entities divorced from the body makes no sense to him. Ideas are essentially carnal. He said,

> There is no vision without the screen; the ideas we are speaking of would not be better known to us if we had no body and no sensibility; it is then that they would be inaccessible to us....They could not be given to us as ideas except in a carnal experience. It is not only that we would find in that carnal experience the occasion to think them; it is that they owe their authority, their fascinating, indestructible power, precisely to the fact that they are in transparency behind the sensible, or in its heart (1968, 150).

In his ontological thinking, Merleau-Ponty holds that, "The essential point is clearly to grasp the project of the world that we are" (1962, p.405). In other words, "It is before our undivided existence that the world is true or exists;...which is to say...that we have in [the world] the experience of a truth which shows through and envelops rather than being held and circumscribed by our mind" (1964a, p. 408). That is to say, the world thinks through us. We do not initiate either life or thought; the world does.

At the same time, it is true that the world does not achieve consciousness except through us and our language. "The world gets defined only in terms of this 'project' which subjectivity itself is" (1962, p. 405). In short, the world and we as subjects are mutually correlated. There is a vague, unexpressed meaning in the world that is never known until we express it.

Merleau-Ponty's definition of Being comes straight from his phenomenology. Being is the "flesh" of the universe. "Flesh" corresponds to the general relational field of the world that was discussed earlier. It is what objects and conscious body-subjects have in common, the fabric that they are cut out of. Yet Being is a kind of yearning for consciousness. Man is the individual, indeterminate, free expressivity of Being. Gary Brent Madison (1981) describes the situation this way:

> Consciousness would be an opening in Being; it would be Being opening itself up. The advent of subjectivity...is a negation of Being whereby Being realizes itself, a negation of Being which is "the miraculous promotion of Being to 'consciousness" (Nietzsche, 1968, p.118). It is thus entirely as though in Merleau-Ponty Being needs man in order to truly be, such that man is the "there is," the presence, the truth, the very logos of Being. If Being is underneath man and only expresses itself in him, human history then possesses an ontological significance because it is the history of the becoming of Being itself (pp. 235-236).

Thus, for Merleau-Ponty as for Nietzsche, reality is basically Becoming. For Merleau-Ponty this becoming happens in a special way in man and exhibits a certain indeterminate teleology. In other words, Being becomes its conscious self through the expression of free human beings. The movement of human history is the cultural history of Being.

The thought of Merleau-Ponty is deep and intricate. There is no possibility of adequately summarizing it here. What has been synopsized is presented as a first grounding in his thought, which provides the context for the argument of this book. In the course of the book, his words are often quoted as they bear on the topics discussed.

**The Body Is the Mind**

We misunderstand the concepts of body, mind, and spirit when we presuppose that they refer to separate distinct things. We pluck these names out of the river of our living experience to identify aspects of who we are. We are badly mistaken when we think of these separate ideas as separate realities that are opposed to each other. "Body," "mind," and "spirit" are all names that refer to our whole self. When we make those concepts separate entities we create enormous confusion. Our culture wallows in that confusion today. It is time to get back to basics.

Merleau-Ponty situates the relations between bodies and souls best. For him, body and soul are terms that make sense only in relation with each other. Body is prior to soul. Soul is a higher degree of organization of body. The process is an ascending one. For the body as a mass of chemical components in interaction, the organism is soul. For the organism, the living body interacting with its biological and social milieu is soul. At the next level, the body as social subject in its group is soul. The process is a dialectic one of creative contradiction where the body transcends itself as soul while not losing its bodily reality. In short, "The body in general is an ensemble of paths already traced, of powers already constituted; the body is the acquired dialectical ground upon which a higher 'formation' is accomplished, and the soul is the meaning which is then established" (1963, p. 210).

Madison explains the relations between body and soul in the following passage:

> The relations between soul and body must then be thought of as relations between two relative and varying terms in a single dialectic where the first term encompasses and surpasses the second, but where the second serves as a foundation and condition of possibility for the first (p. 11).

In Merleau-Ponty's words: "It is not a question of two de facto orders external to each other, but of two types of relations, the second of which integrates the first" (1963, pp.180-181). Merleau-Ponty was saying that the body provides the stuff and the impetus for the soul which, in turn, integrates that stuff and gives it conscious unity. Finally in this regard Madison observed,

> There are certainly not two substances in man, but nevertheless man is not a rigidly monolithic entity. There is indeed a "soul" and a "body," but the body is a human body only in being the very foundation of the soul, the visible expression of a "spiritual" life; and the soul is a soul only by means of the body which is like its very appearance. (p.12).

We are bodies in the world. Our every experience contains both ourselves and our environment, both a subjective and an objective pole. Nietzsche (1962) pointed this out over one hundred years ago. He said, "It is absolutely impossible for a subject to see or have insight into something while leaving itself out of the picture" (p. 83). Heidegger said the same. He decided that every experience that we might have can be described as being-in-the-world. He showed that the ideas of being and world are mere abstractions from that experience. We do not experience our being apart from the world nor the world apart from our being. We have a unitary experience that is somehow also differentiated.

Heidegger tries to put across this idea by hyphenating the phrase, being-in-the-world. Within this joint-but-differentiated experience, our being is our sense of ourselves as we relate to the world. This sense of ourselves, sometimes called I-feeling, is not fixed in a solidified ego. Sometimes we feel tiny and isolated. At other times we feel as big as all outdoors. In either case, the field of outer reality is part of our experience.

From our I-feeling we abstract the ideas of body, mind, soul, and spirit. Body we conceive to be mechanical and material. It is not; it is alive and alert. Mind is thought of as our thinking part which is immaterial. It is not a real part separate from the rest of us and it is not immaterial except as an abstraction. We conceive of spirit as the all-pervading life force of the universe and soul as our own life force. As such, neither is separate from our bodies or immaterial.

It is time to declare that the body is the mind. Doing so clears the air. It is also time to declare that the body is the soul. At the very least, we have to say that mind and soul are simply more developed organizations of the body. Or in the words of Madison (1981),

> Spirit is not a new kind of being but a new form of unity. Since, therefore, spirit is not a kind of substance or a being-in-itself, it would be better to speak, not of a spiritual order and a bodily order, but quite simply of a human order (p. 12).

Soul in our culture indicates the enduring self, our source of inspiration, something in touch with spirit, providing guidance and awareness. This is a description of the body. Only one aspect that we customarily attribute to the soul is not applicable to the body, immateriality. That is a virtue of the body, not a vice. Immateriality is an untestable attribute of an overly abstracted idea of who we are. We are bodies. Our bodies are our souls.

Our bodies make us wise. The unconscious (in our framework, the body), as Freud has shown, has its own language and so speaks to us in dreams, symbols, slips, and witticisms. It tells us what is really important about ourselves, leading us to take care of unfinished business and release our creativity. By listening to our bodies we prepare more quickly for danger and sense what is going on in puzzling situations. Our bodies lead us into romantic liaisons that help us transcend our selfishness and keep the world populated. They act out to make us aware of parts of our childhood that require attention.

In saying, "We are our bodies," "Our bodies are our minds," and "The body is the soul," we are not implying that we are crass material mechanisms. On the contrary, as bodies we are totally awesome. We are live, magnificent, bodily wholes in a transcendent river of universal life. Attending to our bodies in engaged intuition we are open to self-knowledge, awareness of transpersonal reality, and control of our destinies. We commit a grave error in devaluing bodies. In so doing we devalue ourselves.

Our bodies are the crux of existence, the locus of our being-in-the-world. As bodies we experience a world that is molded of the same "flesh" that we are. As bodies we shape that world and bring it to consciousness. Our abstractions need to pay homage to our experience. We dishonor our experience if we segregate ourselves from the world. The honorable course is to accept ourselves as bodies united uniquely in a field of bodies, but as magnificent bodies. In the words of Gary Madison: "Is my body a thing, is it an idea? It is neither, being the measurant of the things. We will therefore have to recognize an ideality that is not alien to the flesh that gives it its axes, its depth, its dimensions" (p. 154).

The body provides our basis for reckoning space and time. As common "flesh" with the universe, it provides us with a universal standpoint. In our pre-personal identity, as body, we are, in a real sense, all that we see. Merleau-Ponty (1962) said, "When I perceive, I belong, through my point of view, to the world as a whole" (p. 329). He also said,

> The lived body...is in the world as the heart is in the organism: it keeps the visible spectacle constantly alive, it breathes life into it and sustains it inwardly, and with it forms a system (1962, p. 93).

and

> My...body is not an object ...it assembles into a cluster the "consciousnesses" adherent to its hands, to its eyes, by an operation that is in relation to them lateral, transversal [i.e., of the same basic quality: not superior]; ..."my consciousness" is not the synthetic, centrifugal unity of a multitude of "consciences of." [i.e., not an aggregate of divergent sensations. Rather,] it is sustained and subtended by the prereflective and preobjective unity of my body (1964a, pp.141-142).

Michael Eigen in his text, *The Psychotic Core* (1986), discusses the breakdown of psychotic patients as they mentally straightjacket themselves into roles in which they become either completely isolated from the world or else lose all sense of themselves as separate beings. He points out that we are both separate from the world and united to it; and we need to incorporate both experiences into a healthy personality. He puts it this way, "Distinction-union appears to be a constitutive structure of our beings. Take away either and the self would disappear" (p.147).

Zen Buddhists have a distinctive perspective on our relationship to the universe. In their sitting meditations they find a reality that is not plural. They sense a oneness that lies behind the appearance of multiplicity. The most terse, or compact, statement of this sense of unity is given in the phrase: "not two." As we reflect on this phrase, as we might on a meditation riddle or koan, we see that even our differences contain a felt, bodily commonness. For clarity, I use a less terse phrase, "not two/not one." By this, I indicate a magnificent harmony of free individuals created in a chaotic clash of opposites. These ideas will be developed later.

At this point it is necessary to state the relationship between body and soul clearly and succinctly. There is a soul. We have bodies and minds. Soul, mind, and body, however, are not different parts of us. The body is the soul is the mind, but all in varying ways. We are one thing, not several. The body is the stuff of both mind and soul. The body, as mind, knows; the body, as soul, is spiritual. The body, of course, is not immaterial—and spirituality does not imply immateriality. Spirituality is, simply, openness to the prepersonal, dynamic creativity of the universe.

We exist separately from each other. We are also one with each other, sharing the same "flesh." In our experience, we are being-in-the-world, that is, not two/not one with it.

The following abstractions are not presented discretely in my living experience: myself, the world, soul, mind, and body. These concepts are abstracted from my being-in-the-world. Therefore the body is one with the soul, with the mind, with the world in our experience before we start separating things abstractly. In our abstraction we first separate self from world and discover that the separation works well in our practical life. We conclude, therefore, that our selves and our worlds are separate things. They are and they are not. We exist in our world as an object in the foreground exists in its background, or better, as a piece of a hologram exists in relation to the whole hologram. We are both one with the universe and separate. We are not two/not one with the world.

Second, we separate ourselves into body, mind, and spirit and find that these distinctions work fairly well. We conclude that we are made up of different parts. We are and we are not. The whole body thinks; the whole body is not two/not one with the universe; it is us; it is our soul. Merleau-Ponty states this truth by saying that we are of the same "flesh" with other people and things.

This book is entitled Body Wisdom because the body is the pivotal locus where we are not two/not one in the universe. Talking about ourselves as bodies is the least abstract, least confusing, most real way to talk.

It is tempting to talk of our bodies, minds, and souls as if they were completely separate things. It is also confusing. When we make abstractions into objects, we create logical contradictions. The fault is not in our logic; it is in our epistemology. That is, we falsely assume that abstractions such as self, world, body, mind and soul represent discrete realities. They don't. That false assumption is what Gregory Bateson, the systems theory pioneer, calls "logical typing."

There is one way out of our confusion that we cannot possibly use. We cannot create a language that is not abstract, nor an abstract logic that handles concrete reality. We are stuck with the same epistemology and logic that Aristotle used. What we can do with this necessary and useful confusion is temper our conclusions with a sense of their half-true nature, especially where slippery concepts like self, world, and being are concerned.

In this book, it is understood that all of my conclusions are half-true. They are true from the perspective of body knowing and connectedness in a not two/not one universe. They are not true in a universe of merely abstract thought, or in a completely individualistic world, or in a world of complete unity. These conclusions expect scrutiny, revision, and contradiction even in their chosen universe. That being said, they need to be stated. We sorely need basic debate to get us back to our intellectual roots. As ungrounded thinkers we cannot maintain a vital culture.

**The Freudian Unconscious**

The unconscious is a slippery concept in our language. We usually consider it in a series containing the terms: conscious, preconscious, subconscious, and unconscious. The implication being that the deeper our ideas, memories, and activities are buried, the harder they are to bring to mind. We think that the things in our unconscious are there because they are repressed, forgotten, habitualized, or simply physical, and so are below the threshold of awareness.

The unconscious, for Freud, is a dynamic part of us with drives, emotions, and logic peculiar to itself. It is contrasted to both the conscious and the preconscious mind. The conscious mind, of course, is the mind that we are commonly aware of. The differences between the unconscious and preconscious minds were described, by the anthropologist, Levi-Strauss:

> The unconscious is...not the reservoir of personal recollections, images, and experiences, for these merely form an aspect of memory and are more properly called "preconscious." The properly unconscious consists of the aggregate of structural laws by which individual experiences are transformed into "living myth." ...The preconscious is the "individual lexicon" containing the vocabulary of personal history that becomes meaningful to the extent that the unconscious structures the vocabulary according to its laws like grammar, "and thus transforms it into language" (quoted by Muller and Richardson, pp. 7-8).

The structural laws of the unconscious grew and revised themselves as Freud developed them over a period of four decades. Of special import for this book is the emphasis that Freud put on language. He showed, for instance, that the unconscious has its own language which is expressed in symptoms, dreams, witticisms, and slips of the tongue. He also described how the conscious mind (the ego) is constituted by a baby's appropriation of language. Language also plays a central role in the central emotions of love and power, which Freud called the drives of Eros and Thanatos.

The Freudian unconscious is tightly circumscribed as an arena of dynamic activity with its own logic. In this, it is unlike the Jungian collective unconscious which contains race memories and transpersonal elements, and numerous cultural myths.

*Eros and Thanatos*

We begin life in symbiotic union with our mothers (and the world). We progressively individuate when we are progressively separated from that symbiosis by birth, by the cutting of the umbilical cord, and by the "blooming, buzzing confusion" of extra uterine life; when we recognize our imago in the presence of our mother and in our reflection in a mirror; when we grasp symbolization and language. In these processes, we create ourselves as separate centers of consciousness that are ex-centric to both our mothers and the world at large.

In doing this we gain something and we lose something. We gain our humanity as creative beings and experience the joy, discovery, and growth of independent life. We lose our felt communion with our source. On the one hand, we have narcissistic love for our egos and are propelled by an egoistic urge for power: we want to get on with our individual lives as ego. On the other hand, we have a nostalgic yearning to return to the scene of our primal intimacy and lose our egos; this is the urge for love.

Freud opened up these avenues of exploration and gave us a sense of the territory when he said that we are driven by the opposing drives of Eros and Thanatos. In so doing, he taught us a lot, but he created a conceptual morass.

> Instead of being a clear delimitation of two domains, the dualism of Eros and Thanatos appears as a dramatic

> overlapping of roles. In a sense, everything is death, since self-preservation is the circuitous path on which each living substance pursues its own death. In another sense, everything is life, since narcissism itself is a figure of Eros. ...[This] dualism expresses the overlapping of two coextensive domains (Ricouer, 1970, p. 292).

Because of this overlapping, I am at times departing from Freud's wonderful terminology of Eros and Thanatos. I use, instead, the terms Love and Power. I do this reluctantly because his terminology has the emotional power to express our life and death struggles. It also demonstrates the wonderful circularity of human existence.

The urge to power (Thanatos) is related to narcissism, egoism, and the drive to individuality. The urge to love (Eros) is related to nostalgia and the urge for intimacy. Thanatos, paradoxically, as death, restores the original community with our source. Thanatos is related to the compulsion to repeat and so to metonymy. It is the drive to experience more and more things, go to exotic places, and achieve great things. With it we strive for personal fulfillment and/or autonomy. With Thanatos we try to resolve the internal ravage of our ex-centricity by making ourselves the center of the universe.

Eros is the drive for intimacy that is symbolized pre-eminently by the sexual act, wherein the original unity is felt as restored. The first urge in this direction is, of course, directed towards our own mothers from whom we have just become separate. Paradoxically, it is also symbolized in the final reunion with our source at death. In either realization, Eros symbolizes total ecstatic fulfillment. That is, insofar as we are living ex-centric, and therefore alienated existences, we desire to be single-centered and merge in our source.

This fulfillment can also be viewed in another way, in which I am both the center and the entire universe and everyone else is both center and entirety also. The model for such a conception is provided by holography and chaos/fractal theory.

Understanding Eros and Thanatos this way makes sense of considering love-making as a "little death," as also of the biblical injunction, "to die daily." We face this death limitation in everything we do, which was pointed out by Heidegger, who calls us "beings-unto-death." Death points out both our limitation and our glory.

In short, the dialectic of Eros and Thanatos plays itself out in our lives. With Thanatos we have boundaries, we compete and make a life for ourselves. With Eros we seek community, love, family, ecstasy, and death. With Thanatos doing the urging, we strive for independence; at Eros behest, we crave intimacy.

The further working out of Eros and Thanatos take place in the developments of childhood, adolescence, maturity, and old age.

# CHAPTER THREE

# Individuation

### First Impressions of Myself-in-the-World

The world met me face to face on March 15, 1936, after we had communicated urgently, but in muted fashion, during the previous nine months. There was light, sound, excitement, and then... quiet. There was being awake in the experience of "blooming, buzzing confusion" as William James described it, then being asleep and immersed in a prepersonal world much like that of the womb. There was being awake... (click)...being asleep. From the first, I was part of what was going on, and somehow separate from it. I separated myself from it all, for example, by going to sleep.

    Clinical psychologists and psychiatrists have strained to express what the infant's world is like at the beginning. The baby is not yet a separate ego. It is "prepersonal" in the sense that it is "an anonymous and generalized corporeal existence," (David Levin, 1988, p. 295) which melds with its environment and is minimally distinct from it. Some authors have called this original state a symbiotic fusion, implying that the infant and its mother (mother = nurturing environment) exist together in a boundless oneness. The English psychoanalyst, Winnicott, described the infant's experience as being, "not mother" and "not self."

    In its prepersonal state, the infant knows its world through a kind of collective-erotic sensing. It senses everything at once: lights, sounds, physical contact, the emotions and attitudes of the people around it. This global, affective engulfing of its surroundings is the basis of what we will be describing as endo awareness.

    A simple description of this infant experience is provided by the Zen expression, "not two." As I grew up, another phrase described my experience," not one." Both expressions are valid. "Not two" points out that my experience of conflict and isolation is not present at the core of my being. "Not one" expresses the fact that I have boundaries which enable me to function in the practical world. The Zen saying "not two" actually encapsulates my experience in its cryptic fashion, but I prefer the less cryptic expression, "not two/not one."

The sense is that there are not two realities in existence, but only a universal one which is not monolithic. In other words, within this oneness there are individuals. More precisely, this whole is a harmony of free individuals. Michael Eigen (1986) says succinctly, "The infant seems both separate and permeable from the outset." (p. 151).

The first thing I came to recognize was myself as reflected in the smile, caress, and embrace of my mother. I drew my sustenance from her. In her mirror, I became me. I was part of her and she, me. When she left I panicked because I was no longer there. My bawling magically brought me (her) back to me. When I did not reappear as my mother, my bawling would blessedly turn to sleeping.

Somewhere between six and eighteen months I saw my reflection in another kind of mirror, one made of silvered glass, (described by Lacan, 1977, pp. 1-8) and was fascinated as to how I could make me appear and disappear. These two kinds of reflection produced an image outside of myself with which I identified. I easily assumed the identity of that image, which is termed the *imago* in the literature. Later with the development of language I separated that imago from my mother and, in so doing, constituted my own ego.

The ego is my relatively stable, boundaried, practical, but alienated game face that enables me to function as an independent entity in the world. It is the first of many bodily creations that populate my dynamic, symbolic, imaginal realm.

Freud and Lacan offer an enchanting account of how Freud's grandson started to appropriate language (described by Freud in *Beyond the Pleasure Principle*, 1920, pp. 14-15). The boy was in his crib playing with a spool that was attached to a string. As he lowered the spool below the side of the crib where he could not see it he cooed "o-o-o- o-o"; when he raised it back to where he could see it he said "Da." Freud perceived that the boy was trying to vocalize the words "Fort" and "Da" which are the German words for "Gone" and "Here."

The boy was just at the age where he had to cope with the fact that his mother would not always be there when he cried. Freud saw that the boy was dealing with his separation from his mother as he played his game over and over. He had learned to cope symbolically with the absence of the toy (and, by implication, his mother) by making it disappear and reappear while expressing absence and presence. In doing this, he was able to possess his mother's presence symbolically, even when she was absent. This exercise made him content and allowed him to let his mother go away without protesting.

Lacan points out what a momentous occurrence this Fort/Da experience was. The child did not only possess his mother symbolically with language; he also became a separate entity (an ego). While he coped with his frustrated desire for his mother in this way, he now had desire in a more articulated sense: He could now express her absence and demand her presence with language. The original unity between mother and child was broken. Lacan (1977) says, the moment "in which desire becomes human is also that in which the child is born into language" (p. 103).

In a strange, but real, sense, language "kills" the mother for the infant. The undifferentiated unity with mother is broken. The experience of the "languaged mother" is not the same as what was sensed in the original mother-me. Merleau-Ponty expresses this same truth in the broader philosophical context when he says, "The advent of subjectivity...is a negation of Being whereby Being realizes itself, a negation of Being which is the miraculous promotion of Being to 'consciousness'" (1968, p.118; Madison, p. 235).

In the Fort/Da symbolization (or its equivalent) and all later speech, I gave birth to my individuality by using the universal subtle reality of language. In symbolizing and languaging, I nested my individuality in its broader reality. For this progress I pay the price of desire. My deepest longing is for the intense unity I experienced as an infant (before language). This longing expresses itself in sexual yearnings among other things. I also have an intense desire to be an individual. Life is the working out of these two, conflicting drives.

Three modern discoveries give coherent backgrounds which situate my not two/not one reality. They are hologram, chaos theory, and fractal geometry. We will next describe these remarkable discoveries. Also we will describe the geography of the Jungian and Freudian unconsciouses and detail some of the ways that the Freudian version speaks to us through our bodies.

## Scientific Analogies of Creation

The body of the universe has found exotic ways to symbolize for us the way it is put together. It presents the microcosm/macrocosm similarities to us in relation to both the little world/big world of physics and the personal world/universal world of psychology and sociology. Recently, through the efforts of the scientists of chaos, it has created exquisite artificial universes by indeterministic and decentralized processes.

These chaotic processes are clues to the constituting process of the universe. They indicate how we function in the grand economy. They also sketch a solution to the freedom vs. predestination debate. They show us, as does the theory of the holoverse (described below), a divine economy in which we are both whole, center, and part.

*The Holoverse*

The high-tech, laser, three-dimensional photographs called holograms give sensual confirmation to our sense of being not two/not one. They demonstrate the relationship of the microcosm and the macrocosm, the age-old theory that the universe is reflected in its every part.

If you take an ordinary photograph of your face and tear off the part containing your chin, you will have two pieces; one will picture your chin; the other will show the rest of your face.

Not so with the hologram. If you take a hologram picturing your face and break off the chin part you again have two pieces, but each one is a picture of your whole face. Break both pieces into two and you then have four complete pictures of your face, and so on. The whole is completely present in each of its parts. Regarding any two pieces resulting from breaking the hologram of your face, it is true to say, "These two are not two."

David Bohm, the physicist, was the first to widely propound the idea that the universe is constructed on a model similar to that of the hologram. Many writers following his lead have proceeded to describe that universe which is dubbed the holoverse. Karl Pribram applied the same holoverse concept to the structure of the brain

Our interest in this theory is its portrayal of ourselves as identical to the whole, yet separate. The whole of the universe is encoded into its every part. This is similar to the way that our body is encoded in the DNA of its every cell. What this means in our context is that our bodies are the universe. What we are is what the universe is and vice versa. These properties of hologram give background to the clinical observations that we are identical with the world and yet distinct. We embody a logical contradiction.

This contradiction is closely related to the subject-object contradiction explicated by Merleau-Ponty. In both, our bodies are found to be "total parts" of the universe. The holographic identity is a physical metaphor of what Merleau-Ponty calls "flesh" or "Being." It is first cousin to the entity that linguistics and Lacan dub "the Subject." The physical hologram symbolizes our experienced reality. It indicates that reality itself and our bodies are structured according to the same specifications. In this holoverse, as Madison has put it, "Each thing is a partial expression (but expressive as such of the totality)" (p. 217).

The coming together of physics, philosophy, and New Age thinking in the hologram is merely one instance of the radical congregating that is brewing a revolution in our dominant Western worldview. It is becoming possible to withstand the Western tradition from within, as counter-traditionalists, who understand and appreciate our heritage and move it in radically new directions, and not just as anti-traditionalists, who just want to junk the tradition.

*The Strange Attraction of Chaos*

Chaos theory provides a rationale for the random exquisiteness of the universe and my free participation in its creation. The strange attractors of chaos are both natural processes and equations. They generate harmony by chaotic processes. They exhibit remarkable characteristics. When their equations are graphed, for example, they often generate beauty of infinite depth and variety. They do this in unpredictable ways that do not seem to coerce the freedom of individual atoms or points.

A non-mathematical demonstration of a strange attractor at work is provided by the rise of cigarette smoke in a still room. The smoke rises but each individual atom within it is free to go wherever it will as each atom is indeterminate (free). The smoke gracefully rises curling at some point into two beautiful plumes which then separate into four plumes, thence to eight and eventual chaos. No two plumes are ever the same, but they maintain remarkable fractal similarity.

Thousands of processes in fields as diverse as biology and electronics follow this same process as they progress from regular to periodic to chaotic. The following discussion relies heavily on Ian Stewart's, *Does God Play Dice?* (1989).

Martin Feigenbaum was intrigued by strange things like cigarette smoke. He made them his life study. What happens, he wondered, when steady dynamic systems break down? He studied ripples on a still lake, for example, and non-linear equations. He discovered that a bifurcation process, that is, one thing splitting into another, underlies all turbulent activities as they move into eventual chaos. He worked out the whole process mathematically. The process can be succinctly stated as 1,2,4,8,16--CHAOS!

This relationship is often symbolized by a bifurcation diagram which Stewart calls a fig tree because that is what "Feigenbaum" means in German. It turns out that the fig tree is a universal phenomenon. The constants it reveals have an importance in chaos theory equivalent to the straight line in geometry. In the mathematics of chaos theory, one of them is called the "irreducible basis of periodicity in chaotic transformation." In other words, it is the nitty-gritty of all chaotic transformations.

Further examination of chaotic transformations and the fig tree reveals that the bifurcations occur in a precise scaling ratio that equals 4.669. All sorts of physical systems, electronic, optical, and biological show a bifurcation pattern with this precise scaling ratio. The preceding bifurcation is always 4.669 times larger than its successor. The constant 4.669 is a number like 3.1416 ($\pi$). This process goes on for three, four, or five bifurcations, then chaos sets in and there is no longer a discernible pattern.

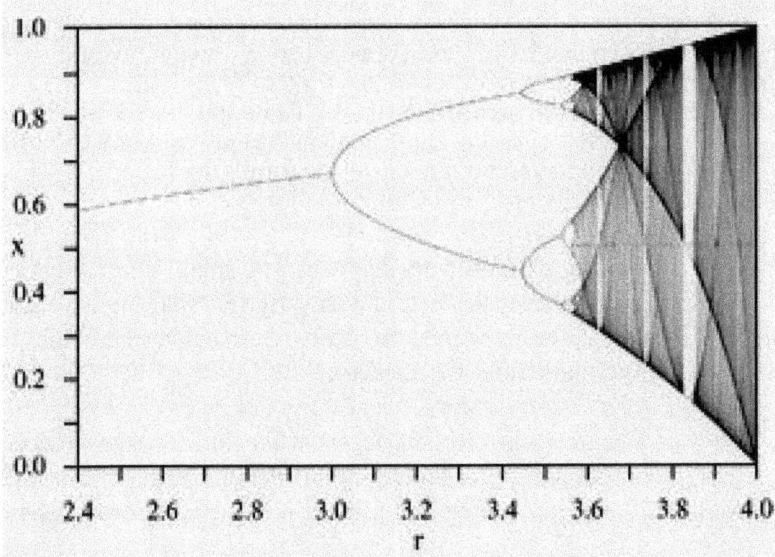

Computers compelled by our curiosity allow us to pursue this process right into chaos, then out of it, and back in again and again. We can generate a bifurcation tree by graphing simple mappings like this logistic one: (Stewart, p.197)

$$x \to rx(1 - x)$$

Performing this mapping for one value of r, then for another (fractional) value, and repeating the process over and over again for values of r between 0 and 4 we generate a fig tree. As r progresses from 2 to 4 a bifurcation occurs and happens four times before chaos sets in at k = 3.58.

Stewart (p.198) points out that 4.669 is a "scaling factor," and says,

> This structure is the shape of the fig-tree itself. The steady attractor forms the trunk. The period-2 attractors form two shorter boughs. From these sprout even shorter period-4 branches, then period-8 twigs, period-16 twiglets, and so on. The size-ratios of trunk to bough, bough to branch, branch to twig, twig to twiglet, get closer and closer to 4.669, the nearer you get to the top of the tree.

Indeed, if you break off a bough, you get an approximate copy of the entire fig-tree (see figure). The same holds if you break off a twiglet. The copy is smaller, and the sizes decrease in a scaling ratio that tends to 4.669. And the further along you go, the closer the similarity becomes. This is self-similarity. (pp.198-200)

At 3.835 something extraordinary happens. A small window appears which exhibits on further inspection a tiny fig tree that branches three times. This tiny fig tree ends in chaos, but again there are tiny windows. In these are tinier fig trees, etc.

Stewart illustrates in physical terms what the iterative procedure just described amounts to by talking about making toffee. You make this candy toffee by stretching and folding it in a precise way. Here is the recipe (p.143-147):

- Take one roll of toffee.
- Stretch the toffee.
- Double the toffee back on itself.
- Stretch the toffee again.
- Double it again
- Repeat this process millions of times registering the position, sequence, and proximity of all points (not just A, B, C, D, & E).

Points that were close together are now far apart and vice versa. Soon tracking the proximity and sequences of points becomes impossible. The process is out of control and random. Yet the generator of this chaos is a simple thing like stretching and folding toffee. To produce creation in this mode, God just makes toffee. The results are:

steady → periodic → chaotic → periodic → chaotic → periodic—randomly generated.

Our knowledge of the chaotically produced universe that we live in mirrors these phases. The periodic phases correspond to our rational grasp of what is going on. The chaotic phases correspond to our incubation of ideas in unconscious processes. The windows correspond to moments of intuition with subsequent rationalization.

The folding involved in making toffee, and generally in chaotic creation, bears remarkable similarity to the folding back on itself performed by the body as described by Merleau-Ponty. This "folding back" results in sensation, perception, thought, language, and culture.

With "folding back," as in the hologram we have an instance where physical processes mirror psychological and ontological ones. With chaos theory we add to the metaphor of the hologram the idea that every atom and every configuration of atoms is not just a microcosm of the macrocosm, but also a free agent which creates the beauty of the whole by practicing that freedom in whatever way.

*Fractal Grandeur*

Fractal Geometry deals with fractional dimensions between our usual one-, two-, and three- dimensional representations of the world. In doing this, it deals directly with jagged lines and crinkled surfaces whereas traditional geometry deals with smooth lines and surfaces. An aerial picture of a rocky coastline, for example, has a fractal dimension of about 1.25 (Stewart p. 219), whereas a protein molecule has a dimension about 1.7 (Stewart p.223), and a crumpled ball of paper has a dimension of about 2.5 (Stewart p.224).

Surfaces in nature are very irregular and have individualistic qualities. Traditional geometry smoothes out the differences and reduces everything to approximations of straight lines and curves in order to compute lengths, areas, volumes, etc.

Fractal geometry, in contrast, tries to come to grips with the uniqueness of observed reality to discover its underlying structure. Using fractal geometry mathematicians can reproduce a fern on their desktop computers by following a few simple rules. Lucasfilms generated the geography of the moons of Endor in this way for the film *Return of the Jedi.* (Stewart p.229).

Visually the most remarkable production of fractal geometry is the Mandelbrot set which is sometimes called the gingerbread man because of its overall shape. Using complex numbers and the simple mapping procedure, (Stewart p. 235)

$$z_{n+1} = z_n^2 + c$$

Mandlebrot plotted the connectedness of every point c in the plane. There is no foreseeable sequence for plotting the connectedness of those points. They occur randomly all over the computer screen. The order is chaotic. Only after thousands and millions of iterations does the pattern appear. It is the gingerbread man.

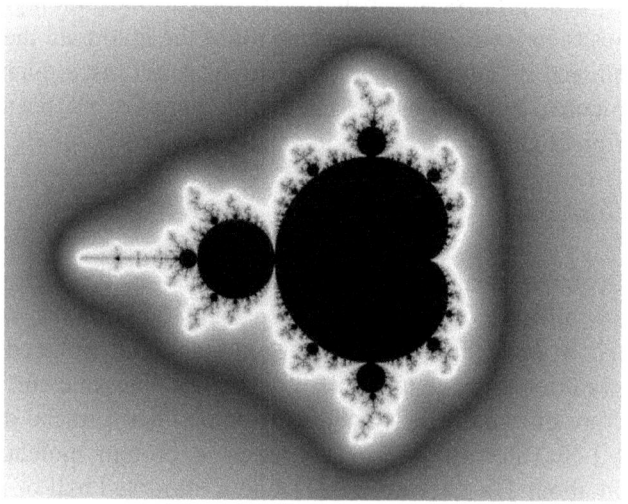

[Black and white representations of the Mandlebrot set cannot do it justice. Google "Mandelbrot set" to see it in all its glory.]

Picking any spot on the gingerbread man we can enlarge it 100 times mathematically and find a design of jeweled splendor having elegance surpassing seashells and sea horses. Again enlarging this portion 100 times we find elegant designs by the same jeweler. Repeating the process we find equally detailed but unique beauty by the same jeweler, etc. The Mandelbrot set has infinite depth.

Searching within this beauty, geometers have found reproductions of the original gingerbread man exact in every detail, with infinite depth just like the original.

One is reminded of the biblical phrase, "God's only begotten son," but in a depth that says he is begotten again and again infinitely. One is tempted to mimic the style of John Lennon singing about the walrus:

God is the Gingerbread Man.
Jesus is the Gingerbread Man.
We are the Gingerbread Men.
Again, the One and the Many.
Again, not two/not one.
Again, infinite freedom and depth
In infinite elegant order
Randomly generated.
God writing straight with crooked lines.

We can place ourselves anywhere we please in this universe and still fit exquisitely into the grand design.

Chaos theory and fractal geometry deal with random (free) events that create remarkable unpredictable beauty. They situate my experience of being one with the world precisely because I am a free individual: I do what I please, and, whatever that is, it is just exactly right for the universe. I am one with the magnificent unity of the universe because I am a free individual.

The workings of chaos and fractals expand on the metaphor of the hologram. They show a likely scenario for the formation of the microcosm in the macrocosm. They also surprise us with the revelation that the universe is free.

God (also known as the Universe) doesn't need to make toffee. He just plays around with strange attractors. They organize chaos for him with gay abandon and infinite wisdom. God creates what he will by typing formulas on his computer, then sitting back and watching his screen to see what develops. Nietzsche and Heraclitus were right, "The world is the game that Zeus plays." They must be laughing together in Valhalla. Nietzsche slaps Heraclitus on the back and repeats one of their favorite quotes, "It is a game. Don't take it so pathetically and—above all—don't make morality out of it" (Nietzsche, 1962, p. 64).

We too play with strange attractors and make toffee because we are the same hologram. Knowing how to use the laws of chaos gives us control of our lives in the way that the laws of physics give us control over our environment.

To master the game of strange attractors we need to grasp how our body communicates to our conscious minds. Sigmund Freud (1856-1939) provided the foundation for this understanding. We will explore some of the workings of the unconscious mind in the next chapter. We also need to appreciate the creative imagination. In later chapters, Carl Jung (1875-1961), contemporary psychiatrist W.R. Bion, and a chronicler of the imaginal realm, Mary Watkins, will be our guides in learning how to focus our imagination. The focused imagination is the strange attractor of consciousness.

# CHAPTER FOUR

# Transcendence and Dynamism

## Big Mind, Little Mind, Beginner's Mind

The Eastern tradition of psychological thought bears marked similarities with Freudian ideas about the unconscious and, more generally with thought that goes beyond narrow Cartesian limits. The concepts of Zen Buddhism, in particular, are very congenial to post-modernist thought and therapeutic practice. John Welwood provides a concise statement of some key Buddhist insights. What follows draws heavily from his article "Psychotherapy as a Practice of Love" (1988).

In Buddhism the words for "heart" and "mind" are one and the same (*citta* in Sanskrit). When Asian Buddhists refer to mind, in fact, they point to their chest. Mind in this sense is not thinking mind, but rather a larger quality of presence and awareness that is intrinsically open to the world. The mind that is one with the heart is a larger presence of being that responds to the world in a wide-open way. Centuries of meditators have found that this big mind, this openness to what is, is much more central to human nature than the thinking mind, which Western philosophers such as Aristotle used to define as the "rational animal."

Big mind is the larger, formless ground of awareness that is prior to the "small mind" of conceptual thinking. Before we can even think about something, we first have to let it into awareness, let it touch or affect us in some way. We tend to overlook this spacious awareness precisely because it is formless (in Buddhist terms, "void" or "empty"), and thought can only grasp and remember what has form. Yet we can sometimes touch big mind in the silent spaces between thoughts, or when a powerful experience suddenly stops thought and we find ourselves for a brief moment wordlessly facing what is. When we respond to things from this open, non-conceptual awareness, rather than from our ideas about things, a full encounter and exchange with reality becomes possible.

We could define "heart" as that "part" of us that makes such an exchange possible. Heart is present in those moments, however fleeting, of complete connectedness, when we reach out to touch some aspect of reality and feel touched by it as well. Heart in the Eastern traditions is nothing sentimental. It refers instead to our capacity to let reality into us, as well as to reach out and make direct contact with what is. Our language expresses this twofold activity. We say, "My heart went out to him," or "I took her into my heart." Just as the physical organ with its systole/diastole, the heart/mind involves both receptive letting in and active flowing out. We touch the depth of our humanness when we experience an unconditional quality of love that arises from the heart and expresses itself in these two movements: letting be and being-with. Welwood quotes Freud as saying that "psychoanalysis is essentially a cure through love." He also relates how,

> When I studied Rogerian therapy in graduate school, I was intrigued, awed, and puzzled by the term, "unconditional positive regard," which Rogers stated should always be the therapist's underlying attitude toward the client. It sounded appealing, but was hard to embody in practice, because there was no specific training for it. Moreover, since Western psychology had not provided me with any understanding of intrinsic healthiness or goodness underlying pathology, I was unclear just where unconditional positive regard should be directed. It was only in turning to the Eastern traditions that I came to understand the nature of a human being's intrinsic healthiness, which helped me understand the role of unconditional friendliness in the healing process (p. 5).

The Buddhist counterpart of unconditional positive regard is the experience of *maitri*, which is an unconditional friendliness toward our very being. *Maitri* develops gradually but very concretely through the practice of sitting meditation, where you can contact and come to know your own inherent goodness underneath all your confused, neurotic patterns.

In the practice of mindfulness meditation, you just sit and be in the moment, without doing anything, without holding onto anything, without trying to concentrate on a mantra, think good thoughts, or even get rid of thoughts. You let your thoughts and emotions come and go, and you learn to be with yourself, without any other project, while using the breath as an anchor to bring the attention back to the present moment. This is quite a radical practice. There is nothing else like it. Normally we do everything we can to avoid just being. When we are left alone with ourselves, without a project to occupy us, we usually get nervous. We start judging ourselves or thinking about what we should be doing. We find ourselves putting conditions on ourselves, trying to arrange our thoughts to satisfy the inner critic. This is quite painful, so we usually reach for something to distract us from the turmoil of our mind.

In meditation practice, you work directly with your confused thoughts. You let them come up and pass through you, and you come back to the breath, which is a literal expression of well-being even in the midst of the most upsetting states of mind. Through this practice, you can begin to realize that being alive is quite wholesome, despite all the turbulence and confusion of your thoughts and feelings. You realize that you have a basic well-being that is not conditional upon doing something good or being good in any particular way. Your intrinsic sanity self-exists no matter what you do. You are basically good for no other reason than that you are awake, responsive, and open to life. In contacting this sense of basic goodness, you are beginning to develop *maitri* toward yourself.

Welwood goes on to describe how he is able to maintain unconditional positive regard towards the being, or big mind, of his clients even while not liking the way they are behaving in their little minds. He says,

> The hardest step in any healing process is to make contact with what is really happening inside a person. The busy thinking mind—in both the therapist and the client—continually interferes with the direct perception of what is. In order to sidestep this busy mind, with its habitual thought/reaction patterns, we must cultivate a beginner's mind that makes no assumptions about what is happening.
>
> Beginner's mind is a willingness to face what is without holding on to any concept about it. As a powerful state of presence that cuts through old prejudices and beliefs, it allows us to perceive things freshly and find new directions. When we can discern what is and bring our full presence to bear on it, the way forward often becomes clear. (pp. 2-7).

Heart and Big Mind, as Welwood describes them, are very similar to heart, body, unconscious. and the Other, as they are described in this book. Little Mind corresponds to the ego. Beginner's mind is the therapeutic attitude suggested by Rogers and corresponds to the phenomenological attitude of categorical attention. It is a highly developed form of endo awareness. It is also what Lacan describes as: the Other of the analyst attending to the Other of the analysand. It approximates what Freud calls "even-hovering attention." W. R. Bion's phrase for this mindset, which we will discuss later is: Faith in the emotional truth of the moment. He abbreviated this phrase in the formula: F in 0.

**Alternating Current: Change Is Constant**

Everything changes. Heraclitus (c. 500 BC) said it best, "Nobody puts his foot in the same river twice." The water that washes one's foot this time is not the water that washed it last time because the former water is already down stream.

From today's biology we know a twist on that truth, "No river can wash the same body twice" because the cells of our bodies are dying constantly and are constantly being born from the food and oxygen that we ingest. The body that washes this time is not the same body that washed last time.

This dying and re-borning has been called the biodance. Most cells of our bodies turn over at least once within seven years. Every seven years we consist of entirely new material. Every five days we replace our stomach lining. We somehow remain the same even though the elements that are now us were not even alive six years ago.

The physical world dances even faster than the biological one. Its cosmic dance is an instant shuffle. In deep space matter and anti-matter switch places over and over again in nanoseconds, billionths of seconds, no time at all. At the foundation of our world, as revealed by quantum physics, matter and energy are indistinguishable. The paradoxes of the quanta are fabled and almost unbelievable. They have often been recounted.

Ervin Schrödinger, for example, proposed a famous thought experiment in which a cat was placed in a box in such a way that its life depended on the results of a quantum physics experiment. The experiment is run in which light is shone on a delicate receptor. The result was that the cat was both alive and dead. If the experiment was interpreted as a wave equation, the cat lived. If it was interpreted as a particle equation, the cat died. Whenever the door was unlocked using the key of wave mechanics, the cat was alive and well. Whenever the same door was unlocked using the key of particle (matrix) mechanics the cat was dead. In whatever key sequences the door was opened the same result occurred. The cat was both alive and dead. Its life depended not on the experiment, but on how the experiment was interpreted.

The contradictions of quantum physics are our contradictions because we are the same hologram. Heisenberg's indeterminacy principle applies to us as well as quanta. We disturb our nature by the questions we ask of ourselves. In the language of phenomenology, we co-constitute our answers by the questions we ask.

Jean Paul Sartre pointed this out in *Literary and Philosophical Essays*, 1955, when he had a young Frenchman ask the question whether he should assassinate Hitler. The priest told him, "Thou shalt not kill." The resistance leader said, "Kill him." The young man could not rely on any outside authority; he had to rely on his own resources, had to be an *ubermensch*. Who he questioned determined his answer.

The same holds for us. Are we material? Are we immaterial? Ask a scientist. Ask a priest. Like the quanta we're both wave and particle. Like Schrödinger's cat we're both alive in the box and we're not. We're individuals and simultaneously we're universal. Schrödinger's cat fits perfectly into the chaotic Mandlebrot set (the equation and geometry of the gingerbread man) that we are. The nuttiness of quanta makes a kind of sense when it is seen in our not two/not one context.

Adjectives for our world are evanescent, fleeting, ephemeral, and insubstantial. Their antonyms also apply. Our world is permanent, stable, lasting, and substantial. Every moment everything changes and remains the same. Nietzsche expressed this truth as the eternal return of the same. By this he expressed that Becoming (life, growth) keeps on revealing itself in our world.

Our world goes out of existence every moment and reconstitutes itself anew. At the sub-atomic level electrons and positrons do their cosmic dance. We can attend to the same dance in our consciousness if we still ourselves. Zen produces some striking descriptive statements of this. S. Suzuki (1970) says, "Everyone comes out from nothingness moment after moment." (p.109) Yet we experience stability. We even write books purporting to state enduring truths about this flickering, alternating-current world. Philosophy, psychology, and natural science make no sense without the assumption of continuity and sameness.

Our understanding of our flickering, alternating-current, stable existence is enhanced if we place it within the not two/not one context of our being-in-the-world. Our very existence is a logical contradiction. Our experience of change/sameness is consistent with that.

**The Sun Within: Implosion at Our Core**

The Sun is a chaotic place heaving with nuclear gases and the transmogrification of hydrogen into helium, with matter and antimatter thunder-clapping in an out of existence, instantaneously, insistently, constantly: Nuclear fusion, implosion, collision of opposites. At the same time, the sun gives warmth and light, makes water and rain possible, sets the stage for life, nurtures plants, animals, and us. Its chaos makes possible our own.

Our heart, our sun within, is the symbolic, essential, sensitive center of our bodies. As bodies we integrate and disintegrate constantly in the biodance. Parts of us die constantly while we create new parts out of the earth. We are our material world and we're not. Our bodies constantly enter and exit existence. We are an alternating current of contradictions, embodiments of logical/existential implosion, sites of chaos in which anything is possible.

Our experience is a contradiction in the abstract world of formal logic. Logic exorcises contradictions with one of its first rules:

$$-(a \cdot -a).$$

That is, it is not allowed that a statement and its contradiction both be true at the same time and in the same sense. Our experience makes logic a liar on the level of concrete reality. Insisting on logic in this case is a profoundly dishonest enterprise. As Lacan puts it, "The radical heteronomy [division or chasm] that Freud's discovery shows gaping within man can never again be covered over without whatever is used to hide it being profoundly dishonest" (1977, p. 172).

In life, contradictions bring about fruitful chaos. Combine a sperm and an egg to generate new life. Combine the One and the Many to generate humanity; the evanescent and the permanent to get the temporal; the discrete and the continuous to get quanta. Combining forward moving electrons with backward moving ones produces alternating current. Experiencing simultaneous division/union makes us individuals. The confluence of opposites in us implodes into life.

Merleau-Ponty, in his own inimitable style, discovered the existence of this Freudian "heteronomy" within the body itself in what he calls the chiasm ("crossing over") between its sensing and sensible modes. He said that, "the undivided flesh of the sensible [the body before awareness of itself] differentiates itself and articulates itself in the sensing-sensible chiasm" (Madison, 1981, p. 231). That is, the human body splits itself into subject and object, becoming both One and Many.

The nuclear fusion in our bodies is our inner sun. It vitalizes us. It provides warm flesh, shadowy light, and living water. It prompts us to explore and appropriate the polarities of our human constitution. Even more, it propels us to complete the very self-transcendence of Being that we are. In the words of Merleau-Ponty, "Transcendence no longer hangs over man: he becomes strangely, its privileged bearer" (in Madison, p. 235).

The world evolves in consciousness through human activity. Body (animal) awareness begins the process. Madison stated it this way:

> Bodily or carnal existence is nothing other than a first articulation assumed by Being in its exploding, and it is thus a power of natural expression because it is Being itself expressing and articulating itself (the definition of the flesh, of man, is the definition, the logos, of Being itself) (p. 257).

The outer sun warms our planet, gives it light, makes water and rain possible, generates life, and encourages civilization. The sun within does the same. The fusion of hydrogen into helium creates the sun and makes possible everything that we are. The implosion of One/Many, evanescent/lasting, discrete/continuous, infinitesimal/infinite creates our personal universe as walking contradictions, as both ciphers and masters of the universe.

The traditional word that expresses our body as a whole and as its essence is the heart. The heart is the locus of confluence of our constitutional contradictions. It is our dark, wet, metaphysical cauldron. From its bubbling depths we arise and face our world.

# CHAPTER FIVE

## Am I God?

I am a body.

I am not two/not one with the universe.

I am a creative, chaotic, metaphysical contradiction as is the universe.

The universe and I and everybody else are the same hologram.

I am the creative force of the universe, especially in my microcosm where my body and environment provide the material limits that creativity requires.

I am free to do and be whatever I will

According to the laws of chaos, I attract a uniquely beautiful constellation into my microcosm and also fit exquisitely into the overall design.

With attention, imagination, effort, and body wisdom, I co-create myself.

In free association with other bodies, I continue designing and producing the universe.

So I am God, - and I'm not.


In later chapters these ideas will be developed more fully.

# PART TWO

# APPROACHES TO THE WORLD, OURSELVES, AND THIS STUDY

## Part 2 examines how we see the world/self relation and how we study it

Chapter 6 explores the world/self relationship

Chapter 7 outlines how we study it.

Chapter 8 examines how our personal orientation affects our thinking, learning, and remembering.

# CHAPTER SIX

# How We See the World and Ourselves

**Three Perspectives**

[This introduction to the ecto, meso, and endo outlooks on the world is derived from *The Ecology of the Body* by Joseph Lyons (1987)]

Have you ever wondered about the pyramid on the one dollar bill, the one with the big eye atop it? That eye has an unobstructed 360 degree view of all four sides and directions. The Freemasons who designed our currency were impressed with that.

This book is about viewpoints and their associated visions. The eye atop the pyramid represents the detached ego gazing dispassionately at reality. This unblinking eye has the perfect vantage point for visualizing objective science. Its viewpoint, which we call "ecto," is the origin and strength of Western theoretic science. This point of view is often called the Cartesian one because Rene Descartes made it his starting point.

The second viewpoint is not so dry and detached. It is in our moist eye sockets. This viewpoint, called the "meso," is wired into our bodies and tied to practical activity. From there, we focus on the push and pull of life. This viewpoint received the resolute attention of Merleau-Ponty when he probed the *Phenomenology of Perception*, which was first published in 1945.

The third viewpoint, called the "endo," is less familiar to us. It is found in our hearts at the dark, vibrant, self/world border of our existence. This deep endo position is immersed in life and its subterranean currents. Visions from here appear in intuitions, feelings, and dreams. Merleau-Ponty probed this kind of knowing in works like *Eye and Mind*, written in 1961, and *The Visible and the Invisible*, published posthumously in 1964.

The ecto view is arid, farsighted, theoretical, and detached from living reality. The meso is sweaty, near-sighted, practical, and harnessed to our bodily adventures. The endo is dark, intuitive, and immersed in living.

We are so accustomed to the ecto viewpoint which was drummed into us at school that we might not suspect that there are other ones. There are. On the practical level athletes, artists, mothers, and babies face their worlds from meso and endo positions. None of us face our everyday lives from a purely ecto position because we have to be involved to be alive. In our everyday lives, we need to be wired into our bodies; detached observation does not work. Even physicists cannot observe an electron from an ecto viewpoint because their every effort to observe results in a distortion of the electron's reality.

On the theoretical level, Eastern thought has never limited itself to an ecto viewpoint. Zen Buddhists, who calmly focus on the content of their perception as they dare to just sit, do not discover themselves as detached souls. Instead they experience little mind and big mind as their consciousness naturally expands and contracts. They know themselves in relationship to this big mind to be not two. Furthermore, they recognize their relationship to other people to be not two also. Big mind is the formless ground of awareness. John Welwood (1988) points out, "We tend to overlook this spacious awareness precisely because it is formless, ...and thought can only grasp and remember what has form." (p.2) Such descriptions parallel closely descriptions of Being by Merleau-Ponty, such as in this summary by Madison (1981): "Consciousness is always consciousness of something, of an object, and thus it cannot see the unitary fabric, the flesh, from which stem both consciousness and its objects" (p.194).

Phenomenologists in the 20th century mounted a concerted attack on the exclusive Cartesian (detached observer) viewpoint. They describe the pre-reflective content of perception, what we perceive prior to the mental actions of classifying, correcting, and distorting. They do not often find a Cartesian self. Instead, they find a self that expands and contracts, that both merges with the world and separates from it.

It is time to declare that we are aware from our hearts, our eye sockets, and from the top of our mental pyramid. A unified perspective for these three distinct styles of knowing is not to be gained from the top of the pyramid; it is to be found within—at the heart. Once we position ourselves there, we possess an unobstructed view of our inner workings and of the underlying structures of our experience.

The beauty of the heart vantage point is its all-inclusive view of all our endo, meso, and ecto realities. Trying to describe life from there, however, is not easy. Establishing what this standpoint is, and how we see from it, is hard to do because the heart locale is inaccessible to unaided meso and ecto enquiry. This inaccessibility naturally raises suspicions about reliability and deception. Nevertheless the view is enthralling.

How should a person express this endo vision? We could just talk about what we see as we do in categorical descriptions, free association, and authentic speech generally. We could fashion explanations of those endo experiences by describing their underlying structures. We could express the view in inspired language and poetry. The answer for me is a disciplined description of perceived structures following the norms of human science. This approach provides an ecto/meso explanation for endo realities.

Of central importance to this explanation is an understanding of personal space, its limits, and its defenses. We begin examining these concepts in the next section.

**I-Feelings and Boundaries Part One**

Lacan uses the word "Subject" in a linguistic sense. In this sense, its signification slides so that sometimes it means just the ego, sometimes just the unconscious as Other. The "Other" is a pre-conscious state of transpersonal knowing. It is the ground out of which we constitute our individual egos. A similar ambiguity surrounds the term "I-feeling" as it is used by phenomenological psychologists. I-feeling, on analysis, is seen to be a linking of the subject "I" with its affective condition, "feeling." I-feeling is the sense I have of who I am at any particular moment. It is what Kohut calls the "self".

We have already glanced at the world of the infant whose I-feeling is global and whose ego-boundaries are but faintly defined. Michael Eigen (1986) sums up the evidence by saying, "The infant seems both separate and permeable from the outset" (p.151). We might wonder how our boundary relationship with the world changes as we mature and become individuals.

Reflection on our adult experience of I-feeling and boundaries shows our I-feeling as expanding and contracting and our boundaries being sometimes porous and sometimes impermeable. At times, nothing is outside our I-feeling; at other times, even our body is outside of it. My body and my world are then both me and not me. This observation again tells us that we are not two/not one with the universe and everything around us.

We used to state as self-obvious common sense that two objects cannot be in the same place at the same time. This is, of course, true of the solid objects of daily experience, but it is questionable at other levels of consideration. We might contend that this common-sense principle still holds in the case of two hydrogen atoms and one of oxygen because we picture them in a certain spatial configuration. At the level of subatomic particles, however, where matter and antimatter switch places every nanosecond, common sense leads us to say that those two things are in the same place at the same time. Human time, after all, is sequential experience. At any one time that we experience, there are many subatomic particles in the same place at the same time.

In our daily lives, we commonly experience two or more things in our consciousness at the same time. For example, I might be simultaneously experiencing a keyboard, a screen, a chair, some words, and various competing ideas. When I say that someone is "getting into my space," I am saying that I do not have control over the contents of my consciousness. At other times, I welcome people into my space to commune with them. I control the content of my consciousness by constructing and regulating my boundaries.

Having good boundaries is important. Many of us, especially those of us who are processing our childhood traumas, find ourselves invaded by outside influences and without protection from them. We usually picture this protection as a wall, fence, cushion, membrane, or skin. Early trauma has left us with inadequate skin and we experience a montage of influences, compulsions, moods, even selves within us that constantly shift as people move into and out of our lives. In the extreme, this lack of skin results in schizophrenia with its rampant hallucinations, mindlessness, reversals, flaming resentment, and inability to practically sort out reality from fantasy. The presence and integrity of personal boundaries has therefore become a litmus test for insanity.

We as a society have a phobia about insanity. We are encouraged in oh so many ways to have solid boundaries. As a result, many of us develop rigid, billiard-ball-like boundaries in order to survive in a dog-eat-dog world. On the other hand, we are urged to be open with the ones we love. Conceptually, imaginally, and symbolically the ideas of boundaries and openness are in conflict.

It is hard for us to conceive boundaries that expand and contract to fit the fluctuations of our I-feeling. It is easier for us to imagine rather rigid ones with a self imprisoned inside them, which we have proceeded to do. Such a simple mistake causes us severe personal and theoretical difficulties. Boundaries are ego defenses which have a somewhat problematic existence because our I-feelings often transcend our egos.

Understanding ourselves as not two/not one, and as other/ego provides a context for understanding boundaries in two ways. They are the present limits of our I-feeling where we come into practical contact with the external world. They are also the practical shields that we sometimes take up as protection to make practical living possible. We open our boundaries to obtain results and intimacy and close them when we need privacy.

Clinical descriptions confirm that our boundaries are not fixed. Michael Eigen in *Psychotic Styles* (1986) describes our fluctuating boundaries as follows: "In normal circumstances, our I-feeling waxes and wanes....In physical illness, I-feeling may contract to exclude the body. In health on a sunny day after a swim, it may include not only the body, but the entire universe as well" (p.143). With approval he states Federn's conclusion that:

> Primordial I-feeling drenches the entire cosmos. Everything is invested or imbued with I-feeling. Original I-feeling is infinite. ...[then] the everywhereness of I- feeling comes up against the hard facts of life. ...[then] a smaller I, more successful in material terms, becomes dominant. But a nostalgia for boundlessness lingers...We live through the tension of our larger and smaller I (pp.144-145).

Later, in his own words, Eigen states:

> Our experience would not be what it is without the double sense of materiality-immateriality. It is part of what gives our

> experience its resonance, depth, and elusiveness. We move in and out of ourselves as if we were air, yet we also meet with resistance. Our thoughts are at once clouds and stones. Our flesh melts, but our muscles hold their ground. We are one, two, three,...infinity. Our mysterious I-feeling spreads through earth and heaven. For Freud it comes from the body, for Federn it moves toward the body. Where is its point of origin? We grow and fade in the mystery of doubleness (p.147).

And,

> The mystery of doubleness is nowhere more intensely encountered than in our sense of self and other. We feel both connected with, yet separate from ourselves and others. In mystical communion (co-union), the self feels wholly in union, yet distinct at the same time. At deep levels of our being, we feel part of others and others part of us, yet we also maintain areas of difference. We may swing back and forth, now emphasizing the dimension of union, now that of difference, whereas the two belong together and make each other possible. Distinction-union appears to be a constitutive structure of our beings. Take away either and the self would disappear (p.147).

Finally,

> The psychotic individual seems to approach zero or infinity by trying to separate union-distinction. The psychotic self may approximate moments of absolute fusion and/or isolation. In either case, the psychological structure breaks down or becomes grotesquely distorted. The individual lives in a swamp or vacuum (p.148).

Thus, clinical observation confirms the conclusions of Merleau-Ponty, the phenomenologists in general, the Zen masters, and also the experience of mothers, poets, and athletes throughout the ages: We are both separate from other people and, yet, one with them.

Phenomenology provides a method for further understanding boundaries and their relation to the ecto, meso, and endo styles of living. In the next chapter, we will explore how that method works.

# CHAPTER SEVEN

# Methods of Study

**Phenomenology**

*Phainomenon* is a Greek word that means the appearance of something. It is contrasted with *noumenon* which is the word for the essence of a thing. The quest of Western philosophy until this century was to get to the essences of things and to think logically about them. The Platonic world of *noumena*, the eternal essences of things, was, in some shape or form, taken for granted. The phenomena, the appearances, were not considered reliable; the essences were the stuff of serious thought.

Edmund Husserl, at the turn of the 20th century, began to change all that. He proposed to study perceptions as they appeared to us, as phenomena. With his new science of phenomenology he hoped to overcome the subject-object dichotomy that located the thinker in an immaterial mental box and treated objective reality as alien material stuff. He observed a very simple fact: Our perceptions never appear without some content; they always point out or intend something. He proposed that this intentionality was basic to our experience. Therefore, all philosophical thinking has to start from that experience and focus on it. As a result, the mind-reality dichotomy is bogus.

All of philosophy, in his view, required rethinking. In this rethinking one is required to pay minute attention to the content of his or her experience, to both its objective and subjective elements. This content is primary to any theoretic formulation, and supersedes theory when there is a conflict. Philosophy is stood on its head. In phenomenology lowly phenomena are trusted while abstract essences are suspect.

Martin Heidegger in 1927 generalized this insight to the whole self-world relation when he described consciousness as being-in-the-world. With this phrase, he indicated that we are not isolated atoms of existence but beings irredeemably enmeshed in the world. His formulation gave depth to the observations of both Gestalt psychology and systems theory: we are always part of a field and do not exist without it.

Maurice Merleau-Ponty, as we have seen, delved deeper into this relationship. He described how we are the expression of Being itself through our bodies. In our bodily activity, art, and language, we are simultaneously the expression of Being and its creator in space and time. The works of Husserl, Heidegger, and Merleau-Ponty express the high points of phenomenology as a philosophy of knowledge.

Phenomenology is, however, much more than a philosophy of knowledge. It is also a general philosophy, a first cousin of Existentialism as it is seen in the work of Jaspers, Heidegger, and Sartre. It is also a preferred method for psychology and an attitude adopted in scientific and therapeutic situations.

As a psychological method, phenomenology owes its roots to W. Dilthey who in 1894, pointed out that the methods of objective science "are not suited to psychology" (quoted by van den Berg, 1972, p. 126). He initiated the development of phenomenological psychology. Karl Jaspers developed these thoughts and urged a method of describing what we see by introspection as the one suitable for psychology. Introspection remains an important part of the phenomenological method, but its method has been refined to emphasize first impressions. Introspective statements, made after a reflection which has fit observations into one's reality system, are relegated to secondary importance.

Binswanger in 1923 used a distinction made by Edmund Husserl in 1900 between "objective" and "categorical" realities to create this refinement. In the words of van den Berg (1972):

> The objective (better generally valid) perception is the perception of the "closer investigation," the perception of the physicist and physiologist. The categorical perception, on the other hand, is the perception as it takes place in everyday life. In categorical perception, there is no gap between man and world; the world is human nature's dwelling place, and the dwelling place of nature's peculiarities (p.129).

Binswanger held that phenomenology originates from the categorical perception and not from precise introspection. Since his time, the meaning of phenomenology has become the "elucidation of prereflective existence" (van den Berg, p. 130). He advocated the paradoxical truth that we find out about ourselves by looking outward instead of inward. As van den Berg expresses it, "True introspection is effected by means of the physical sense of sight; we are seeing ourselves when we observe the world—in which sentence the words 'seeing' and 'observe' are concerned with categorical and not objective thought" (p.130).

As an overly simple example, consider the situation of a man who categorically describes the scenery as "just like any other day" while other people are flying kites and tossing Frisbees on a gorgeous day in spring. That man is describing his restricted, depressed inner state. On reflection, that is, as an objective observation, he might be able to describe a pretty day to us. His categorical description tells us about him, while his objective one is filtered through his reality-testing and conventionalized-ego thought mechanisms.

Phenomenology, as an attitude of inquiry, ties into the idea of phenomenology as a method. Using it as a therapeutic method, one pays attention to the sound and demeanor of the client, how he or she relates to time, space, the world around him or her, other people, and himself or herself. By accurately describing these things, one comes to an analysis of how the client is put together. In more general psychological inquiry, one pays attention to the same things: always interested in the categorical experience, honoring it, and shaping concepts to experienced reality. One does not curtail reality to fit pre-established concepts.

Much of philosophy and science mimics the activity of the mythical Greek innkeeper, Procrustes. He was both a good host and an awful one. As good innkeeper, he offered hospitality to every traveler, never turning anyone away. As awful host, he had only one bed in his inn, and "one size fits all." He made the bed fit by stretching his shorter guests and by lopping off the legs of the taller ones. In a similar way, philosophers and scientists are prone to making reality conform to their pre-conceived concepts and methods.

Phenomenologists disdain the use of a "Procrustean bed." They try to let the material under observation prescribe the method for describing it. Merleau-Ponty (1962) described phenomenology in the following terms:

> The whole universe of science is built upon the world as directly experienced, and if we want to subject science itself to rigorous scrutiny and arrive at a precise assessment of its meaning and scope, we must begin by reawakening the basic experience of the world of which science is the second-order expression. Science has not and never will have, by its nature, the same significance as a form of being as the world which we perceive, for the simple reason that it is a rationale or explanation of that world ...To return to things themselves is to return to that world which precedes knowledge, of which knowledge always speaks, and in relation to which every scientific schematization is an abstract and derivative sign-language, as is geography in relation to the countryside in which we have learnt beforehand what a forest, a prairie or a river is.
>
> It is because we are through and through compounded of relationships with the world that for us the only way to become aware of the fact is to suspend the resultant activity. ...Reflection does not withdraw from the world towards the unity of consciousness as the world's basis; it steps back to watch the forms of transcendence fly up like sparks from a fire; it slackens the intentional threads which attach us to the world and thus brings them to our notice; it alone is consciousness of the world because it reveals that world as strange and paradoxical (pp. viii - xiii).

In short, Merleau-Ponty endorses a spirit of "wonder" in the face of the world. (In Zen this is called beginner's mind.)

An American phenomenologist, Ernest Keen (1975), essayed a description of his field in this way:

> The goal of phenomenological psychology is to reveal—for our explicit understanding—ourselves to ourselves. We must do that by observing ourselves and one another. Such observation, of self and others, may be taken roughly to correspond to introspective and behavioral methodologies respectively. Phenomenological work is limited to neither of these two but presupposes both, depends on them, and uses them. Beyond observing ourselves and others, phenomenological work involves disciplined reflection upon our own observation. Naturally, good scientists have always reflected, but it has never become a method with a goal of its own, questions of its

own, answers of its own, and an orderly procedure for moving from one to the other.
More particularly, the goal of phenomenological psychology is to reveal for our explicit understanding those things we already implicitly understand (p.130).

In this book, the phenomenology of perception and knowledge, as developed by Merleau-Ponty, is accepted and built upon. It is accepted that we are beings-in-the-world. The attitude and approach taken is phenomenological, although it does not pretend to be exhaustive. Instead, the work of others is reported and strung into an overall vision of how we actually exist as living bodies in our material, mental, spiritual, and transpersonal dimensions.

Of particular relevance to the subject of this chapter (the ecto, meso, and endo styles of functioning) is a statement by Joseph Lyons (1987). He proposed that: "Phenomenological philosophy, insofar as it is basic and introductory to all the sciences (as Husserl boldly claimed in 1910), is an attempt by way of meso style to undercut the dominance of ecto-style thinking in science" (p. 35). Until Lyons created full-blown descriptions of endo, meso, and ecto intelligence it was difficult to distinguish the endo and meso modes.

For example, introspection is not necessarily an endo exercise. We can observe feelings from ecto and meso viewpoints. We describe them from an ecto viewpoint when we have already conceptualized a proper response to a situation. For instance, in the midst of a heated argument we might state, "I'm not angry." We describe our feeling from a meso viewpoint when one of us says, "I want to kill you." In the endo mode, the statement might be, "I feel it in the pit of my stomach." The ecto statement is made from a head detached from experience. The meso statement is made from a head attached to an active body. The endo statement is simply in tune with the body.

Endo statements of introspection come from the heart. They have both authenticity and incompleteness. They are authentic in that they derive from our inner feelings and intimations. They are incomplete in that they never encompass all that we have to say. They are explicit statements about implicit, unconscious feelings. Merleau-Ponty calls this originating speech. In the words of Madison (1981),

> Beneath constituted speech, which only functions as the vehicle for already discovered thoughts, there is an "operative" or "originating" speech, which is precisely the coming to light of thoughts in search of themselves. New ideas are born and become fully conscious of themselves only by "speaking themselves out"; before being expressed they are only a vague feeling of dubious value (p. 58).

Most of phenomenological study deals with meso reality. It describes our mutuality with other people and things, how we experience them, how they experience us, and how we feel about our interaction. Such study makes explicit what is going on in our meso experience; by indirection it shows what is going on within us.

In this book I try to make clear what is going on in our endo experience. Our hearts and their comprehended objects do not have hard boundaries. They know each other by communing. In Lacanian terminology, heart language is Subject to Subject, and so bears the possibility of the Other in me communing with the Other in you. How can one talk about such things in a disciplined, scientific manner?

The scientific method for doing phenomenology is specified by the discipline of human science. Next, we will start spelling out the specific methodology employed in this book.

**Methodology Part One**

There are several considerations about method which need to be spelled out. One concerns the methods used in composing this book. A second is the paradigm, or point of view, from which this book's observations are made. A third is the procedure used to clarify the meaning of endo awareness. A fourth answers the questions: "How do we know what the unconscious is saying?", "How do we attend to it?", and "How can we express and utilize its messages?" A fifth methodical consideration regards how this book will, in its final section, use conclusions drawn from endo awareness to explain things such as visions, empathy, time, space, language, death, and the geography of human imaginal existence.

The present chapter deals with the way this book was put together, with its paradigm, and the way its ideas are presented. The methods for attending to the unconscious and explaining paranormal and universal reality are saved for a later chapter.

Carl Jung is reported as saying, "All psychology is autobiographical." In stating my standpoint, I recognize the validity of his remark. As a result of a less than perfect childhood with loving and "optimally failing parents" (Kohut, 1977, p. 179), I possess(ed) modest schizoid and borderline traits. The schizoid ones are tendencies to withdraw into myself and be out of contact with vital reality, which tendencies I have satisfied with spiritual and religious striving. The borderline traits manifested as not having a vital self of my own. As a result, I sought to identify with other people's lives in order to feel alive.

In addition, I had a stubborn streak of individuality and was determined to be my own man. My way to that was the path of intense intellectualization and moral rectitude. Somewhere along the line this intellectualizing saw through itself and recognized values outside of abstract conclusions. I began to trust what I called "Spirit." Through the years, this Spirit became less fettered with dogmatic, organizational, and abstract chains. It came to dwell in me. In fact, the Christian dogma of incarnation, that Jesus was both totally God and totally man, expresses the paradigm of this book about as well as does the Zen phrase: Not two/not one. Nowadays, the rather amorphic terms of Subject, Other, flesh of the universe, personal guidance, and authentic speech, express for me what Spirit did in more dogmatic contexts.

In broad personal terms, then, this book was composed in bits and snatches as it was authentically spoken through me by the Other. I mulled over these images and ideas; tested their reality against my overall perceptions; and organized them into a coherent whole. I did this within an accepted context of unconscious knowledge, logic, and language. In addition, I had an appreciation of the body as a process of conscious evolution; I believed that all knowledge was involved in human emotion and concern; and I experienced reality as not two/not one.

The proximate method of discovery for this book was a series of psychology courses which I enjoyed at West Georgia College. William Roll taught a course on "Zen and Psychology." Mike Arons probed the collective unconscious using Joseph Campbell's, *Power of Myth*. Raymond Moody delved into the history and rationale of visions. Robert Masek imparted an experiential, phenomenological understanding of "Psychotic Styles." Tip Schumrun introduced me to family and systems theory. Richard Alapack introduced me to Lacan. Of primary catalytic importance was a course on "Values and Meaning" taught by James Burrell in which he explored the ramifications of ecto, meso, and endo body types. His text was Joseph Lyons', *The Ecology of the Body*.

In this course every individual in the class endeavored in a structured sequence:

- to define his or her body type in the areas of head, upper trunk, and lower body;
- to give both categorical and objective descriptions of themselves in terms of interests, activities, and modes of operation;
- to discuss their interests, etc. with a group of class members who possessed a similar body type;
- to ferret out similarities.

In this phenomenological investigation, the evidence supporting Dr. Burrell's hypothesis of a link between body types: head→interests, torso→ activities, and lower body→mode of operation was compelling, but not overwhelming.

What grabbed my attention was the Lyons/Burrell attention to three different ways (ecto, meso, and endo) of knowing, learning, remembering, acting, and being in the world. This distinction sorted out and made sense of previously conflicting convictions that I had regarding how we and our world are put together. Thus, this book was conceived and began to grow.

The heuristic used in composing the thoughts of this book is familiar to every author faced with overwhelming complexity of data. First, gather information, opinions, and perspectives from many sources. Then select the material that seems relevant. Sort out the relevant material into groups that cohere. Mull over the material to discover some underlying pattern (F in 0 work). Continue the process until it reaches a tentative closure. Try to describe the pattern from different perspectives. Decide on a perspective and define the pattern of experiences. Fit this pattern into a general system of theory and try it out from different perspectives. Correct it. And so on.

Over a lifetime I have been grappling with the concepts of this book, trying many ideas by living them, trying out combinations of ideas, trying to find the "center of my circle" (Heidegger). Lyons work provided a glimpse of that center.

The paradigm of this book is the vision from the heart, endo awareness, body wisdom, unconscious knowledge, call it what you will. As proposed earlier, the vision from the heart puts into proper perspective not only endo awareness but meso and ecto knowledge as well. The primacy of unconscious knowledge shows the relativity of rational and practical knowledge. It also solves the old western philosophical problem of bridging the gap between the detached observing mind and a physical reality "out there" somewhere.

The body develops the ego by creative identification with its mirrored image, and by developing language. As both subject and object the body creates itself as mind and spirit. As mindful, spiritual bodies we are not two/not one with our universe.

The distinctive phenomenological observations made in this book are made from the heart. The heart is that feeling center in us that responds empathetically to the emotional reality of our situation at any moment. It intuitively grasps the meaning of a situation, and forthrightly engages us in action. The heart is the center of our endo awareness and activity. It is the locus of our highest dignity and individuality.

The heart is the place where we are everything and everything is us, yet we are still individual in the manner of hologram and Mandlebrot set. As bodies, we are not one/not two with the world. Our hearts, as our symbolic and feeling centers, exist at the confluence of the evanescent and the eternal. The unique location of our heart allows us access to both our individual and universal aspects.

How observations are made from the heart center is not easily described. They are dark observations and feelings of rightness. Physical (meso) vision with our eyes will not penetrate to our hearts. Rational (ecto) vision detached from our lived reality is impotent also. Only the heart can experience the heart. The heart is our radiant source of vitality, intelligence, and creativity. It is a radiance dark and warm. We experience it constantly through our endo awareness.

At our heart center our endo awareness is not at one moment in eternity and at the next in evanescence. No. Abstractions such as these are the business of ecto intelligence. Endo awareness presides serenely inside the chaos of our not two/not one temporality. From its identity with our temporality, endo awareness attends at times to its universal situation and at other times to its fleetingness. This process is directed by our attitudes and attention, but its experience is holistic (always awareness-in-the-world) and not discrete in the fashion of ecto intelligence.

The descriptions in this book represent endo observations taken from the heart center which have been formulated with meso and ecto intelligence. The observations regarding endo, meso, and ecto are for the most part derived from Joseph Lyons. They capture (stop) the dynamic flow of experience giving it conscious form and revealing its underlying structures. They are descriptive, structural, endo-generated, and given from the standpoint of the heart.

The theory (vision) presented in this book provides a coherent background which situates our sometimes puzzling experiences. The vision, a composite of observations taken from a central standpoint, enables us to center at that point, our heart. From there we gain a radiant inner comprehension of our lives and a functional understanding of how to employ our endo faculties. The endo awareness that we gain provides us with night goggles to attend to and interpret our hunches, intuitions, and feelings.

The adoption of the heart as observation point and of endo intelligence as night goggles is a choice whose worth is proved or disproved by the quality of the vision. This book professes to offer a coherent and comprehensive theory that describes our experience of being not two/not one, and explains how we function in this specifically human realm. In a later chapter, we will spell out specific ways to test its validity.

This, in short, is the heuristic and paradigmatic method of this book. Beyond these is the need to present endo consciousness in an understandable way.

The first way this is done in this book is the locating of the unconscious subject in the realm of common discourse. It is located in the thought systems of Nietzsche, Heidegger, Merleau-Ponty, Freud, Jung, Lacan, and clinical psychology as exemplified by Kohut and Eigen. This endo awareness is also situated within Zen, Vedanta, New Age, and chaos theory.

In the following pages, endo awareness will be accurately described. It will be contrasted with ecto and meso awareness in a variety of contexts. In this way, the distinctiveness of endo thinking, learning, remembering, etc., will be made evident. This description will facilitate the statement of specific methods for discerning the message of the Other with its structures of communication, and its relevance for understanding transpersonal realities. A later chapter will spell out some of these methods.

**Interviews with Three Me's**

> The endo motto might be: "I'll take whatever I can get." The meso motto is: "Go for it." The ecto motto is: "Let me think about it." (Lyons, p. 45)

Describing my world has always been a baffling task for me. My observations always changed. For instance, I would start saying how I love competition, but I would begin to think that it was pretty stupid. Then I would try to decide when competition was good and when it was bad, and on, and on. Even I got bored with myself.

Recently, with the discovery of Lyon's work, I can describe my world with ease. The trouble is, I am three people: #1 is ecto, #2 is meso, and #3 is endo. Therefore, I interviewed all three people. Here are the results.

*Interview with Me #1, Ecto*

As ecto, I picture myself and my world in Cartesian fashion. I am a thinking box separate from the people and world around me and not quite sure how to connect with them. Accordingly I am distant and aloof. I like people that I can share ideas with who are embodied intellects that have roles in my life. They are recognized as flesh, blood, and emotion only in an abstract manner. They are categorized, studied, and navigated around. I see them as interchangeable and have little commitment to anyone.

In my ecto mode, objects are not appreciated as unique, nor perceived vividly; instead, after their essential natures are determined, they are generally ignored. Things are identified with their names, the more univocal the name, the better.

For the person whose style is predominantly ecto, something is so if it resembles thought. In this mode, expressions that carry values are always suspect, and an emotional coloring to thought or word is a sure sign of its limited value in discourse. (Lyons, p. 99)

My ecto contact with concrete reality is tenuous. I operate on things from a distance; processing information, playing with permutations, looking at things from different perspectives. My world is a world of ideas organized in systems, similar in form to the courses taught in universities, full of computers, push buttons, and fax machines. I plan ahead finessing situations, getting my rewards. I accumulate money, experiences, and knowledge.

In my ecto mode I live in my head and not my body. I talk and read theoretical stuff for hours and hours, curious and absent-minded, collecting knowledge and second-hand experiences. I am always looking for unusual experiences and tend to scatter my attention over many things at once. I feel no identity with my body but I take good care of it (as I do my car and my computer). My own interpersonal feelings are blunted and the feelings of others are objects of curiosity, not empathy. Beauty for me is a drawing done in perspective or the preparation of a gourmet meal, things intricate and geometrical. I set long-term goals and plan how to achieve them. I deliberate, getting everything in line, before acting. Then I move in quick and jerky manner. I am impatient with slow people and slow results.

My mind in ecto mode roams happily over all of the past and all of the future. I revel in rapid change, variety, excitement, and new experiences. I dream far into the future, strong on planning but weak in execution.

*Interview with Me #2, Meso*

As meso, I am a self-contained individual in a world of similar people, taking care of myself with strength and forthrightness and expecting others to do the same. Others are my equals: coworkers and competitors. I like people that I can work with. I use them to get something done and measure myself against them. The possibility that they and I are one does not enter my head.

The meso world is an arena of action. "It is resistive, effortful, conflicting, and hard at work for its own ends, no matter what we do in it or against it—or perhaps just because we are constantly acting in it and against it" (Lyons, p. 101). In this world, the focus is on the job at hand, getting it done. There is little concern for long-range effects such as environmental destruction. Events are forced; broken things are just nuisances.

As meso I am a hands-on accomplisher. As soon as one project is completed, I look for another. I hate ambiguity, faulty tools, impractical procedures, and deferred gratification. I distrust our pushbutton, computer, and at-a-distance work world. I dislike things abstract and mystical. Beauty for me is functional, for example, a machine that works beautifully or a chair that someone can sit on.

In my meso mode I am a doer, a competitor with hard boundaries. I live in my body, but not in the sense of relishing pleasure and avoiding pain. Instead, I use my body to test myself. I climb mountains over and over again loving the rush of excitement and danger, reveling in the feeling of being alive. I move straightforward with force to do a task often getting lost in my work. I am proud of my accomplishments and my ability to get things done. I fume at immovable objects in my path and lack subtlety in dealing with them.

I enjoy talking and reading about sports, mechanics, and adventure. I am baffled by theoretic arguments and disgusted by vapid wallowing in pain and pleasure.

I am not interested in the long ago or the distant future. I live in the present using the recent past to create the near future. I judge the pace of events and adjust my efforts accordingly. I like fast change because it provides challenges, but hate it when I am no longer able to cope with the speed of its overwhelming complexity.

*Interview with Me #3, Endo*

I was most endo as an infant. As endo I am immersed in the world with porous boundaries. I resonate readily to the feelings of others. I have their experiences in natural empathy with them, sensing them to be either safe/familiar or disruptive/weird. The familiar ones are divided into care-givers and care-receivers. In them I value kindness, generosity, and receptiveness. I like people who feel appealing to me.

I am immersed in the world with my boundaries down. I flow in it naturally and with grace, feeling situations as friendly, safe, hostile, depressing, exciting, and so on, sensing the health and feeling of even animals and plants. The singular and peculiar so appeal to me that I can get lost in the contemplation of a leaf.

My home, car, and workplace are extensions of myself and I keep them safe and familiar. I am gentle with my tools and protective of the environment, massaging situations and feeling my way to solutions. I am careful not to destroy the existing balance of situations. I enjoy the process of doing things and appreciate how the result enhances my personal ecology.

In my endo mode I am grounded in my body, sensitive to pain and pleasure, very much in touch with my feelings. Yet I take my body for granted, often not taking care of its nutrition, grooming, and conditioning. I am involved with the people in my life. I am sure that I am not an island and shrink at the idea of being isolated from friends and familiar surroundings. I always see the background even when I put myself in the foreground.

I enjoy the more passive forms of activity, like reading, especially sentimental literature. I get absorbed in feelings of unity with my surroundings. I feel my worth through the approval of friends.

Time goes slowly for me. I live in the traditions of the past, liking the steady routines of work, family, seasons, and traditional holidays. When I act, I move in a flowing, usually slow, manner. I relish doing the old things and want my future to be like my past.

\* \* \*

I am not really three distinct persons, but sometimes I approach being the stereotypes I have just portrayed. I find that I can be intensely ecto and still be moderately meso and endo. When I am intensely ecto and endo, as I am in writing this book, I am minimally meso and have trouble supporting myself. And so on.

The following chapter will sharpen and elaborate our understanding of endo intelligence by contrasting it with our more familiar ecto and meso intelligence.

# CHAPTER EIGHT

## Ecto, Meso, and Endo Modes

**Thinking**

Thinking is different in the endo mode than it is in the meso and ecto. So are the methods of learning and remembering.

*Ecto Thinking*

In our familiar ecto mode of thinking, we start by abstracting from a situation those facts that we consider important. Then we manipulate our abstractions until we accomplish our purpose. In all this thinking we are dissociated from the real world. In familiar classroom experience we solve a word problem in algebra by abstracting the speed of a train and the distance it has to go in order to determine the time needed to take a trip. This kind if thinking is usually described as being linear.

Ecto thinking is based on the familiar Cartesian dichotomy between subject and object. Using ecto thinking, we schematize our world and make rational the jumble of our lives. We locate ourselves in patterns of time, space, and causality. We nimbly play with combinations and permutations of possibilities leaping blithely between future, past, and present.

The "what" of ecto thinking is anything and everything . It varies and reverses from moment to moment having no necessary ties to lived reality; in fact, it functions essentially in the absence of lived reality. Abstractions in general are its "what."

Ecto thinking has its weakness in this same ungrounded flexibility. It does not create the abstractions that it manipulates nor by itself establish truth or falsity, reality or unreality. Its contribution to reality testing is the test of coherence. (Is this statement compatible with other statements that I hold to be true?).

*Meso Thinking*

Meso thinking denies an absolute dichotomy between subject and object. Instead it lives the interdependence between the external world and the thinking body. It is involved with the world in an effort to control the subject's destiny.

We think with our muscles as did Einstein, who felt his mathematical equations in his musculature. We engage reality in emotional, perceptual, and cognitive ways that involve both our muscles and our nerves. We think with our whole bodies.

When we join in a serious discussion, for example, our eyes behave in a definite chaotic way. When we are not very interested our eyes move back and forth in the horizontal plane as if they were spinning randomly on an LP record. When points are striking home we look down, sometimes staying down and moving horizontally on a lower level. Chaos researchers have recorded an analogous pattern in computer-enhanced images of EEG's. When they are mentally challenged, subjects have a rich strange attractor that "looks vaguely like the Starship Enterprise" (Paul Rapp quoted by McAuliffe, 1990, p. 86). When they are bored, "the strange attractor flattens out in one plane, resembling a Frisbee seen from the side" (idem.).

With meso thinking we gain a special type of mastery over our world. We use it to gain peace of mind and to perfect skills. At times we calm ourselves down by stopping to take a few deep breaths. In so doing, we allow our bodies to speak their calming message. We take ourselves from the condition of out-of-control ecto and reground ourselves in our meso (and endo) awareness.

In our efforts to perfect an athletic skill, say bowling or shooting a basket, we find that our (ecto) thinking gets in the way. So we tell ourselves, "Don't think about it, just do it." When we are successful we find a spot of tranquility within ourselves. From this spot we "go with the flow" (Alan Watts).

When we think meso we are not abstracted from our world; we are involved in the push and pull of active living. Some meso thinking is meso-ecto, resulting in some insight that is of use to our ecto thinking.

Some is meso-endo, resulting in a change in our being that is immediately incorporated into our lives. For example, when we learn to dance the gracefulness of our movements becomes part of who we are.

Meso thinking is practical and short-term. Combined with ecto reasoning, it produces practical applications for ecto speculations, giving them focus and power. When combined with endo awareness, meso thought gains intuitive ease, functional beauty, and ecological elegance. Meso thought's contribution to reality testing is the pragmatic one (does it work?). Things are real if they have influence.

*Endo Thinking*

Endo thinking dissolves the subject-object dichotomy. It merges with its surroundings and moves from a perception of contextual awareness of the whole situation. It does not recognize firm boundaries between self and others or self and the world. It is an activity that is largely subconscious or unconscious for us.

When we think in endo mode we are completely involved in some activity that is not characterized as thinking. The thinking is coincidental and usually unobserved. If we are talking to a friend, for example, our mouth and larynx form words; our eyebrows, eyes, and facial expressions accompany the words like an orchestra in a concerto, showing remarkable intelligence and dexterity—evidence of endo thinking.

We do not usually pay attention to such thinking, taking it for granted. On reflection we see how amazingly clever it is. What we know in our bones and innards is our unattended treasure of enlightenment—our body wisdom.

When we think endo we immerse ourselves in a situation and do what comes naturally. We let hallucinatory fragments join with experiences, join with activity, join with ideas in un-self-conscious play. We let ourselves live with something contemplating different angles of it, handling and caressing it, juggling it, sleeping on it. The thought then just grows on us.

Sometimes the result of endo thinking is an explicit thought or theory. The story of Kekule, the chemist, who dreamed of a serpent swallowing its tail during a period when he was struggling to express the atomic structure of benzene, is well known. He was enabled by the endo thinking of his dream to formulate the universally accepted theory of the benzene ring.

Often the result of endo thinking is a growth of general competence and awareness. Examples abound. For instance, I move to a new city. In a matter of weeks, I know places (friendly, hostile, useful, fun), ceremonies (lunch time, quitting time, happy hour, rush hour), people uniquely attractive or repulsive, and so on. All the while, the focus of my attention has just been on doing my job. Furthermore, I find myself moving at ease in situations that once were foreign, giving my activity no conscious thought. This intelligent natural activity is meso and endo thought at work.

Endo thinking gives us personal mastery of familiar situations and activities. By making the routine habitual it frees us to attend to new growth and adventure. Endo thought gives the inspiration for discoveries when combined with ecto thought. Also it generates inventions when combined with meso. By itself endo thought is mystical and impractical because it recognizes no boundaries.

The contribution of endo thinking to reality testing is the feel test. Some things we know in our bones. Situations either feel right or they don't. This feel test works in areas inaccessible to ecto coherence testing because our endo awareness is transpersonal and is vastly more complicated and better informed than our rational elaborations.

There are numerous examples of endo thinking in the writers we are dialoguing with in this book. There are also numerous descriptions of thinking that are rightly to be judged as endo. There are also statements that reveal the proximity of meso and ecto thought.

Nietzsche, for example, in a famous quotation, offered a very meso valuation to thought. "Truth," he says, "is not something that is there to be found and discovered, but something that must be created and can be called a process, or better, a will to conquer which has no end, ...a process ad infinitum. ...It is a word for the 'will to power'" (quoted by Pfeffer, p. 93).

Nietzsche saw in the "will to power," the basic "truth" of life, its affirmation. He valued a style of facing life that loved its randomness. His hero, for this robust lust for life, was Dionysus, the god of exuberant living, dying, and birthing. He proposed as a model:

> A Dionysian Yes-saying to the world as it is, without deduction, exception and selection. ...It is the highest attitude that a philosopher can reach: to stand Dionysiacally toward existence: my formula is *amor fati* (in Pfeffer p. 185).

For Nietzsche, the will to truth was the most spiritual will to power, but the truth he sought was the truth prior to the ego's creation. He looked for a way to "shatter the *principium individuationis* (the ideal of a self-contained individual)." The path to truth that he advocated was intuition. This was his "new road to a 'Yes'...a philosophy which does not negate any more. It wants to achieve the opposite...to say Yes to the world as it is" (in Pfeffer p. 194).

Heidegger followed Nietzsche in this and advocated the thinking style of the Pre-Socratic philosophers who functioned quite well without Socratic and Aristotelian logic. He described the "thinker's thinking" (endo) in this famous quotation.

> Whereas scientific thinking, figuratively speaking, always runs along a line and can continue from the place where it stopped earlier, a thinker's thinking must in advance make a leap into the whole for each step it takes and collect itself in the center of a circle (Heidegger, 1987, p. 12).

Freud described how our unconscious bodies speak to us with their own logic and language in dreams and symptoms. This is proto-logic and proto-language because it is not oppositional in the manner of abstract logic and conscious language.

Lacan expressed this reality by stating that the expressions of our unconscious are "the discourse of the Other"; that is, our dreams, symptoms, etc. express an unconscious knowledge and logic. He remarked, in this regard, on Freud's studies of telepathy. Freud had noted a

> coincidence of the subject's remarks with facts about which he cannot have information, but which are still at work in the connections of another experience in which the same psychoanalyst is the interlocutor... It is a case of resonance in the communicating networks of discourse, an exhaustive study of which would throw light on similar facts presented by everyday life (Lacan, 1977, p. 56).

Lacan speculated that, the omnipresence of human discourse [the continuous communication of both conscious and unconscious mind] will perhaps one day be embraced under the open sky of an omnicommunication of its text. That is, everyone will understand what is being said by both conscious and unconscious language. Lacan fervently desired this "open sky" that gets beyond positing the structure of reality in "merely dual terms." He locates telepathy in the "omnipresence of human discourse." In the terms of this book, he advocated endo awareness and communication.

Merleau-Ponty refers to endo knowing in speaking of the painter's "inspiration":

> We speak of "inspiration," and the word should be taken literally. There really is inspiration and expiration of Being, action and passion so slightly discernible that it becomes impossible to distinguish between what sees and what is seen, what paints and what is painted (Eye and Mind in 1964a, p. 167).

Madison dramatically points out the endo character of Merleau-Ponty's work in the following invitation to study him.

> Let us then return with Merleau-Ponty to the things themselves and to our shadowy life, to that source beneath us full of inexhaustible riches, and let us attempt with him to wrest from it its secret. Let us follow his thought in its constant attempt to awaken a primordial, covered over, and forgotten logos and make the "voices of silence" speak (Madison, 1981, p. xxxii).

A casual reading of the experiences of seminal thinkers such as Descartes, Einstein, Van Gogh, Jung, Yeats, and Nietzsche reveals that their genius was endo.

**Learning**

Learning is a kind of thinking that is less active than creative thinking. In learning we appropriate the attitudes, skills, or knowledge of someone else. Learning is not totally passive, however, boring classroom lectures not withstanding. For centuries, it has been presupposed in many academic circles that knowledge had to be poured into the heads of vertebrate sponges. Sponges learn facts in the ecto mode. People, in addition, can learn in the meso and endo modes.

We use endo skills in learning to love, meso skills in learning to build a house, and ecto skills in learning geography. In learning some skills, say taking photographs, we proceed in all three modes. We start in endo mode, as we feel the mood of a shot before we shoot it. We learn in meso mode, as we rapidly snap pictures of events evolving around us. We act in ecto mode, as we compute light and distance, adjust stops, and engineer perspectives.

*Endo Learning*

Endo learning, like endo thinking, is coincidental with some ongoing activity. As the baby suckles, it learns that it is loved. As a boy tries to be grown-up by copying his father's actions, he internalizes his father's values, skills, and demeanor. As a child mimics its parent's sounds, it learns to talk. Endo learning is rapid and intuitive. As described by Lyons, it is "a period of growth that is immediately buried in the person's ongoing development." It is personal and non-goal directed.

An example of endo learning is provided by forms of animal therapy in which troubled children and teenagers are given the company and care of animals. The troubled youths become more grounded, sociable, and responsible. What they learn is personal and unforgettable, a part of who they are.

I began my life learning in the endo mode, absorbing things and letting them grow within me. I was one with my surroundings, acutely aware, had minimal boundaries and structures of experience. I accomplished very complex personal growth with amazing speed.

Of interest is the way I mimicked the behavior of adults who were smiling at me or sticking out their tongues. I stuck out my tongue, too. The process used was endo: I absorbed the situation and became one with it. Placing myself in their position, I simply performed their act.

*Meso Learning*

Unlike endo learning, meso learning is very goal-directed. Learning this way I am insistently active, straining to know what is almost in my grasp. After achieving success I drill myself so that I won't forget.

When I am learning in the meso mode I am concerned about overcoming some gap in my knowledge that I ought to know or need to know. I chafe at obstacles blocking my vision.

In meso mode, I am a good test taker, especially if the questions have a right and wrong answer, as in programmed learning where I know from question to question how I am doing and gradually accumulate mastery of the material. I like to have my problems broken down into small chunks so that I can solve them one piece at a time. I build my knowledge incrementally.

As infants we learned to talk with meso attentiveness as well as by endo awareness. Lyons (1987) put it this way:

> When there is required of the infant some form of learning rather than simply an appropriate response, as occurs when the stimulus is the speech of older persons rather than their smiling faces, then the infant displays behavior best termed "participative grasping." As films of infants have shown, the baby now goes through a series of quite well defined movements—although they may be seen by observers as mere random thrashings—that keep time to the accented portions of spoken words. It is in this way that one begins, almost from birth, to build into one's body the very sounds and rhythms of one's native language (p. 199).

Lyons notes that the examples we have shown and many others on young infants point to an original, underlying, endo, animal-like intelligence. He cited Arcredolo and Goodwyn's (1985) study, "Symbolic gesturing in language development." These authors, in Lyon's words,

> suggest that there is an underlying, foundational mode of intelligence in humans prior to what is termed the emergence of self toward the end of the first year. It grows out of that mutual interpenetration of movements and feelings, most often engaging mother and child that constitutes much of the behavior of young children. This endo intelligence cannot be dismissed as simply an early phase through which the infant passes on its way to something higher or better, leaving the early style behind as the snake leaves the skin that once served it well. It cannot be defined as the absence [of meso and ecto intelligence] but as the presence of a [different] form of intelligence.

> How and when this endo intelligence forms, and what it contributes to the totality of the child's developing personality, are issues that can hardly be avoided in a comprehensive theory of development. Piaget began such a study, but he chose to begin with what really constitutes a next stage of development, which he termed sensory-motor and which I have called meso (p. 199).

Lyons continues his account of the developmental stages of childhood learning by briefly describing the most active years of meso learning:

> Following the earliest months of life, which constitute an endo burst, the child begins to develop and elaborate forms of motility and physical action. The picture during the second half of the first year as well as the twelve months or so that follow is one of an upsurge of the meso component. The child becomes semi-erect in a sitting position, learns to move volitionally by scooting or crawling and then walking, and becomes occupied, often to the distraction of parents and other adults, with moving, grasping, holding, pulling, handling, whatever can be accomplished motorically vis-à-vis the resistance of the world. In all, it is a meso burst that lasts, in individually varying form and emphasis, for the next three or four years and that will not again be experienced until the years of mid-adolescence. In Piaget's terminology we may say these are the sensory-motor years. In David McNeill's formulation of the language learning process, they are the years during which the child builds upon a primary "functional unity" that links Piagetean sensory-motor schemas with the movements involved in speech (pp. 199-200).

Lyons details the development of ecto intelligence from animal (endo) consciousness through meso consciousness. He solves the mystery of how we come to be what we are. He gives substance and articulation to the phenomenology of perception traced by Merleau-Ponty. He shows how our bodily intelligence creates our language and logic.

Our physical activities are learned in the meso mode. Things learned by ecto or endo processes are also carried in the meso mode; as is revealed when body therapists find knowledge and emotion locked in our musculature.

*Ecto Learning*

When we talk of learning, we almost always mean ecto learning, the kind that we did in school. In thinking this way, we are in accord with traditional academic practice, which considers the term "ecto learning" to be a tautology; it is assumed that all learning is ecto. Such is not the case. As we have seen, there are three learning styles. Lyons notes the following distinctions between these learning styles:

- Ecto learning begins with questions about ideas or concepts. Endo learning begins with a personally felt riddle or problem. Meso learning begins with a goal that is sensed as somewhere ahead (p. 121).
- Our "control of ecto learning is absolutely limitless." In our meso learning, we find the "world is present and resistive to our biologically determined limits." In our endo learning, we "pay a price for control in the necessity to first absorb" whatever we are learning (p. 123).
- The ecto learner has some new knowledge and can lose it, while endo and meso learners "are their new knowledge, for they represent it and have been changed by it to become the persons they now are" (p. 125).

The "ecto learner is so far removed, at least in principle, from the real world of what is encountered and overcome, absorbed and rejected that it is hard for us to conceive of behavior done in ecto style" (Lyons, p. 123). As an ecto learner, I am uninvolved in the living reality of what I study and do not connect to concrete unique reality. Instead, I function with second-hand abstract material, and process it in a detached manner. I often appear to be an absent-minded, uninvolved, ineffectual dreamer. As a result of this detachment, I am slow to catch on to the nuances of interpersonal relations.

In the area of grasping and processing abstractions, however, where there is a distance between myself and reality, I shine as an ecto learner. In my intellectual curiosity, I search out facts that will fit into theories, which can be manipulated into a coherent pattern, which is presumed to be a true picture of the world.

In attending to the different ways that we think and learn, we have developed a clearer idea of how the body knows: by endo processes. In the next section we will specify how the body remembers with endo processes. Once we clearly see how the endo processes work, we will be able to appreciate the body's role in depth communication, empathy, creative imagination, visions, hallucinations, dreams, perception, and language.

**Remembering**

What we usually call memories are the products of ecto remembering, but they have shadings depending somewhat on personality type. Ecto memories can have an endo quality when they are immersed in lush feelings and have lots of atmosphere. Ecto memories with a meso quality are of activities and conflicts. Ecto memories with an ecto quality are of ideas and interconnections. In remembering a childhood experience of riding a bike, for example, endo, meso, and ecto personalities would remember different things. The endo would feel the rush of the wind and the strain in the legs. The meso would recall exploits and races. The ecto would retrace the routes he or she used to take.

In addition to memories of this sort, there are meso and endo rememberings that are of an altogether different nature. They are our next focus of attention.

*Ecto Remembering*

Aristotle described remembering in terms of traces (engrams) of experience imprinted on the mind. This has remained the preferred psychological model for memory till this day. This model is well adapted to ecto modes of thinking because (1) it relies to a minimum extent on contact with lived reality; (2) it is valueless and emotionless; (3) it is neatly filed away; and (4) it is readily accessible to our ecto mind.

When we remember in this Aristotelian (ecto) mode, there is always a gap in time between when we first learned something and when we remember it. When I remember what I ate last night, for instance, I remember now that I had turkey and dressing then. If there is no gap, we do not say that we (ecto) remember.

Remembering nonsense symbols is an ultimate form of ecto memory. Lyons (1987) described ecto remembering in this way:

> It is concerned entirely with neutral units of memorized material in the form of value-free content closely resembling the symbols and abstractions of ecto-type thought. ...Just as in the case of ecto learning, what I have remembered is what I now have, not what I now am, for I am no more defined by the content of my memory store than a library is defined by some of the books on its shelves. (p. 136)

Ecto remembering is what Hegel described as *Gedachtnis,* which is rote, mechanical memory. The contrasting form of memory, *Erinnerung,* which he describes as interiorizing memory, is the equivalent to what Lyons calls meso and endo remembering (cf. Derrida, 1991, p. 219).

*Meso Remembering*

In recent years it has been shown that we do not acquire our memories mechanically. Even in impoverished learning environments, we automatically process an object that is presented to us "in terms of its belongingness in clusters of meaning. ...We make sense of what we hear even when the experimenter has arranged that there be no sense in the material" (p. 137). Even in remembering nonsense material, we impose sense and purposes upon it (meso intentionality). Also, we score better when we connect doing to memorizing (meso reinforcement). This active form of memory is called meso memory. In Lyons words:

> This kind of remembering requires that the person be actively engaged in an ongoing situation and be permitted, even encouraged, to make sense out of the situation, to be involved in it, even to take some first steps toward constituting the situation as personally significant (p. 138).

An everyday example of meso memory is sometimes exemplified in my searching for lost or misplaced keys. I will scour my memory. I'll go look in everyplace I (ecto) remember being. Then, likely as not, I will go absent-mindedly roaming about the house, perhaps being interested in something else, and presto, there are my keys in front of me. My muscles remember for me and save my day.

*Endo Remembering*

Endo memories are not readily accessible to ecto consideration. A painful example of our endo memories is given by our constant acting out of experiences which we had as infants and toddlers. This acting out is an endo remembering that is trying to bring an experience and a need to conscious (ecto) awareness, so that we can deal with it in a useful (meso) fashion. Making endo memories conscious is a major concern for both self-growth and psychotherapy. In an important (ecto) sense we do not know things like this about ourselves until we verbally express them.

Expressing memories that come from our infancy is especially difficult because we had no language or concepts at that time to express what was happening to us. When we try to recall those things, we experience only feelings (sometimes traumatic) with occasional flashbacks in the manner of photographs or silent movies. Because we do not sense a time gap in these experiences, as we do in ecto remembering, we have difficulty accepting them as memories. They are not ecto memories; they are endo memories.

There are other things which make us what we are that are endo memories. They include things like our native language and our regional accent. We never say that we "remember" our native language. Our accent is just part of who we are. We learned these things in the endo mode and repeat them over and over. Do we "remember" our accent each time that we use it? We do not even know that we have it unless someone points it out to us.

To understand how we "remember" our accent, Lyons uses the distinction between declarative memory and procedural memory.

> The essential characteristic of declarative memory is that it can be recalled at will and that it can be "declared" or talked about; equally important, it can be lost, as by a stroke, or can be forgotten. As regards procedural memory, on the other hand, it is not really recalled but rather re-expressed or brought back into play, as we do when we use a cognitive or motor skill or behave in terms of a habit that may have become rusty from disuse. The procedural memory thus cannot be forgotten in the

same sense, and is rarely lost in the usual course of injury. Procedural memories are brought back by a kind of recognition process, declarative memories through a process of recall (p. 143).

Summing up endo remembering, Lyons says:

> Experiences that we have in the endo style seem...to be outside the province of memory in its ordinary sense. They are experiences that require us to redefine both memory and learning. ...We need to understand them in the special sense of something being laid down beyond recall, leaving behind as an effect only a remembrance of something alive, underpinning everything we do or recall later (p. 148).

There are, then, three distinct modes in which we live. Understanding this, we can see that the "upright position" (in which mind is glorified and body is scorned) is both egoistic and mistaken. As bodies, we have developed all three modes. We function best when we integrate them.

Lacan says that we are three intertwined circles of Ego, Other, and Language. Lyons dubs those circles meso, endo, and ecto respectively. Authentic ecto communication that integrates endo and meso learning is the activity that makes us human. It is the dynamic, strange attracting goal of evolution, what Nietzsche calls the "will to power."

# PART THREE

# THE DEEP STRUCTURES OF EXPERIENCE

**Part Three relates body wisdom to history, depth communication, identity, and chaos. It sums up what we have covered so far.**

Chapter 9 places our discussion in a large historical context.

Chapter 10 probes the positive and negative aspects of language, which makes human progress possible and posits artificial splits between mind and body, self and other. This chapter develops terminology that symbolizes both that split and the process of healing it.

Chapter 11 examines how we fashion a sense of identity from the chaos of our raw experience. It also identifies shifts in our ego boundaries based upon how we relate to our bodies, to others, and to the universe.

Chapter 12 gathers up all the observations made thus far into one list.

# CHAPTER NINE

# The Big Historical Picture

The endo, meso, and ecto modes of living have influenced the broad sweep of human history. Each of these modes has been dominant in various periods. During some wonderful periods all three modes have existed in harmony. As we might expect, the endo mode prevailed in our earliest known history.

When we reflect on the descriptions of primitive peoples, made by Mircea Eliade and others, we conclude that those peoples are endo. They live close to nature, in harmony with its rhythms, and in circular time, as they forage, hunt, and farm. In these respects, they seem similar to what we know of our pre-archaic forbears. At the origins of Western civilization, we know from archeology that the people of Old Europe, starting about 18,000 years ago, began a civilization. By 5000 B.C. they lived in villages where they were housed in buildings with some architecture, with artistic furnishings and inventions such as swinging doors. They were a peaceable people who tilled their fields and had a primitive type of writing. They also cared for their dead and honored the Great Mother.

There are two intriguing accounts of what happened next. In *The Chalice and the Blade*, Riane Eisler (1987, pp. 16-59) describes the matrifocal (mother-centered) nature of this early advanced civilization. She recounts the invasions by tribes of patriarchal Indo-Europeans, called the Kurgans, who were fierce and warlike and had little culture or sense of community, other than their tribal warrior fealty. They killed, plundered, enslaved, and destroyed. These warriors had great advantages over the woman-centered Goddess cultures that they invaded: (1) they rode horses, (2) they had copper and bronze weapons, and (3) they were ruthless. Where the Kurgans went, civilizations were abased and destroyed.

The Kurgans, attacking in successive waves over thousands of years, eventually obliterated the old European matrifocal civilization. By 1500 B.C., patriarchy had the ascendancy. One of the last holdouts was the remarkable island of Crete, which had no fortifications and proudly maintained the old rites of the Mother and the Bull. One surmises that Crete was a holy sanctuary that won survival by gaining awe and respect. Mycenae, c. 1500 to 1200 B.C., the proto-Greece that Homer was to hymn centuries later, had a written alphabet based on the Cretan alphabet. It would seem that the Mycenaean barbarians appreciated culture and wisdom more than did some of their cousins.

Joseph Lyons examined roughly the same period of history but from a different perspective. In examining the artifacts of Cro-Magnon civilization, its artwork, and especially its representations of the Mother Goddess, he found their civilization to be very endo. These representations of the Great Mother, sometimes called Venuses are statuettes that will fit in one's hand of a very round, fertile woman with diminutive arms and legs.

Lyons also examined another school of art, produced in northern and Mediterranean Spain, which was developed much later. These drawings are known as Levantine art. In Lyons words,

> They are monochrome black or red, done in swift and lively strokes, and restricted entirely to groups of humans and animals engaged in vivid scenes of hunting or battle. In a typical drawing...we see what must be a battle scene in which dozens of figures, most of them male, are shown in swift, almost violent action; they are all armed with bows, all in movement, and all have exactly the same physique. This is what is most striking about Levantine art, that just as in the tradition of the Venuses, the bodies all look alike. The bodies of the Venuses are female and heavy, with pronounced emphasis on the structures associated with the gut and pelvis. The bodies in Levantine art, by contrast, are all male, quite tall, with almost abnormally long thin waists, quite muscular shoulders and chests, and with wiry legs dressed in what appear to be pantaloons. Indeed, in the Levantine males the waists are so attenuated as to have almost disappeared, by contrast with the very evident stomachs but disappearing hands and feet of the Venus figures; whereas in the Venuses the energy seems concentrated at the middle, in the Levantine figures all the strength and energy is concentrated in the puffed-up chests, muscular shoulders, and active arms and legs (p. 30).

It would seem that Eisler's matrifocal civilization is Lyon's endo one. Her patriarchal Kurgans are his Levantine meso warriors. They are describing the same history.

Male meso values prevailed over female endo ones generally by the middle of the Iron Age, c. 1500 B. C. The dominance, of course, was not total. We see an example of how a balance was struck if we observe the culture of Greece as it came out of its Dark Age, c. 800 B.C.

We see endo and meso values in equilibrium. On the meso side, the Greeks were a very individualistic and warlike people who were never able to maintain a political unity for long. They were cantankerous individuals who were not to be bullied. In their Mycenaean past, *habrosyne*, conspicuous display, was a dominant virtue. Yet under the influence of the Sages, especially Solon, *sophrosyne*, "moderation in all things," became their motto (cf. Vernant, 1982, pp. 83-87).

On the endo side the Greeks were a very religious people. Their whole civilization engaged in the mystery rites at Eleusis; flocked to the oracles at Delphi, Delos, Claros, and Didyma; honored the Great Mother; frolicked with Dionysus; and healed themselves in dream sanatoriums (the *asklepia*). They listened to their visions and trusted signs and omens. They were a very endo people.

The Greeks emerged (c. 800 B.C.) from their Dark Age with three revolutionary things: the *polis*, the *agora*, and the goddess Eris (strife). These three functioned as a unit. The *polis* put the protective wall around all the people instead of just around the royal palace as before; and it centered town life on the *agora*, the public square of marketing and meeting. *Eris*, the spirit of contention, was exercised in the *agora*. Everyone contended on equal grounds there. From this triadic unity democracy emerged as a very contentious meso society, but one hemmed in by endo rules of equality and fairness.

As the Greeks harnessed their meso energy with democracy, they quickly developed their endo, meso, and ecto abilities to a superlative degree. Their endo achievements include the poetry of Homer and Hesiod; the plays of Aeschylus, Sophocles, and Aristophanes; and classic pottery, artwork, and architecture. Their meso achievements were a world-class citizen army and navy, a great merchant fleet, colonies throughout the eastern Mediterranean, and magnificent cities. Their ecto achievements, starting with figures like Thales and Pythagoras, including Plato and Aristotle, are the foundation of Western philosophy, science, and history.

In controlled turbulence, Greeks of the classic era maintained the vitality and cohesion of endo sensibility. They channeled their meso spirit of contention and became even more adventurous, vigorous, and defiant. Their balance of endo, meso, and ecto was self-nurturing and productive of a grand civilization.

Eventually, because of its (meso) contentiousness, Greece declined. Afterwards culture had its ups and downs. Generally, however, religion, democracy, and philosophy spread to a broader global base. Life proceeded this way for centuries with endo and meso influence roughly even.

With the Renaissance the balance began to change. Merchant (meso) culture arose. Greek ideas as diverse as the philosophy of Aristotle and the mysticism of Hermes Trismagistrus were imported and absorbed. There arose a more general sense of personal independence. Foreign commerce began to flourish. Meso values were definitely on the ascendancy.

Ecto values were also gaining currency, but in a conservative fashion that was respectful of ecclesiastical and Aristotelian tradition. This was about to change. Erasmus decided to interpret scripture for himself. Men like Descartes and Galileo wedded their meso and ecto traits and thereby embodied a drive for knowledge that demanded practical results and practical certainty. The scientific revolution was on.

The scientific revolution is still with us and still going strong. The universal validity of the scientific method, however, is under intense challenge. The authors cited in this book, for example, contest the claim that the meso-ecto scientific method is the only fruitful, trustworthy approach to truth.

Scientist themselves, having pushed the method to its limits, discover that their statements do not tell us what is real. They accept that the fundamental viewpoint (paradigm) that they adopt determines both what they see and its importance. They accept that their seeing distorts (even destroys) at the atomic level what they are looking for before they are able to see it.

Freud, Heidegger, Merleau-Ponty, Lacan, and legions of other thinkers from West and East declare that our basic experience is unitary. We never experience anything that is not in the world, and we never experience the world without it being our bodies that experience it.

In terms of the images we have already used, the scientific ideal of pure objectivity is represented by the ecto eye atop the pyramid. The view of the phenomenologists is primarily located in the meso eye sockets of active, inquiring people. This book, using the observations of Lyons as a springboard, endeavors to describe reality from the (endo) heart: our warm, dark, wet, turbulent/still, and not two/not one core, where we converge as individual and universal, evanescent and eternal.

In the next chapters, we will examine, from an endo perspective, some of the basic structures of human living and depth communication. We will describe chaotic faith and ego as a strange attractor. We will examine how we modulate our boundaries so that we can be both separate and connected to our world. Finally, we will collect in one place what we have learned so far.

# CHAPTER TEN

# Depth Communication

This chapter develops shorthand expressions for the actors involved in depth communication and creates models to symbolize the murky unconscious operations that generate those actors and bring their operations into consciousness.

**The "Subjects"**

Newborn infants, as we have seen, are almost undifferentiated from their nurturing environments. As such, they approximate what are called "Original Subjects," symbolized as "Subject0." As infants begin to differentiate themselves through processes like mirroring, they imaginatively create imagos of themselves. As they continue to develop their imaginations and language, they create rifts between themselves as independent imagos and their nurturing environment; that is, between the ego, symbolized as "Subject1," and the remainder of Subject0, which remainder is symbolized as "Subject2." The contents of Subject2 are two-fold: the external nurturing environment and all unconscious bodily functions and awareness. The gap created is then symbolized with language in the act that makes the Subject specifically human.

Because of this primal split there is a built-in ambivalence every time we use the word "I" as the subject of a sentence. "I" can theoretically express the standpoint of Subject0 (original subject), Subject1 (ego), or Subject2 (my unconscious, which Lacan dubbed, the Other). In addition, "I" can also stand for Subject3 (which is a communion of other and ego).

It is in this context that Freud's famous dictum, "*Wo es war, soll Ich werden*," (where it was, there I am to be) finds its proper place. After careful analysis, Lacan (1977) concluded that this dictum signifies, " 'There where it was'... I would like it to be understood, 'it is my duty that I should come to being'" (p. 129). The first "it" in Lacan's translation stands for Subject2. The meaning then would be that Subject1 (the ego) is to enter into dialogue with Subject2 (the other) and create Subject3 (the communion). In notation, this could be expressed as:

$$\text{Subject1} + \text{Subject2} \rightarrow \text{Subject3.}$$
$$\text{or}$$
$$\text{Ego} + \text{Other} \rightarrow \text{Communion.}$$

**The Language of the Unconscious**

Lacan describes how the unconscious talks to us by first mentioning the historical records of its speaking to us in the past, and then explaining how those records are to be interpreted as a text. He said:

> The unconscious is that chapter of my history that is marked by a blank or occupied by a falsehood: it is the censored chapter. But the truth can be rediscovered; usually it has already been written down elsewhere. Namely:
> - in monuments: this is my body [In physical and hysterical symptoms];
> - in archival documents: these are my childhood memories, just as impenetrable as are such documents when I do not know their provenance;
> - in semantic evolution: this corresponds to...[my] stock of words and [the way I use them];
> - in traditions, too, and even in the legends which, in a heroicized form bear my history (p. 50).

We tune into our unconscious body language by translating dreams, transference and counter-transference, witticisms, slips of the tongue, symbolic acts, and jokes into conscious language. The language of the dream, symptom, or slip of the tongue is often to be deciphered as a rebus,

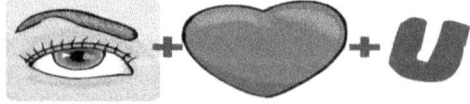

or a hieroglyphic and not just decoded as a collection of signs. For this reason, the science of linguistics is important to help us interpret the text presented by the unconscious.

Freud and Lacan found that figures of speech are especially valuable for interpreting the language of the unconscious. Of special value are the rhetorical devices of metonymy and metaphor. Metonymy "is a figure of speech consisting of the use of the name of one thing for that of another of which it is an attribute or with which it is associated (as in 'lands of the crown')" (Webster, 1975). Metonymy is expressed strongly in the repetition compulsion, wherein a series of similar objects are passionately desired but never satisfy. The reason these objects fail to satisfy us is our metonymic misidentification of those objects with the real but unrecognized object of desire. All desires for objects are expressions of the power wish (Thanatos). As such, they are metonymic expressions of the primal erotic wish. This futility in seeking fulfillment in objects is the truth behind Augustine's famous statement, "Our hearts are restless until they rest in you."

Metaphor, on the other hand, is "a figure of speech in which a word or phrase literally denoting one kind of object or idea is used in place of another to suggest a likeness or analogy between them" (Webster, 1975). Metaphor illuminates the likeness between things and fosters their harmony. With metaphor, we unite with others in a spirit that reflects our unity with our source.

Both of these figures of speech are used in a statement such as "Watergate was Nixon's Waterloo." The term "Watergate" properly describes a building in Washington, D.C.; by metonymy it designates the political scandal that began there. Waterloo was a battle where Napoleon suffered his final defeat; by *metonymy* it designates "final defeat." In the sentence, "Watergate was Nixon's Waterloo," however, "Waterloo" is also a *metaphor* for "final defeat" because it says that Nixon's final defeat was like Napoleon's.

A good deal of human fun and trouble results from our confusion of metonyms and metaphors. Metonymic striving for happiness is expressed in materialism and hedonism. Metaphoric participation in the fulfillment of life is expressed in love and cooperation, the expressed harmony of the One and the Many.

Our bodies also communicate with us more directly as when they produce pain or delight in the pits of our stomachs. They sometimes seem to create demonstrative incidents in our lives and thereby force us to face up to face aspects of ourselves that we have repressed.

In addition, there are ways that we can actively prompt our unconscious to speak. Active imagination, as encouraged by Jung, is one example. There is lucid dreaming and the programming of dreams, as when we say, "Let me sleep on it." There is creative doodling which is sometimes called automatic writing. These are all ways that can get our bodies to talk to us.

Free association is another active way to access the unconscious. To engage in it, one formulates feelings and intuitions as they boil up from the unconscious depths. One engages in what Merleau-Ponty calls "originating speech" which brings to light thoughts in search of themselves. One talks categorical, pre-reflective expressions, not the objective expressions based on closer investigation.

In free association, Subject1 (ego) relaxes its boundaries to attend to Subject2 (the body, the unconscious) in order to bring forth Subject3 (communication between ego and the body).

$$\text{Subject1} + \text{Subject2} \rightarrow \text{Subject3}.$$
$$\text{or}$$
$$\text{Ego} + \text{Other} \rightarrow \text{Communion}$$

In terms of endo, meso, and ecto, we (egos) heed feelings and gain intuitions as (endo/communion) Subject3, and strive (meso) to articulate them in language (ecto) thus making these feelings and intuitions specifically human, that is, symbolically expressed. Only when thus stated do the feelings and intuitions become fully human. The desired end of this effort is to create a union of Subject1 and Subject2 in Subject3 (of ego and other in communion). *Wo Es war, soll Ich werden* (where other was there ego should be).

Paul Ricouer (1970) expresses the project that is consciousness in terms of first naiveté and second naiveté. Both naivetés consist of an acute awareness of immediate, vibrant, physical reality. The first naiveté is our timeless, inarticulated unconscious (the other). The second naiveté is the goal of evolution, the conscious, concrete, symbolic expression of the unconscious (communion). He says, "The concreteness of language which we border upon through painstaking approximation [by our use of language] is the second naiveté of which we have merely a frontier or threshold knowledge" (p. 495). He continues,

Let us not be mistaken about the meaning of this last stage: this return to the immediate is not a return to silence, but rather to the spoken word, to the fullness of language. Nor is it a return to the dense enigma of initial, immediate speech, but to speech that has been instructed by the whole process of meaning. Hence this concrete reflection does not imply any concession to irrationality or effusiveness. (pp. 495-496).

The unconscious body other (Subject2) is naive and illiterate. Communion (Subject3) is naive, also, in the sense of wide-eyed wonder about the world, but it is not illiterate. It is literate and more; it is the goal of our self- reflection.

Freud, in discussing Leonardo Da Vinci's statement that Nature "is full of countless reasons [*ragioni*] that never enter experience," said, "Every one of us human beings corresponds to one of the countless experiments in which these '*ragioni*' of nature force their way into experience" (quoted from Ricouer, p. 551). We each are experiments of Nature in which the unconscious becomes conscious uniquely, chaotically, strangely.

**Interpersonal Depth Communication**

When you and I engage in intimate conversation (as lovers, as friends, as patients/therapists, as intellectual seekers, etc.), your Subject2 and my Subject2 "get down" with each other. We lower our boundaries and let our bodies express themselves. Your other and my other engage each other.

In this kind of conversation, vague feelings and ideas take shape as intuitions, images, meandering stories, hunches, and half-baked ideas. This kind of communication requires us to listen to our bodies, let them express themselves, and mutually decipher their messages in order to achieve mutual understanding and/or cooperation. This process can be symbolized in the same notation developed above:

$$\text{Subject1} + \text{Subject2} \rightarrow \text{Subject3}.$$
$$\text{or}$$
$$\text{Ego} + \text{Other} \rightarrow \text{Communion}.$$

Lacan pictures the process of deep communication, as it is accomplished in analysis, as a game of bridge in which there are four players. They are the analysand's ego (A) and other (B) and the analyst's ego (C) and other (D). In this game, it is agreed that the egos of both analysand and analyst are dummies that can act as organs of speech and hearing but are not allowed to speak and hear as such. In other words, the other of each of them both speaks and listens while the egos of each act as only transmitters and receivers of language. The anticipated result of this game of bridge is understanding (communion) and personal growth.

Lacan's analysis of psychoanalysis holds for deep communication in general. When we are really talking to one another, we rummage in our shadowy unconscious and pull out the things we find. We share them as incomplete thoughts, as feelings, or as crystallized insights. In other words, we share our pre-reflective thoughts and we engage in authentic speech. By expressing our murky unconscious in words, we clarify its messages. In this authentic sharing, we project the communion within us upon the world at large. So, we create civilization and culture. Communion (Subject3) is a cultural goal as well as a personal one.

**The Necessity of Separation**

The necessity for separation is recognized by us in many activities that are metaphors for each other: the birthing process, the cutting of the umbilical cord, the weaning, the child's learning to be physically absent from its mother, the first day of school, the going away to college or work, the first apartment, the marriage, the death of parents. Lacan pays special attention to the way that language brokers these separations, especially as the child's way of coping with the physical absence of its mother.

In the "Fort/Da" ("Gone/Here") episode already described, Freud's grandson symbolized his mother's comings and goings by the visual absence of the spool when lowered outside his crib and her visual presence when he lifted it back up. He accompanied his action with his attempts to pronounce the words, "Gone" and "Here." Freud was watching his grandson enter the specifically human world of language. Ricouer (1970) describes the meaning of this event as follows:

> [In] *Beyond the Pleasure Principle*...Freud sketches the genesis of signs starting from the mastery over privation in the game of fort-da. By alternately voicing the two words, the child interrelates absence and presence in a meaningful contrast; at the same time, he no longer undergoes absence as a fit of panic massively substituted for a close and saturating presence. Dominated thus by language, privation—and consequently presence as well—is signified and transformed into intentionality; being deprived of the mother becomes an intending of the mother (p.385).

With his use of language, the grandson accomplished some things and suffered a backlash from those accomplishments. He was able to make his mother (symbolically) present whenever he wanted her with language, but in so doing he put an end to the symbiotic unity he previously enjoyed with her. Freud used the phrase, "He [symbolically] killed her." The result is that his fresh new ego harbors a sense of alienation.

With language, the grandson was able to situate himself as an individual independent of the physical presence of his mother. Thus, he was able to become truly human, sharing in the great symbolic universe of language. Language, however, demands separation as the necessary partial ground of communication and articulation of the unconscious. Because of language, Freud's grandson lost his all-consuming unity with his mother and with the unconscious being of the world. In other words, he lost his Subject0. This seminal event created our universal existential situation for the grandson.

Freud expressed that situation as a dialectic of "eros" and "thanatos." Underlying these drives are two facts: (1) We are "not two" because we are at our root (Subject0) and in our destiny (Subject3) one with each other and the universe. (2) We are "not one" because we (out of evolutionary necessity) have divided ourselves into ego (Subject1) and other (Subject2) with language. In short, we are not two/not one with each other and the universe—and there's the rub.

This existential situation brokered by language enables us to traverse life making it uniquely our own, and then to reunite with our Source as an aware, consciously articulated being. In other words,

$$\text{Ego} + \text{Other} \rightarrow \text{Communion}.$$

# CHAPTER ELEVEN

# Chaos and Ego

**Chaotic Faith**

The British analyst, W.R. Bion (1970), expands our understanding of what listening is in depth communication. In the course of his practice, he worked with a patient who refused to speak in words and whose only vocal communications were strings of modulated nonsense syllables. In sitting with this man, Bion found himself listening to those syllables as a kind of music. He attended to that and concluded (hesitantly) that the man was "doodling in sound." He felt that he gained some rapport with the man through this doodling, especially when he reciprocated by doodling himself.

Bion formalizes this approach to listening in the expression as

$$F \text{ in } 0.$$

In this expression, "0" is the emotional truth of a situation as it is unfolding. It is a symbol for the existential and phenomenological reality of the moment, prereflective, here and now. The proper response to 0 is "F" (Faith). By Faith, Bion means an attitude of steady attentiveness and openness to the play of unconscious free association. The formula, "F in 0," expresses the proper attitude of any person trying to come to grips with the immediacy of life.

The authentic way of F in 0 is the way of all the beautiful things. Authentic speech, for example, is speech proceeding from our feelings and our depths that formulates where we are at that moment in a way that hasn't been said before. It is the opposite of any kind of patter: small talk, shop talk, cultural and intellectual chitchat, or exhibitions of philosophic and psychological sophistication. As such, authentic speech just has to be real, not necessarily profound or extraordinary, certainly not necessarily free association. Authentic speech is Subject3 talk. It is the emergence into language of our unconscious voices, surprising even to us at times, tuned in, right on, categorical.

**"Faith" as a Strange Attractor**

Words in authentic communication have a magical quality. Levi-Strauss called it their "inductive property." The attention and the intentions directed to the unconscious through F in O generate our creative imaginations. In describing authentic speech as F in O, we facilitate a somewhat scientific explanation of its creative character. This kind of speech is creative speech because it programs the unconscious in the manner of chaotic attractors.

**F** plays the role in **O** that the strange attractor plays in chaos. It sets an intention to work that randomly generates the desired expression or work of art. **F** is the essence of creativity, the loosely focused intention hovering over the chaos of the unconscious, which lets ideas, images, memories, feelings, and half-baked intuitions burst into and out of consciousness, sometimes peacefully floating, sometimes in a maelstrom, and allows the logic of the unconscious to work.

This unconscious logic is the logic of chaos, skipping about in the manner of individual plottings in the solutions of non-linear equations. As we observe these plottings in the graphic coordinates provided on the computer screen we see no discernible sequence. Only after hundreds and thousands of iterations does a pattern slowly emerge from the mist. Such is the process of unconscious logic as it is observed on the viewing screen of our pre-reflective mind.

The specific character of the strange attractor, **F**, is determined by the circumstances, intention, and attention of a person. In Bion's originating example of the analyst with the analysand, **F** is an open intention to understand the patient. **F**, in this situation, is the equivalent of what Freud called, "even-hovering attention"; what Lacan termed the other of the analyst attending to the other of the analysand; what Kohut called empathy; what we in everyday parlance call "being with" someone. As the analyst's attention evenly suspends itself over the messages it receives from the analysand's unconscious, it instills in those messages an intention to understand. This intention functions as a strange attractor. Then, as both analysand and analyst trust their unconscious logic, understanding gradually appears from the unconscious mist.

In the course of our personal journeys of self-understanding and growth, **F** works in the same way. How often have we said something like, "I really want to know why I did that," in a situation when we are perplexed by some recurring personal behavior? Then to our dismay we find our bodies acting out symptoms in bizarre ways, thus providing an experience that forces us to recognize why we were doing that. The statement vocalized the **F**. The body (the unconscious, the other) is the **0**. The symptoms are the speech of the other. The other will also speak in a dream, by way of a chance encounter with a person, book, or unfamiliar word, or through a random consultation with the bible or some other book by opening it and reading the first passage that is seen. Any authentic statement of intention of this variety chaotically generates a unique personal constellation of unconscious language in response. The statement, "I really want to be free" will generate its own chaotic constellation. The statement, "I'm no good," will generate a different one.

One persistent theme of creative people, when they discuss the processes they use in their work, is that they fill themselves with material while holding some flexible idea of what they are looking for. Then they let that material percolate until a coherent idea, image, tune, story, theory, or invention shows itself. This aspect of creativity is an endo process operating under the principle of F in 0 in which the flexible idea, **F**, acts as the strange attractor in the chaos of information and feeling. The end result of such a creative incubation reveals the inherent logic, beauty, and language of the unconscious.

Carl Jung advocated the use of active imagination in therapy. He encouraged his patients to talk to their moods as if they were persons and to put words into the mouths of figures in their dreams or from their childhoods. He would ask them to fill out their dreams and scraps of memory with imaginative elaboration. In effect, he asked them to freely associate ideas, scenes, and feeling in an imaginative context in order to make those experiences more real, vivid, and revealing.

Creative imagination as a tool of self-growth and healing has blossomed in recent years. As it is discussed today, it is descended on its paternal side from Carl Jung. On its maternal side it is descended from countless generations of metaphysical thought, stretching back past the Gnostics, to a belief in the magical power of speech. Speech does in fact have this magical property, as is demonstrated by Claude

Levi-Strauss. Here is a summary of one of his works, "The Effectiveness of Symbols," provided by Muller and Richardson (1982):

> Levi-Strauss interprets an 18-page South American shamanistic text, a long incantation whose purpose is to facilitate difficult childbirth. How is the cure effected? Levi- Strauss sees it as a matter of making an emotional situation explicit in words and thereby making acceptable to the mind pains that the body refuses to tolerate. The transition to this linguistic expression that the medicine man provides induces the release of the physiological process—not unlike the work of psychoanalysis. In both cases, unconscious resistances are made conscious, and conflicts materialize in an orderly way that permits their free development and leads to their resolution. In the one case, a social myth provided by the healer specifies the patient's actions; in the other, the patient constructs an individual myth with elements drawn from her past. In both cases...structures of organic processes, unconscious mind, and rational thought are related to one another through the "inductive property" in which the effectiveness of symbols consists (p. 7).

Thus, the magic of words is in their "inductive property," their ability to act as strange attractors. Words direct the body to generate a sense of meaning and wholeness. Thus is the effectiveness of Freud's "talking cure" explained.

Creative imagination is packaged under many labels today: guided imagery, directed meditation, hypnotherapy, neuro-linguistic programming, miracles, quantum healing and, of course, the old standbys: affirmations, positive thinking, mind control, etc. Some methods claim to provide spiritual peace and transpersonal experiences. Some offer mental and emotional peace or freedom from compulsions. Others are said to promote physical health. Still others promise prosperity and power. The power of some of these techniques in certain situations is undeniable. In all of these techniques it is the "inductive property" of the image or word that provides the impetus. This inductive property is a close relative to the strange attractor of chaos.

The way of F in 0 is the way of chaos, the way of authentic speech, the hearing of "evenly hovering attention," the process of creativity, and the magic of symbolization. As such it is not something new. It is what the Chinese call simply Tao (the Way) one of whose most practical adages is *"Wei wu wei"* (Doing without doing). This is the way described in Buddhist thought as "letting the arrow shoot itself." In the circles of Alcoholics Anonymous this way is translated as "Let go and let God." It is the way of beautiful things.

**The Ego as Strange Attractor**

We, as unconscious body-subjects (Subject0), began to create our egos at birth when we first sought our mother's breast. At that moment, we declared that growth was not possible without other people. We were already identifying with the image of ourselves as it was mirrored by our mothers.

In profound empathy with our parents as they cuddled us, fed us, and gave us needed relief, we absorbed a feeling-idea (image) of ourselves as beings of worth. We were totally dependent on our mothers at that time and our self-images were embedded in her physical presence. We absorbed with unconscious endo processes the behavior, feelings, and thought processes of our mothering objects. We also absorbed their language. Our first use of that language is a momentous event.

(1) We become fully human.
(2) We become individuals.
(3) We separate our imagos (self-images) from the physical presence of our mothers thus creating our egos.
(4) We destroy the undifferentiated unity we previously enjoyed with our mothers and with our environment (including our bodily unconscious).
(5) Our use of language creates the separateness that is necessary for the practice of thought and language. Language is the separation of opposites (as in the Fort/Da experience of Freud's grandson). Further it rends unconscious unity, and requires separateness for objective (ecto/meso) observation and expression.

Many other shifts occur at this point.

(6) Being creates consciousness. Equivalent statements to this are: The body creates the mind; big mind creates little mind; Nature begets Reason; the unconscious creates the ego; The primary Subject before separation develops its conscious self; that is,

$$\text{Subject0} \rightarrow \text{Subject1}.$$

(7) Being, the body, big mind, Nature, the unconscious, and Subject0 become conscious. They transcend themselves as their first leap toward historical, cultural fulfillment.
(8) The body now observes itself and expresses itself.
(9) The rift in the undifferentiated body-subject (Subject0) that separates ego (Subject1) and the unconscious other (Subject2) sets in motion the drives of Eros and Thanatos (Love and Death/Power).
(10) Conflicts set in.
(11) Creativity is unleashed.
(12) Our I-feeling (what Lacan calls the Subject and Kohut calls the Self) is created along with the ego. This Subject is equivocal in its content. It locates itself all over the conscious and unconscious map. Schematically it can be assigned to either Subject1, Subject2, or Subject3 (ego, other, or communion). That is, our I-feeling both expands and contracts.
(13) The ego remains relatively stable although it has a great capacity for growth toward both individuality and communion.
(14) Subject0 → Subject1 + Subject2. That is, our primal animal conscious develops into ego and other
(15) The plan of life and of Being is implemented: Subject1 + Subject2 → Subject3; that is. ego and other develop towards communion.
(16) The pre-eminent chasm of phenomenological description is created (the split between ego and other).
(17) The ego becomes a strange attractor over the unconscious that creates our life.

(18) Our Faith (F) obtains its optimum locus, Subject3, communion, where it straddles the chasm between other and ego, alert to both sides, making the other conscious and cluing in the ego to what is really going on.

We did not end our endo absorption, however, with our attaining language. We continued to learn from our mothers in the same way that we did before we had language and arranged our egos in accord with theirs. We did the same with our fathers, our siblings, and with the traditions of our families and the culture of our people. We grew by leaps and bounds.

Only occasionally was this a conscious process. What unconscious processes did we use? How did we select which influences to build into our egos? With the language of chaos theory, we can improve upon the standard "absorbing" metaphor used to explain this process.

Briggs and Peat in *The Turbulent Mirror* (1989) introduce this line of thought. They ask,

> Could the brain's overall expression, the personality, also be a strange attractor? A psychiatrist at the University of California at San Diego argues that we each possess a unique identity that is written in everything we do. Arnold Mandell claims he has studied individuals' patterns as reflected in the firing rate of dopamine receptors, serotonin receptors, and single cells in EEG activity and in the oscillating of behavior—and that he has found a fractal self-similarity among all these indicators (p. 168).

In the context of the ideas we have been discussing, we can offer the following explanation of what that strange attractor might be, how it arises, and how it operates.

Our attention (Faith, **F**) makes the whole process work. We begin life learning in the endo mode incorporating the moods, feelings, attitudes, and actions of other people as our own. With the principles of F in 0 (Faith at ground zero, the immediacy of the moment) and chaos at work, we develop mental and emotional structures much like theirs. The Faith of our nurturers along with our own Faith produces a harmony of sensation and organization.

As we become more separate individuals, our imaginatively formed and symbolically identified egos provide the controlling attractors directing our growth. Our complex ego images become the main attractors in our lives. They routinely select moods, personality traits, companions, and careers that are compatible with themselves. Most of the attractor's selections never rise to the level of our conscious understanding or decision making.

Like every other strange attractor, the ego flows along with the randomness of events producing its own pattern, intricately, beautifully, and uniquely organized. The ego is the strange attractor, par excellence, in the chaos of our unconscious. It plucks out of our myriad possibilities just those that fit our image of ourselves (which it is).

What we have control of in this unfolding drama is the nature of our attention, or Faith (**F**). If we are negligent, we allow the drama to play out in its inevitable fashion by not paying attention and not wanting to know. Even then, the conflicting drives of Eros and Thanatos force us to face up to some crises in our lives and to take stands. By being vigorous in our F in O we can intervene directly and so take charge of our lives. We are free in our **F** to make real for ourselves the potential union of Ego and Other.

The structural elements in our makeup that make **F** possible are $Subject0$ (the original body-subject that started the process, but has now dropped out of the scene); $Subject1$ (the ego, which embodies one cliff of the chasm); $Subject2$ (the Other, which is the other cliff); and $Subject3$ (sitting in the catbird seat conversing with both $Subject1$ and $Subject2$).

Briggs and Peat (1989) offer another model for visualizing the chaotic/rational interface at work in our brains. They describe the work of Matti Bergstrom who has worked for years on what he calls the "bipolar generator" model of the brain:

> The model divides the brain into an "information" end and a "random" or chaos end, and Bergstrom says it is the interaction of these ends that produces thought and behavior. When the retina or other sense organ is stimulated, Bergstrom argues, the input goes in two directions. One direction is through the cortex, which is organized to convert the stimulus into limit cycle attractors—that is, into an organized form of information. Input is also circuited through the "random generator." This end is located in the brain stem and limbic system; it takes input from the sense organs and vegetative activities—including the systems controlling digestion and heart rate—and

adds them all together. The random generator input is "nonspecific," unstructured—or at least its structure is so highly complex that it contains no information that can be decoded (p. 168).

The "information" end of the brain corresponds to conscious, conceptual, ecto thinking. The "random generator" end corresponds to unconscious, creative, chaotic, endo thinking.

Briggs and Peat also offer a different slant on how the brain processes non-linear thought as it is offered in the work of the systems scientists William Gray and Paul LaViolette. They say:

> [These scientists have] proposed that thought starts as a highly complex, even chaotic bundle of sensations, nuances, and "feeling tones" which cycle from the limbic system through the cortex. During this feedback cycling, the cortex selects out, or "abstracts," some of those feeling tones. These abstractions are then reinserted back into the loop. The continued abstracting process has the effect of nonlinearly amplifying some nuances into cognitions or emotions, which become organizers for the complex bundles of nuance-filled sensations and feelings.
> "Thoughts are stereotypes or simplifications of the feeling tones," says LaViolette. "They're like cartoons of reality." According to this model, the abstracted thoughts-or-emotions become associated with each other to create larger structures of abstracted thoughts-or-emotions, which become "organizationally closed." Organizational closure means that the richness of nuance has been summarized (simplified) by thoughts-or-emotions that have a feeling of closure about them. Most of our opinions and knowledge are organizationally closed.
> We have ceased to pay much attention to the many feeling tones associated with the things we think about or the nuances of our emotional likes or dislikes. But beneath each thought or simple emotion lie layers of sensation and feeling which keep cycling in the brain's feedback loops. Because these nuances keep cycling, the possibility remains that some chaotic or highly charged situation could cause a different nuance to be abstracted and amplified, becoming the organizing thought. Through this process organizationally closed thoughts and emotional responses can sometimes be changed (p. 170).

This conception of thought exemplifies the endo, meso, and ecto modes of thinking with an unconscious mind, a conscious one, and a selection process.

In short, the ego acts as a strange attractor to organize our conscious and unconscious lives. It crafts a unique intricately organized human being out of a chaos of flashes, clamor, and kaleidoscopic imagery.

## I-Feelings and Boundaries Part Two

The ego is an imaginative creation of the original subject, Subject0. The result of this creation is an ambiguity in the use of the pronoun, **I**. In a sentence, **I** can stand for Subject1 = ego, Subject2 = other, or Subject3 = communion of the two.

Subject0 is never really present in our individual perception. It is us without individuality. We are closest to being Subject0 as a zygote. By birth, as we have seen, we are already both "separate and permeable." The process of separation begins, perhaps, before birth in the third trimester when we become viable for premature birth. Physically, symbolically, and psychically we become progressively more separate in childbirth, in the cutting of the umbilical, and in the periodic absences of our mothers as our nurturers and cuddlers. We progressively take charge of this process as we identify more and more with our images as mirrored in our mothers and then as seen in a regular mirror. With the advent of language, as exemplified in the Fort/Da experience of Freud's grandson, we establish that independence.

How does language change infants into individuals? According to Freud and Lacan, children absorb the language of their families and use that language to symbolize the presence and absence of their mothers. In doing this they free their self-images from enmeshment in their mothers, and so transform themselves into individuals. They transform themselves as body-subjects and become egos (Subject1).

The way Freud's grandson used language signified many things. In particular:

1. It signified the symbolic death of his mother; that is, it showed that his mother was no longer necessary for his survival.

2. It signified the "name of the Father;" that is, the rule of law which is the function of language. Lacan (1977) expressed this truth as follows, "the law of man has been the law of language since the first words of recognition presided over the first gifts" (p. 61). Language is a signifying realm, in which opposition is of the essence (e.g., Fort/Da); in which one cannot have his cake and eat it too. Lacan illustrates this thinking by showing that our phonetic system is composed of groups of oppositional pairs. The human condition is bound by the laws of language. If you talk, you are bound by rules that you cannot escape. You are tied to your culture. In other words, the limit imposed through societal language both enables us and forces us to be free individuals.
3. It signified that the boy was symbolically castrated; that is, he lost his phallic connection to his mothering source. This is a restatement of the effects listed above. In other words, the child found that he was separate from his mother and did this by acknowledging "the name of the father" (the law of distinction/ language).
4. It signified that the boy had begun to exist more fully outside of the primal union of Subject0. (Ex-ist – to be outside of.)

The boy's speech also enabled and forced him to have human desire. In Lacan's (1977) words, the moment "in which desire becomes human is also that in which the child is born into language" (p. 103). Up until the Fort/Da experience Freud's grandson was engaged with his mother in an essentially dyadic relationship in which the mother was the infant's "All."

Then, in the words of Muller and Richardson (1982),

> With the Fort! Da! experience that tie is ruptured. Ruptured, too, is the infant's illusion of totality, its presumption of infinity. It experiences for the first time the catastrophe of negation (it is not the mother), the trauma of limitation, the tragedy of its finitude—in other words, its own *manque a etre* (pp. 21 - 22).

The phrase *manque a etre* literally means "lack of being," but Lacan suggests that it be translated as "want-to-be." Desire erupts in the rupture of the primitive union with the mother, and the principal signifier of desire is the phallus. And so on.

Muller and Richardson set the stage for our having a life filled with desire with these words:

> Wrenched away from a dyadic relationship with its mother in the world of inarticulate images, the infant must now relate to her through a dialectic of desire, in which the subject's ultimate quest is for recognition by the desired. Traumatized by its want, the child wants, i.e., desires, to recapture its lost plenitude by being the desired of its mother, her fullness—in Lacananian language, by being the phallus for its mother (p. 23).

In short, language makes us human. The web of language is the specifically human world in many senses. First, as we have been observing, it brokers our full-fledged entry into the human race. Second, language both sunders our original unity as Subject0 and makes possible our reunification as Subject3. It also makes possible the expression of our unconscious moments of shadowy insight; that is, it is the means whereby our faithful attending to the personal truth of the moment (our F in 0) bursts into consciousness. In this way, it fulfills our destiny.

Looked upon from a social perspective, language allows us to progressively create a culture that articulates more and more of our world, thus making it more human. What does this mean? We create our egos with language. With language we come to understand the world as our culture understands it. Language acts as a strange attractor selecting from the chaos of categorical experience what is meaningful from what is not, in-forming our judgments, our perceptions, and our egos. Over time we co-create with our cultural heritage a culture that is richer than our inheritance. In turn, this richer culture further enriches our lives.

Language does expand our knowledge of the world, but it also cannot really get us intimately in touch with reality. Lacan, using the insights of Saussure, points out the arbitrary nature of our language. Contrary to our usual understanding, words do not directly signify objects. They merely place the signifying word for that object into a web of other words. Lacan symbolizes this relationship as,

$$\frac{S}{s}$$

That is, the signifier (the large S, the word) is always separated from the thing signified (the small s, the object).

According to Saussure and Lacan, the only things that are really ever grasped in language are the words not the objects. All of our poetry, philosophy, science, economics, mathematics, and practical computations are just systems of signification that say nothing directly about external reality, but only situate it in a web of signification, thus making it meaningful. This does not make language completely arbitrary because the structure of language displays the logic of the unconscious, but it does expose our reality as being a web of significations created by us.

Our culture and language have lives of their own, independent of the bodily reality from which they were born. They have a subtle reality which is nonetheless material, being words, artifacts, customs, and so forth. Human reality is a co-created, subtle, trans-individual reality.

Now to attend directly to the notions of limits/boundaries. If we consider Subject0 in the abstract, it has no limits/boundaries because it possesses no subtle human individuality. Subject1 (the ego), on the other hand, considered in the abstract as the isolated individual ego, has hard rigid limits/boundaries. Subject2 (the other), in the abstract, like Subject0, has no limits/boundaries. So far, everything is straightforward.

Subject3 (communion), however, refuses to be considered in the abstract because it is the living human being. It is a communion of Subject1 and Subject2 and, therefore, is an existential, not an essential reality. We are always some kind of mixture of Subject1 and Subject2.

Thus our I-feeling, as we have noted, wildly fluctuates as we emphasize now Subject1, then Subject2, and then Subject3; or as we switch back and forth between our ecto, meso, and endo modes. That is, the place where my gut self contacts the world depends on the size and configuration of my I-feeling at any moment. If my I-feeling holes up in the Cartesian box (the detached, incorporeal observer) then my limits are tight indeed. In meso body awareness my limits approximate my epidermis and the effective range of my tools. In endo awareness my limits are polymorphous. They can include a loved one so that she and I have a common limit. They can take in a country that I feel impelled to defend as I would myself.

Limits are not exactly the same thing as boundaries. Limits express a declaration of just how far out my I-feeling is at any time, a concept of undefended boundaries. Psychology usually talks not of limits, but of boundaries that we erect to defend our space, the kind we need to function as autonomous persons. Boundaries need to be high-tech wonders because of the demands put on them: (a) They have to expand and contract instantly to match the configuration of our I-feeling, and (b) as the situation warrants, they must be permeable, semi-permeable, or impermeable. Needless to say we are not always in balance as we shift our I-feeling around and try to defend it.

Schizophrenics and to a lesser extent persons with narcissistic and borderline disorders do not receive sufficient mirroring (either because of the quality of their mothering or their capacity to receive it) and/or do not sufficiently identify with their reflected image, thus they fail to develop full egos. Without sufficient ego strength, they lack a sense of inside and outside, of skin, of limits, and have no border on which to set up protective boundaries. Thus they are vulnerable and often fall victim to all sorts of external influences. Authors point out that inside/outside and skin are fictions when it comes to human personality. They are not strictly fictions, however, they are imaginative creations of the same nature as the ego itself. Without sufficient Subject1 (ego) and its boundaries, one cannot maintain a satisfactory Subject3.

People who do create healthy egos have a sense of their limits and usually have healthy boundaries. They are enabled to actually inhabit their space with their thoughts, moods, and urges. They can be effective, dynamic people. It is possible, however, for them to identify so completely with their egos that they produce rigid boundaries. In this condition they are well-adapted to meso competition or ecto rationalization, but are crippled in their ability to love another person, to be a responsible member of the community, or to achieve much fulfillment as Subject3.

We have the freedom to concentrate our I-feeling on exclusively meso, competitive, and cut-throat endeavors. We can erect barriers to our hearts and decency, and we sometimes do. In so doing, we put our life source, Subject2 out of bounds and our life force shrivels. Fortunately, we cannot maintain impregnable boundaries to our hearts.

We can also concentrate all our I-feeling onto Subject2, either because of insufficient ego strength, or for metaphysical and mystical reasons. In so doing, we erect boundaries around our heart center and put active living and rational thinking out of bounds. Doing so in moderation makes us meditators, mystics perhaps, or very centered people. If we cut off in this way, consistently and completely, we become ersatz mystics who are of no use to anyone and are a burden on society. Without a healthy Subject1 (ego) we have little to offer as human beings.

The modulation of our I-feeling by Faith is the key to endo awareness and creativity. How do we see with the dark light of the heart? How do we know what we are seeing? What do we see? What is the endo landscape? These are the questions addressed in the fourth part of this book.

# CHAPTER TWELVE

## Theses

Having come this far, let us take a moment to collect our thoughts. Thus far, we have discovered that:

- Western philosophy considers us to be a kind of wedding cake: Body-Mind-Spirit. This concept has served us well, but no longer does.
- Since Descartes, Western thought has struggled for objectivity using the model of the detached mental observer.
- In the nineteenth century thinkers no longer could believe in Plato's layer-cake world. Nietzsche declared the obvious in dramatic language by stating, "God is dead."
- Nietzsche, searching for a new paradigm to replace the layer-cake, found it in the River of Becoming where Heraclitus had found it before the time of Plato. Becoming and therefore growth and death have become central to our post-modern viewpoint on the world. Heidegger was stating this same truth when he defined us as beings-unto-death.
- Nietzsche also saw the impossibility of a detached, objective, mental observer of the River of Life. He saw instead a bodied observer swept along by the river and mooring himself so that the river rushes around him.
- Freud recognized the importance of the body as our unconscious mind. He urged a new Copernican revolution that would place the unconscious instead of the ego at the center of our personal universe. Lacan has developed these ideas. Our heart center (the body, the unconscious) is the true center of our universe; by understanding that, we will create a revolution in human science similar to that of Copernicus in astronomy.
- Merleau-Ponty demonstrated how the body perceives its world by folding back upon itself so that it is both Subject and Object to itself. He also described how the body recognizes itself by

its contact with other bodies (especially people), how the body creates the mind, and how body and soul are correlative terms for different stages of human organization.
- The-Body-is-the-Mind-is-the-Soul in the gradations and developmental phases as described by Merleau-Ponty. This reality underpins the functioning of much alternative medicine.
- Clinical psychology and phenomenology agree that we are neither identical to the universe nor separate from it. A phrase from the Zen tradition states our condition succinctly: Not two/not one.
- According to Freud and Lacan, the ego is ex-centric to the unconscious; in other words, our ego-center is not our unconscious-center. The unconscious is transpersonal.
- We create our egos by identifying with our image as mirrored by our mothers, other people, and reflecting surfaces such as mirrors. This creation of our egos causes an essential split within us between our egos and that part of us that created the ego but remains unconscious, which part Lacan calls the Other.
- By this imaginative identification and our symbolization of it in language we become truly human. Also we become torn by conflicting desires: Thanatos, power, the drive to individuality; and Eros, love, the drive to intimacy and a return to the now sundered original union. The goal of life is to unite ego and other in communion so that the original union which was unconscious may be restored as conscious. In formula form, the original separation can be expressed as:

Original Subject (unconscious) → Ego + Other,
or
$Subject_0$ → $Subject_1$ + $Subject_2$.

The goal of life can be expressed as:

Ego + Other → Communion,
or
$Subject_1$ + $Subject_2$ → $Subject_3$.

- The hologram, chaos theory, and fractal geometry give us physical representations of what Communion and Subject3 might be. They also indicate the kind of universe we live in: one with many non-competitive indeterminate (free) centers of activity. One that is dynamically organized by the principles of chaos and is exceedingly beautiful.
- The unconscious communicates with consciousness with its own logic and language.
- The observations made in Zen, concerning big mind and little mind fit comfortably in the schema developed above. The beginner's mind is an attitude that can be described as categorical (phenomenology), even-hovering attention (Freud), positive regard (Rogers), Faith toward the emotional truth of the moment (Bion), or as just plain wonder.
- Change is constant in our lives and universe. Contradiction is the rule, and not the exception.
- Contradictions within us implode in enormous energy and are the force behind our growth and creativity, much in the way that the atomic fusion of the Sun makes abundant life possible on Earth.
- I am God and I'm not.
- There are three ways to look at life: ecto, meso, and endo. The eye atop the pyramid symbolizes the ecto; our physical eyes in their sockets, the meso; and the heart, the endo. The heart is the place to stand if you want to see the whole panorama clearly.
- I-feeling is the sense I have of who I am at any moment. This feeling is constantly expanding and contracting. Lacan points out that the Subject, **I**, has a sliding meaning depending on the context in which we use it. **I** sometimes stands for Subject1, sometimes Subject2, and sometimes Subject3.
- The concept of boundaries as limits merely describes where we interface with our environment at any one time. As limits our boundaries have to expand and contract to stay configured to our I-feeling.
- The concept of defended boundaries indicates the protection that we erect on our limits to guard our subjective space. Sometimes our boundary defenses are hard and impermeable as

when we are engaged in conflict. At other times they are very permeable as when we are in love.
- Theoretically, Subject0 and Subject2 have no boundaries. Subject1 has hard boundaries. Subject3's boundaries are the ones that fluctuate with I-feeling. As Subject3 we are always in something of the same space with other Subjects3.
- Distinction-union is our constitutive structure. Take away either and the self would disappear. (Eigen)
- The description of our pre-reflective, first impression, categorical experience is one of the surest and quickest ways to arrive at unconscious reality.
- The whole universe of science is built upon the world as it is experienced, and if we want to subject science itself to rigorous scrutiny and arrive at a precise assessment of its meaning and scope, we must begin by reawakening the basic experience of the world of which science is the second-order expression (Merleau-Ponty).
- All of us can realistically describe ourselves to some extent as three people: one ecto, one meso, and one endo.
- Ecto thinking is our familiar schoolroom mode: abstract, logical, valueless, flitting about. Meso thinking is practical, short- term, competitive, dead serious, and involved in the push and pull of active living. Endo thinking dissolves the subject-object dichotomy; it merges with its surroundings and moves from a contextual awareness of the whole situation; its workings are seldom consciously attended to.
- Ecto learning is the sponge-like activity that is usually discussed in academic psychology. Meso learning is insistently active, straining to know what is almost grasped, and drilling what is learned so that it will not be forgotten. Endo learning is coincidental with some ongoing activity; it is a period of growth that is immediately buried in the person's ongoing development (Lyons); it is very personal and non-goal directed.
- Ecto remembering is conceived of as reclaiming engrams from our memory banks; its content is neutral, and there is a perceived gap in time between when we first learned something and when we remember it. Meso remembering is driven by values and active associations that fit the content into

significant situations and activities. Endo memories are not readily accessible for ecto consideration; examples of it are symptoms and acting out; memories without speech that occurred before we could talk; the way we "remember" our native tongue and our regional accent.

- Civilization began with endo consciousness in ascendancy and was supplanted by a dominant meso culture. In Greece, meso and endo reached a balance that enabled a blossoming of ecto consciousness. Today our culture is very meso-ecto. But an endo rebellion is brewing.
- The formula, Ego + Other → Communion, expresses the meaning of Freud's famous statement, "*Wo Es war, soll Ich werde*" (where it was, there I am to be).
- In deep communication my Other and your Other communicate using our egos as mere speaking and listening devices (Lacan). My Subject3 talks with your Subject3.
- **0** for Bion is a symbol for the existential truth of a situation as it is unfolding. **F** is his symbol for Faith, which is an attitude of steady attentiveness and openness. **F** in **0** is the proper attitude for coming to grips with the immediacy of life. **F** in this situation is the strange attractor working in the chaos of **0** randomly selecting those notes that compose the emotional tune being played by our unconscious.
- In general, our Faith acts as a strange attractor in all our acts of creativity. It also works to bring situations into our lives especially when it is reinforced with the "inductive property" (Levi-Strauss) of symbols. The efficacy of both the shaman's rituals and Freud's talking cure are based on these principles.
- The ego is our identification with an image of ourselves, which is socially institutionalized through language. As such, it is the strange attractor which creates our human life. It is capable of adaptation and is, in fact, designed to be modified into Subject3.

With these principles in mind, we proceed to examine what is revealed by our body's vision.

# PART FOUR

# HEARTSCAPES

## Part Four opens the vistas revealed by faith and heart thinking.

Chapter 13 dwells on how calm attention (faith) in chaos manifests endo awareness in our lives. It explains intuition as a mutual lowering of ego boundaries. It also examines the similarities between visions, hallucinations, and dreams.

Chapter 14 considers how heart knowing is harvested, translated into language, and validated. It probes the connections between Perception, Creativity, Language, and Reality.

Chapter 15 explores different conceptions of time and space. It defines the nature of phenomenological time and space.

Chapter 16 declares that the imaginal realm is where we formulate what we believe about reality. It examines the origin and vigor of two myths concerning the Virgin Mary.

Chapter 17 probes the mystery of death and presents several ways of considering survival after death

# CHAPTER THIRTEEN

# Heart Knowing

**The Heart**

The heart is the traditional seat of unconscious knowledge. It is the symbolic, essential, and sensitive center of the body. To be precise, the heart is the home and reality of Subject3 because it is both unconscious and individual, being not two/not one, just as we are. The heart is where we focus our Faith (**F**) and contact the total meaning of the moment (**0**). The heart offers us the wisdom of our bodies and of the universe, but it functions in a world that is dark, wet, and tumultuously still.

What is the view from the heart? It is glimmerings and glows of light in a dark unconscious ocean. The unconscious knows all and knows nothing because knowledge only really happens when it becomes conscious. The heart is the locus where the unconscious reaches consciousness. We decide and create the content of the unconscious by the attention and symbolism of our **F**. By our Faith, we chaotically attract what we need from it.

Being both One and Many the heart has access to universal and particular reality. It does not, of course, know everything for several reasons. First, everything is not yet unfolded in our indeterminate universe. Second, reality is infinitely vast, vaster by far, for example, than the infinite Mandelbrot set of fractal geometry. Third, each of us is a unique gingerbread man specialized by our bodies, whose microcosm freely incarnates the macrocosm. The knowledge of the heart as activated by our Faith is intensely personal. Fourth, the grand design prescribes that each of us concentrate on our own microcosm. In this way the macrocosm experiences fully-individuated replicas of itself in magnificent, chaotic harmony.

Our spatially, temporally, environmentally, and personally defined bodies know what is important. We can attend to them with Faith and bring their wisdom to conscious awareness. In a crucial sense, our hearts do not know until our ecto and meso minds interpret their messages. This interpretation is our symbolic representation of otherwise misty inchoate heart truths into meso and ecto modes. Without this symbolizing, the treasures of our bodies are unknown to us in any practical sense. Truth is embedded in our bodies, but it is born into our human world by our symbolizing Faith.

What we receive from the unconscious is communicated to us in a variety of ways which have already been stated. The communication is always by way of image and symbol. Feelings themselves are part of the language of the Other. We can attend to and understand this communication from the unconscious. With practice we can become good at it.

This is, of course, endo knowledge, but it is mediated by (ecto) language. It is done, however, with minimal ecto input, especially when one is just going with the flow of his or her feelings. When people are working in the deep endo mode they move almost by instinct. The language that they use in their communication with their other is perhaps subliminal. This explains their fluidity of movement, their sureness of step, and their charisma.

If we are centered in our heart we find it easy to work from a sense of the whole. The more we are comfortable functioning as Subject3, the more we find the holistic viewpoint natural, and the more human we become. If we are locked into our ego-centricity (Subject1) we find this kind of communication and activity very difficult.

The heart knows by immersing itself in reality. With boundaries lowered, it incorporates a situation and reads it from the inside. Our heart does this when it precedes us into a room on a social occasion and reports back on the mood of the company inside. It does the same when it dives into a sea of confusing information and, from it, abstracts understanding.

How does the heart communicate to our conscious minds? As directed by our attention and the exigencies of our lives, the heart, having found understanding in our jumble of experiences, creates symbols in the form of dreams, chance occurrences, urges to do something, and so on. The heart, for example, might place me in front of a newspaper whose headline unlocks a personal problem. It might lead me to drive to a different supermarket one day and there meet the girl of my dreams.

Vocalized words are not necessary for heart to heart communication. Words can either assist or hinder the process. Hearts, with their boundaries down, understand each other. Words that express what is truly experienced enhance and deepen the intimacy. Words that mask and lie block intimacy.

Reading and interpreting feelings, one's own and those of other people, is an art, the culmination of heart knowledge.

## Empathy

In our everyday language we express the conviction that we can inhabit someone else's space. We say that we see the world through another person's eyes, walk a mile in her shoes, or get inside his skin. Our empathy is easily understood in a not two/not one bodily world with its endo ways of knowing. We simply lower our boundaries and allow our I-feelings to merge. My Subject3 and your Subject3 allow each other to share some of their being, thoughts, and feelings.

Empathy is a common phenomenon among us as infants, as lovers, as parents, and just as humans. Sometimes, however, we talk about it as if it were weird. In our early years, we immersed ourselves in our family chaos. With our Faith we absorbed and assimilated it. We learned incredibly complex things in almost no time. Our empathy sustained us and made us human.

Imaginatively putting oneself in another's shoes is a way of identifying with the other person. This is a source of insight and understanding. The reason we can do this is that we share a common unconscious. My Subject3, in touch with my other, can contact your Subject3 that is in touch with your other. Your Subject3, in touch with your other, can communicate with my Subject3 on that common ground. Empathy in this sense is not between my Subject1 (ego) and your Subject1. The most I can do to get into your system as Subject1 is to imagine how I would feel in such a situation. This is useful, but it is not true empathy.

In true empathy my Other attends to your Other in even hovering attention. I see the world as you see it, not as I imagine I would see it in your situation. This communication is brokered by the language of the unconscious and formalized in spoken (ecto) language. The model employed here is fidelity to the moment (F in 0) as we listen to both our own hearts and the words of one another.

Empathy can be foiled by rigid ego boundaries or by insufficient ones. With our boundaries too rigid we give too little attention to our Other (Subject2). As a result, we are neither in touch with our own unconscious nor that of others. We are imprisoned within walls that we have co-created and so are unable to communicate on transpersonal levels.

Good empathic therapists, who communicate from an ecto viewpoint, are curious in this respect. They function superbly in an endo mode that they advocate. Heinz Kohut, for example, states, "The empathic understanding of the experiences of other human beings is as basic an endowment of man as his vision, hearing, touch, taste, and smell." He locates the source of this ability in the following passage.

> The groundwork for our ability to obtain access to another person's mind is laid by the fact that in our earliest mental organization the feelings, actions, and behavior of the mother had been included in our self. This primary empathy with the mother prepares us for the recognition that, to a large extent, the basic inner experiences of people remain similar to our own. Our first perception of the manifestations of another person's feelings, wishes, and thoughts occurred within the framework of a narcissistic conception of the world; the capacity for empathy belongs, therefore, to the innate equipment of the human psyche and remains to some extent associated with the primary process.(1977, p. 116).

He states, "The presence of an empathetic or introspective observer defines, in principle, the psychological field" (1977, p.32).

Yet, he does not seem to see empathy in the terms that we do. In explaining empathy he restricts himself to saying that the therapist is empathic only with his own inner life and just imagines how he might feel in the other person's situation. He says,

> Even hovering attention...should be defined as the responsiveness to be expected, on an average, from persons who have devoted their lives to helping others with the aid of insights obtained via the empathic immersion into their own inner life (1977, p. 252).

Empathy is also foiled if personal boundaries are inadequate. In this situation, I might experience what is going on in your life because your consciousness would be present in my awareness, but I would be unable to sort out your experience from my own. There would be lots of unconscious merging but no empathy. Empathy requires a healthy Subject1 in addition to Subject2 in order to exist because those two together create Subject3. Empathy is between two Subject3s.

The following schemes indicate in which relationships empathic information is passed and in which ones it is not. In my personal life,

- My Subject1(ego) does not communicate empathically with my Subject2 (other) directly:
  Subject1 ←/→ Subject2.
- My Subject3 does communicate empathically with my Subject1 and Subject2:
  Subject3 ←→ Subject2 and Subject3 ←→ Subject1.
- My Subject1 communicates to my Subject2 via my Subject3:
  Subject1 ←→ Subject3 ←→ Subject2.

The rules for your internal empathy match mine. In empathetic communication between you and me,

- My Subject1(m) communicates with your Subject1(y) and your Subject3(y):
  Subject1(m) ←→ Subject1(y) &
  Subject1(m) ←→ Subject3(y) &
  Subject1(y) ←→ Subject3(m).
- It is probable that my Subject3(m) communicates directly with your Subject3(y):
  Subject3(m) ←→ Subject3(y).
- It is questionable whether my Subject2(m) communicates with your Subject2(y)
  Subject2(m) ←?→ Subject2(y).
- Our Subject3s do not have access to each other's Subject2s:
  Subject3(m) ←/→ Subject2(y) &
  Subject3(y) ←/→ Subject2(m).

Lacan puts these facts into a curious form. He says that we do not have a "third or fourth [mystical] ear." That is, my Subject3 does not have a special channel to your unconscious other. Empathic communication takes place primarily between my communion (Subject3) and your communion. It also occurs between my other and your other, but it is questionable what kind of useful or enlightening knowledge is passed between unconsciouses without the intervention of Subject3 and some form of language.

The typical way that empathic communication occurs can be schematized in a slightly different form as follows:

$$\text{My S2} \leftrightarrow \text{My S3} \leftrightarrow \text{Your S3} \leftrightarrow \text{Your S2}.$$

If Subject2s can communicate empathically, end arounds are also possible. In other words:

$$\text{My S3} \leftrightarrow \text{My S2} \leftrightarrow \text{YourS2} \leftrightarrow \text{Your S3}.$$

You will notice that these two chains are indistinguishable if you connect their ends.

There are limits of our ability to know the self of another. Kohut states them in the following passage:

> We cannot, by introspection and empathy, penetrate to the self per se; only its introspectively or empathically perceived psychological manifestations are open to us...we will still not know the essence of the self as differentiated from its manifestations (1977, p. 311, quoted from Masek in Aanstoos, 1991, p.35).

Merleau-Ponty makes a similar observation,

> But at the very moment that I think I share the life of another, I am rejoining it only in its ends, its exterior poles. It is in the world that we communicate, through what, in our life is articulate. It is from this lawn before me that I think I catch the sight of the impact of the green on the vision of another, it is through the music that I enter into his musical emotion, it is the thing itself that opens unto me the access to the private world of another (1964a, p.11).

Lacan, Kohut, and Merleau-Ponty are in agreement, I believe, in saying that the use of language and reference to external reality are necessary for empathic understanding. They are also saying that we do not have empathy as mere egos. Kohut's empathic analyst, for example, is not pure Subject1; he is an ego that is in profound communion, Subject3, with his own unconscious, Subject2. Thus, although Kohut limits his theorizing to the scientific, objective, ecto viewpoint, and declares that empathy is merely "vicarious introspection," that is, "I can know the other's psychological life indirectly as mediated through my own self knowledge" (Masek, in Aanstoos, p. 35), still his practice can be seen as an endo empathy that is careful not to fall into a tempting mystification.

The absence of sufficient ego is a source of severe heart trouble. In extreme cases, it is the cause of schizophrenia. In less extreme cases, it is found in the personality disorders described as schizotypic, schizoid, narcissistic, or borderline. It is often the source of delusional and paranoid states as well. In the extreme situation, the thoughts and feelings of others are experienced as alien presences in my mind that I have no power to keep out. In this situation it is very difficult to have a functioning Subject3. It is well known that helping patients to build a missing ego structure and to erect boundaries on it can be good long-term therapy.

Of course, even schizophrenics have some ego structure and sometimes can use it to startling effect. John MacGregor (1989) displays artwork done by people who were certifiably insane. Their artwork is sometimes spectacular and full of archetypical symbolism. Like other true art, it has an unconscious logic and symmetry, but seems to have little practical relevance in the person's life. It is as if they were adrift in the sea of the unconscious, categorically recording what is going on within them as a camera might. In this situation their Subject3 is less an artist perceiving the symbolic meaning of his or her experience and more like a video camera dumbly recording what it sees.

Sane artists inhabit the same unconscious territory as the insane and sometimes get lost in it. Great thinkers such as Freud and Jung allowed themselves to be lost there for a time. Nietzsche, at the end, lost himself hopelessly there. Sanely creative people express not only the symbolism they encounter in their unconscious, but also the sense that their Faith (F) extracts from the experience. F in O informs their creativity in its integrative sense.

There is creativity defined as symbolic representation in the art of the insane. There is also creativity as integration of personality (and culture). The second is the true expression of the Other. One can be creative as a video camera and still be crazy. To be creative in the integrative sense one needs sufficient ego strength. One cannot be a strong Subject3 unless he or she has sufficient Subject1.

That said, a certain relative underdevelopment of personal boundaries does seem to be a persistent trait of most creative geniuses. As Kohut (1985) says,

> The creative individual, whether in art or science, is less psychologically separated from his surroundings than the noncreative one; the "I-you" barrier is not as clearly defined. The intensity of the creative person's awareness of the relevant aspects of his surroundings is akin to the detailed self perceptions of the schizoid and the childlike (p. 112).

These characteristics may hinder them in practical living, but place them close to their unconscious source of creativity.

Empathy, as F in O, is creativity in the integrative sense and therefore requires egos that can enter a co-union according to the formula,

$$\text{Ego} + \text{Other} \rightarrow \text{Communion}.$$

Some people develop their empathic power professionally. They are pastors, social workers, and therapists. There is a price to pay for such intense and persistent empathy. One can easily drift from a state of merged consciousness to a state of enmeshment. For that reason understanding endo processes, discipline, and training are very important for such people.

Heinz Kohut considered empathy to have archaic and pre-rational roots. For that reason, he called it "primary process." He even said that it has a narcissistic and animistic component.

Empathic observation may indeed be archaic. However, as we have seen, it is just this primitive quality that qualifies it as categorical or pre-reflective observation. As such, it is at the basis of all reality according to the phenomenologists.

Kohut described the origins of our empathic ability as coming from the narcissistic self (Subject0) of our early development. He said:

> Our early closeness to the mother in empathy becomes the starting point for a series of developmental steps which lead ultimately to a state in which the ego can choose between the use of empathic and nonempathic modes of observation, depending on the realistic requirements and on the nature of the surroundings that it scrutinizes (p. 118).

As lovers and family members, we often have our boundaries down to each other and so merge consciousnesses. In this empathic state, we sometimes read each other's thoughts as when we complete one another's sentences. In times of trauma, we sometimes are alerted, over great distances, that one of our loved ones is in danger.

Mind readers, to the extent that they are not faking it, tune in through empathy. If they try to force their way in through someone's boundary system, or worse, if they try to manipulate somebody, they pay a terrible price. Joseph Lyons (1987) explains that a person controlling someone in this way "pays a price for control in the necessity to first absorb whatever one has to deal with" (p. 123). This absorbing is debilitating. It explains the exhaustion experienced by psychic readers and healers, and the relative ineffectiveness of metaphysical manipulation. In the jargon, "witchcraft, both black and white, is bad karma."

Empathy and other forms of endo awareness are all-pervasive in our lives whether we recognize them or not. Even our advertising is based on it. Yet we lack the vocabulary to talk about it in a serious academic way. There is a kind of scientific and academic taboo against such basic human inquiry.

Romantic love is a uniquely powerful form of empathy. It is the symbolic physical reuniting of two individuals into the intimacy that existed before they separated from primitive unconsciousness by creating egos. The umbilical cord is re-attached. The original Desire is consummated. Two become one flesh. *Wo es war, soll Ich werde.* (Where it, the other, was; there I, ego, would be.) The process is outlined as follows:

$$\text{Subject1} + \text{Subject2} \rightarrow \text{Subject3}.$$

Each partner takes this journey becoming one with his or her Other and with the Other of his or her partner while retaining a certain separate consciousness. Together the partners symbolize this especially in the formulation,

$$\text{Man} + \text{Woman} \rightarrow \text{Child}.$$

Thus is seen the symbolism of romantic love and its absolute centrality to human existence. Human beings do not come to be except through separateness and union.

The wonder of romantic love cannot be described in this book as I possess neither the talent, the time, nor the space. The topic deserves a marvelous book all of its own. Fortunately, such a book is already written. It is *Dreams of Love and Fateful Encounters: the Power of Romantic Passion*, by Ethel S. Person. She presents an extraordinary phenomenological description of the intricate and powerful phenomenon of romantic passion. Her book is a model of phenomenological research.

Person's observations are made from the heart. She approaches her material from experience, observation, discussions, and literature and has had it thoroughly critiqued by her psychiatric and academic peers. Her work fits comfortably into the framework of a not two/not one world.

In summary, empathy is the endo version of interpersonal communication. In one form, our unconsciouses communicate directly with each other and we read each others feelings and thoughts by attending, as Subject3, to our own unconscious. In another form, we share our unconscious states with each other through language. In either case, I experience (vicariously) what you are experiencing. On analyzing my pre-reflective experience, I see that I am not just imagining what it must be like for you; instead, I am sharing your experience.

In this light, it is clear that empathy is a profound everyday experience. It is not esoteric. It is mystical only in the basic sense that the body itself is mystical; that is, it is an experience of being not two/not one with another person.

**Visions, Hallucinations, Dreams**

Visions, hallucinations, and dreams are variations of endo knowing common to everyone. They are communications from our bodily unconscious that have their own logics and languages. They have been described from different perspectives: primary process thought (Freud), pre-reflective experience (phenomenology), symbolic thought (Jung), the discourse of the Other (Lacan), right-brain activity, and imaginal dialogues (Watkins).

Freud considered primary process thought to be primitive and secondary process thought to be more mature. Primary process thought is incomplete, symbolic, and unrealistic. According to him, secondary process is rational and reality-tested; it is real thinking, not whimsy.

Pre-reflective thought is a term used by phenomenologists. It focuses on the content of perception before we take a second look. We adjust our perceptions later to fit into our conceptual reality. The content of this pre-reflective experience is described as gestalts and symbols. Gestalts, because we experience wholes and not discrete unconnected sensations; that is, before we ecto/meso think about what we perceive we have already endo organized the perceived reality. Symbols, because our first perceptions have a connection to us and a meaning for us; that is, we make sense of our individual realities before we grow into an ecto understanding of what they are. We are not isolated from our world in the manner of the Cartesian box (a disembodied soul with an impossible task: to contact and make sense of a totally other and material world).

Symbolic thought, according to Jung, arises from our innate [meso] quest for meaning. Symbols (personages, animals, physical organs, myths, etc.) well up from both the individual and the collective unconscious. They are valued keys to a person's and a culture's identity. They have a validity of their own as communications from the unconscious. They provide a standard against which conventional reality is to be understood and not just vice versa.

Lacan, following Freud, sees these activities as communications from the unconscious, speaking a language of signs in the manner of a rebus (e.g. eye-heart-U). The language is to be deciphered by interpreting the signs as figures of speech.

Right brain thinking is symbolic, creative, non-linear, and irrational. As such, it is endo thinking and utilizes Faith (**F**) as a strange attractor in the chaos (**0**) of the unconscious. In recent years, Faith has been recognized as the source of artistic creation and intuitive insight. Its current high evaluation is a kind of revolution because it had been denigrated for years by behaviorally oriented scientists and psychologists.

Mary Watkins, who writes a great deal about imaginal realities, has demonstrated that human thought is universally dramatic; in other words, we are always talking to ourselves. Anyone who recognizes the human truth in the works of Shakespeare is compelled to agree with her. In our imaginal dialogues we make sense out of our worlds. These dialogues are, of course, not solely verbal. They are often in the symbolic language that Jung, Freud, and Lacan have described.

Watkins points out that the term "hallucination" became current only after the arrival of psychoanalytic thought in the nineteenth century. Before then people talked of visions. Visions and hallucinations are basically the same thing.

In the Middle Ages, theology had many classifications for visions; today psychology has similar classifications for hallucinations. In theology's main distinction, good and bad, visions are better defined than are hallucinations. Because of our rationalistic bias, that regards all hallucinations as bad, we denigrate an important part of our psychic makeup. Some sort of distinction between toxic and non-toxic hallucinations needs to be established.

With her term "imaginal dialogues," Watkins makes it clear that hallucinations are normal and often salutary experiences. The test for pathology cannot be the presence of hallucinations because they are universally present. The test is the quality of the hallucination. She provides these signs of pathology in imaginal dialogues:

1) Lack of autonomy for self or imaginal other; either self or other feels like a puppet, is told what to do and say;
2) Passivity of one with respect to the other; one enacts or suffers the other's wishes without successfully asserting his/her own agency or wishes. This impotence may be reflected in such

things as not being able to terminate an imaginal dialogue when desired.
3) The mode of relation is egocentric, where one figure is known only insofar as he/she affects the other; depth of characterization, where a figure is known from more than one perspective, is lacking;
4) Absence of a reflecting ego (a self- reflective representation or narrative voice) who notices the difference between figures of the perceptual world and those of the imaginal, who appreciates the latter metaphorically, and who can communicate these distinctions when necessary to others (Watkins, 1986, pp. 146-147).

The core of the pathology of hallucinations is well expressed in the following quotation:

> [The] patient is denied any spontaneous and free survey of the world; his thoughts being heard, his mind being read, denote that the barriers of his intimate life have been leveled off, that the innermost sphere of his existence has been invaded (Erwin Strauss, quoted by Watkins, 1986, p. 142).

Unhealthy dialogues cannot be assimilated; they lead to delusional beliefs that dominate a person's life.

Ordinary hallucinations/visions, on the other hand, are the means we use to explain our world to ourselves and to pose problems to ourselves. "To be or not to be" is the address given by Hamlet to his unconscious other. With it he places a strange attractor in his personal chaos, the necessary step toward creative problem solving. The apparition of his father's ghost had previously been a communication from his unconscious that brought into focus his distress at that time. These imaginal dialogues of Hamlet mirror dialogues that go on in us constantly.

Watkins (1986 pp. 149-150) proposes formal criteria for differentiating imaginal dialogues as they occur in "private speech, hallucinations, imaginary companions, praying, the writing of fiction, dreams, fantasy, and play." She demonstrates the richness of the dialogue between what we are calling ego and other in the communion that is Subject3. In particular, she related the Persian, Sufi mysticism of Ibn Arabi for whom to return to one's Lord is to "return to his self." Watkins wrote:

> In Ibn Arabi's words, "We have given Him to manifest Himself through us, whereas He has given us (to exist through Him). Thus the role is shared between Him and us....If he has given us life and existence by His being, I also give Him life by knowing Him in my heart" (1986, p. 73).

If we remove the theological trappings of these thoughts and replace them with psychological clothes, we have the drama of Subjects0, 1, 2, and 3.

In her 1976 book, Watkins draws distinctions between waking dreams, daydreams, and hallucinations. The waking dream is one manifestation of what we have termed Subject3 activity. It is the somewhat meditative activity of withdrawing from ecto and meso immersion in experience. According to Watkins, it is:

> an attempt to get our awareness [out of immersion so that]...we can then discriminate what is moving. This does not mean one steps out of the experience, becomes unrelated, and begins to analyze. It means that our sensitivities and awareness are freed to participate independently as themselves and to bring their unique qualities into the situation (p.16).

This kind of attention can be employed while awake, in reverie, or, with practice, in lucid nighttime dreaming. It is serene F in 0.

Merleau-Ponty contributes this observation about waking dreams: "What one too deliberately seeks, he does not find; and he who on the contrary has in his meditative life known how to tap its spontaneous source never lacks for ideas and values" (1964b, p.83).

Daydreams are like waking dreams in that they deal with imaginal material. They are unlike waking dreams in the laxity of their attention; in their attention they are simply involved in what is going on in the imaginal realm with the same kind of attention that they fasten on external concerns. Watkins says, "In daydreaming, the ego's attention becomes attached to the imaginal contents in the same way it does to our daily concerns. There is no awareness during it or memory afterward of what was going on" (p. 18). The quality of F in 0 distinguishes Subject3 attention from both daydreaming with imaginal realities, and immersion in physical and social reality. The Sufis held that the imaginal world (the *mundus imaginalis*) was the sacred realm of the soul, and that it required rapt attention to dwell there. As Watkins put it:

> In the Sufi idea of creative imagination it was believed that whenever the imagination is allowed to "stray" and to be "wasted recklessly, then it ceases to fulfill its function of perceiving and producing the symbols that lead to inner intelligence," the intermediary world (that of the *mundus imaginalis* and of the soul) can be considered to have disappeared (p.18).

The idea of hallucination has been used to discredit the imaginal. Watkins points out that, "Waking dreams and hallucinations...rely on two distinctly different psychic functions: imagination and perception. Hallucinations purport to deal with external material and perceptual reality, whereas waking dreams and dreams pertain to imaginal reality" (pp. 18-19). She claims that the "hallucinator is asleep" with regards to awareness of the imaginal. If a person obtains Subject3 awareness he or she is no longer the victim of hallucination.

This point is well-taken, yet it is necessary to point out that all perception is hallucinatory in the broad sense. We perceive wholes (gestalts) which have meaning for us (symbols) and initiate a dialogue about their friendliness/unfriendliness, importance/ unimportance, clarity/density of meaning, and so on. The dialogues that generate these gestalts are often under the threshold of consciousness. For various reasons we often do not perceive things that are sensibly presented to us. We have already glanced at Merleau-Ponty's exposition of perception. In the next chapter, we will examine the relationship between perception and language.

Dreams give sway to our imaginal dialogues often turning them into full-scale dramatic productions. When these dialogues and dramas occur in the hypnagogic state between sleeping and waking they are called visions. Almost all remarkable visions occur in this state which is induced by a variety of methods: sleeping, meditation, dancing, reverie, sensory deprivation or overload, exhaustion, fasting, epilepsy, migraines, medication, drugs, etc.

Imaginal dialogues are grounded in our bodies, our histories, and our cultures. They gather their material and intensity from the preoccupations of our waking life, which act as the strange attractors of perception, hallucination, dream, and vision. In the conflict-resolution dream, they give emotional release to our day's unresolved tensions and also clue us in to the nature of those tensions. In problem-solving dreams, they present us with answers which are arrived at while our rational minds are asleep.

Because our boundaries are porous in endo awareness we may sometimes dream for someone else or dream for our society, especially if we are caught up in their concerns. Again, our attention or Faith acts as the strange attractor in these dreams. Also, because we are not two, our imaginal dialogues sometimes have racial and universal significance, especially in the form of archetypical themes: birth/death/resurrection, war and peace, creation, the quest, etc.

Our imaginal dialogues are usually tied to our time and place for their raw material. For reasons of survival, we do not often obsess on events of another place and another time. If we did, we might have flashbacks to earlier historical events, and so breach the relative divisions of space and time. Likewise, if we were to intensely focus on spiritual matters in the context of a dominant mythology, we would create the strange attractor that would draw religious visions from our unconscious. Ordinarily, however, we focus on our personal, familial, and social concerns, and for good reason. Focusing for no reason on existentially irrelevant concerns creates a scattered unconscious, which fosters personal and societal disorganization or disintegration.

The immersion we experience today in the sea of media/information/ entertainment dilutes the focus of our imaginal life. On the one hand, this is good because we enter into imaginal dialogue with so many different viewpoints, cultures, and situations. On the other hand, we lose the focused mythology that sustained our ancestors and their societies. In our global village we are forced, more than ever, to attend to the quality of our F in 0.

During situations of great urgency breaches of time and space are more likely to occur as, for example, in the documented premonitions and visions of plane crashes. When there is a strong human bond, and therefore a certain steadiness of the strange attractor, spatial boundaries sometimes fade, as when a mother knows from a distance that her daughter has died. Sometimes physical dysfunction is the catalyst. While such visions possess remarkable clarity, many are not so clear, especially when they are induced by mind-confusing chemicals or when they are experienced by people whose attention is not disciplined.

In summary, visions, hallucinations, and dreams are closely related endo experiences that have a limited freedom with regard to space and time. Their content is determined by the focus of our conscious and vital attention. The clarity of their content depends on the single-mindedness of that focus and the steadiness of attention (Faith) with which it is endowed. The principle at work is that of the strange attractor in chaos. These endo experiences have their own logic and language.

**Methodology Part Two**

We have already noted that the preferred standpoint for viewing the material of this book is the heart. I will now make explicit the qualities of heart vision: How it is possible, how it works, how heart vision communicates to conscious reflection, how we are to interpret what the heart says, how we can make conscious use of the feeling communication from the heart.

Heart vision is a natural correlate of our holographic unity with the universe. Our bodies are privy to the universe's unspoken secrets. Our attention attracts elements of the unspoken vision that manifest as feelings, images, verbal slips and annoying recurring experiences that enable us to pay attention to important issues. Language brings these symbols into conscious awareness. We interpret the messages we get on the basis of their clarity and pertinence to our situation. We make conscious use of our heat feelings by acting on them and evaluating the results.

I will describe how our descriptions are arrived at and how they are to be understood. Finally, I will propose tests for verifying and validating the theories arrived at in this book.

*How Our Descriptions Are Arrived at*

Heart vision is both universal and individual. The heart is where we are Subject3, where we are both universal and individual. When we lower our personal boundaries the vast expanse of unconscious knowledge is available to us. In our openness to unconscious chaos (**O**) we send out a signal of Faith (**F**) loosely focused on what we want to see. That signal acts as a strange attractor, garnering those things from the unconscious that are most relevant to our request. The heart then communicates that information to us in a variety of ways. Lacan mentions some of them: bodily symptoms, dreams, chance encounters, and slips of the tongue. He explains that these communications are symbolic, and are to be interpreted by means of metaphor and metonymy. The heart also communicates by feeling which is a basic language expressing either approval or disapproval.

We interpret what the unconscious is saying with its symbols by means of metonymy and metaphor *a la* Lacan and Freud. We also utilize the insights of Jung and others. Taking directions from our feelings is both an art and a learned skill. To utilize these feelings we trust them, go with them, and see where they lead us. We test them as we go along and make corrections where we need to do so. The deviations that we make from a direct course are useful to us in that they allow us to tack back to the preferred course. If we were not moving with our feelings we would neither go anywhere, nor know where the course was, nor be able to use our deviations as our guide. We learn that it is best to feel ourselves going off course early and to correct promptly. Allowing too great a variance to our proposed course causes aberrations so wild that we tend to get swamped and are forced to make corrections without knowing what the proper correction might be. Symptoms of illness are obvious aberrations of this sort. If we lock ourselves into ecto and meso modes of being we can easily lose our bearings and risk swamping ourselves. To attend to our feelings we need to nurture our endo awareness.

Many of the descriptions made in this book are my own. Many more are derivative from other thinkers. In two senses these descriptions are original. One, they are original to the person who made them. Two, they are original to me in the sense that I made the other person's description my own, appropriated it, and interpreted it as it made sense to me. The authors that I quote would not necessarily agree with the use I make of their descriptions.

These descriptions are derived from endo-feeling observation at the heart center. Endo intelligence provided symbols, urges, ideas, and chance events to consciousness. Meso intelligence struggled to make sense out of this material using ecto intelligence to express and organize its insights. The quality of attention that our conscious intelligence provides in this situation is part of the method called phenomenological reduction. This is an explicit and disciplined process for arriving at accurate descriptions.

> Phenomenological reduction is a conscious, effortful, opening of ourselves to the phenomenon as a phenomenon. ...We want not to see this event as an example of this or that theory that we have; we want to see it as a phenomenon in its own right with its own meaning and structure. Anybody can hear the words that were spoken; to listen for the meanings as they eventually emerged from the event as a whole is to have adopted an attitude of openness to the phenomenon in its inherent meaningfulness. It is to have "bracketed" our responses to separate parts of the conversation and to have let the event emerge as a meaningful whole (Keen, 1975, p. 38).

As we listen in this way, we first encompass the whole in an intuitive way and let the inherent logic of the discourse we are hearing reveal itself. The effort required in doing this is well-described by Lacan when he discusses how the Other of the analyst listens to the Other of the analysand.

The listening involved here is a very active process both in the original intending to what is being said and in the effort to understand what is meant. Our understandings are developed by meso/ecto intelligence. They are understood as coming from a specific endo perspective. They are seen against a background of a not two/not one world, within a bodily consciousness that has three modes: endo, meso, and ecto.

We then examine the statements thus produced from a multitude of other viewpoints. We systematically tack between endo immersion and ecto/meso reflection, culminating in a new "totalization" of the experience.

The descriptive statements in this book, then, are an accurate portrayal of the totality of body wisdom as I see it. It has been tested against, and fits into, a worldview that I find compatible.

## How Our Descriptions Are to Be Understood

Phenomenological understanding is defined as a presentation of the necessary and sufficient reasons for phenomena with nothing missing and nothing left out, with an elegance of economy. The phenomena fit into a theory and the theory fits the experience. The explanations clarify our experience making it more amenable to our control and enjoyment. The theories help us to see good, to work well, and to feel good.

This book is an effort to provide a coherent description of myself as an intelligent, spiritual body in an intelligent spiritual world with which I am one in the nature of hologram and Mandelbrot set. This description, taken from the heart perspective, provides an understanding far deeper than the understandings I get from isolated meso and ecto viewpoints. I assume, because I am not two/not one with you, that these insightful descriptions will be enlightening, useful, and enjoyable for you readers of this book.

## Tests for our Theories

There are three general tests of statements. Do they feel right (endo)? Do they work (meso)? Do they fit with accepted facts and theories (ecto)?

The descriptions provided in this book seem to pass the endo test. They feel right (to me). They possess a certain centrality and balance. They put into perspective parts of life that otherwise seem disparate. They promote peace of mind, tolerance, and delight in diversity. They open up new possibilities for understanding lots more of life.

They also seem to pass the meso test. They provide a description of the playing field of life that allows us to pursue both our Eros drive and our Thanatos drive with equanimity. They provide the natural goal for our life-long striving, to be Subject3. They help us use and master our endo capabilities.

These descriptions can also be verified and validated in the ecto mode. They do not, however, fit into the methods of an empirical science which excludes endo awareness from the realm of knowledge. Each description and the entire description can be confronted with all of the following questions:

- Does it fit the facts?
- Does it explain or situate them?
- Does it cover the ground of discussion?
- Is it sufficient to explain them?
- Is it necessary to explain them?
- Does it fit coherently into a larger theory?
- Can it predict or uncover new facts?
- Does it show relationships between disparate facts and processes?

In addition, these descriptions can be proved wrong or flawed by a negative response to any of the questions above. They can also be proved wrong by an affirmative response to the question: Does it lead to inconsistencies?

It seems to me that the descriptions in this book pass the tests shown above. You are invited to make your own judgments.

The method of the presentation of this fourth and last section of the book is to develop a geography of the imaginal realm and to fit it into the auto-genesis of our human reality. In other words, it will be shown how our whole world, both the part called objective and the part called imaginal, are products of our divine bodies.

# CHAPTER FOURTEEN

# Language

## Perception and Language

This section briefly restates Merleau-Ponty's phenomenology of perception and adapts it to the ideas informing this book especially those of Lacan, chaos, and Lyons.

*The Context of Our Lives*

The context of our lives is exuberant and self-transcending. Merleau-Ponty called the "stuff" from which we have sprung "Being" or "Flesh." Freud and Lacan called it "the unconscious," or simply, "the world." Without their transcending quality, Being and the Unconscious would be mute: both unintelligible and (ecto/meso) unintelligent. In its exuberance, the world projects holographic facsimiles of itself in the manner of the Mandelbrot set: facsimiles that are individualized and indeterminate (free).

As the most individualized and free creatures in the world, human beings are the most fully holographically similar to Being as a whole. We began our separate (projected by Being) existence as zygotes and developed an ever more convoluted interface between parts of ourselves as embryo and fetus, developing by those convolutions organs of sense, sight, hearing, and communication. In birth, and in the severing of the umbilical, we physically separated from our physical mother and symbolically separated from our general nurturing source, "Being."

.   In this separation we attain the condition of all the higher forms of animals. We have a circumscribed separateness of action. In one sense, we are in a less advantageous position than other animals because we are born prematurely. They are physically and mentally more fully developed at birth than we are, more quickly able to face the world on their own. We are dependent on our mothers and our nurturing environment for a very long time.

Our prematurity, however, turns out to be a plus for us. Because our minds are premature as infants we mature in a extended, sight-and-sound, interpersonal world and absorb that world (by endo processes) instead of absorbing just the relatively boring world of the womb as do other animals. As a result, our minds are much more complex and agile than other animals, and probably capable of deeper feelings.

Kohut states the same truth in his own distinctive context. He directs our attention to what he called "self-objects." These are the family members and the society with which the child identifies. He wondered,

> ...whether it is correct to say that man is born helpless because he is not born with a significantly functioning ego apparatus. [Rather he thinks,] he is born powerful because a milieu of empathic self-objects is indeed his self (1977, p. 249).

A critical event in our becoming operational human beings is situated in the process of "mirroring" which has been described earlier. We, like other animals, identify with our image, as reflected to us by our mothers, and model our behavior on hers. But because of our immaturity at birth and, therefore, our more complex, active, and alert minds, we take this identification one step further. We signify with language a separation between our identified-with image and our mothers. In this way we create our own egos.

The language we use in performing this separation need not be formal or even vocal. It can be a symbolic action such as the one Lacan describes in which a child is fascinated with his image appearing and disappearing in a mirror. It can be the Fort/Da experience of Freud's grandson. In every case, the basis of that language is the oppositional dyad, such as, Fort/Da (Gone/Here). All language is built on a separation of opposites (as is all logic). "The bipolar nature of language is present throughout every language, all the way down to the twelve pair of phonemes that are its foundation" (Muller and Richardson, p. 11).

The oppositional nature of language is reflected in the oppositional nature of the ego that it creates. Egos (Subject1s) are definitely not one with other egos. The original body-subject (Subject0), on the other hand, before it was split by language into Subject1 and Subject2 was one (not two) with the world, and necessarily so. The reason is this: Two (2) is not a possibility in a consciousness that does not symbolically oppose (with language) the number One (1) with the null set (0) because our whole counting system is built on the system:

$$\text{One plus the null set gives us 2 units;}$$
$$\text{or}$$
$$1 + 0 \rightarrow 2;$$
$$\text{and}$$
$$1 + (1 + 0) + 0 \rightarrow 3;$$
$$\text{and}$$
$$1 + (1 + 0) + [1 + (1 + 0)] + 0 \rightarrow 4;$$
$$\text{etc.}$$
(cf. Schneiderman, 1983, p. 5).

You can sometimes see this process at work when a child is learning to count on his/her fingers. As for the Other, that which is left of the body-subject after it identifies and falls in love with the ego, it (as Subject2) is one (not two) with the universe.

Our Subject3s, which are ourselves as living, intelligent, individual beings, who are the Communion of ego and other, are complex entities. As subject3, we are not two/not one with the world (with Being, with the Unconscious).

As Subject1 (ego) we are the imaginative, linguistic creation of the world (Subject0):

$$\text{Subject0} \rightarrow \text{Subject1} + \text{Subject2};$$
$$\text{or}$$
$$\text{Unconscious} \rightarrow \text{ego} + \text{other}.$$

As Subject3 we are the co-creation of ego (Subject1) and the other (Subject2).

$$\text{Subject1} + \text{Subject2} \dashrightarrow \text{Subject3};$$
$$\text{or}$$
$$\text{ego} + \text{other} \dashrightarrow \text{Communion}.$$

Subject3, Communion, is simultaneously both a necessity of human living and its goal. We cannot be totally other (Subject2) because we use language. Language makes us egos (Subject1). We are not totally ego because we are of the same "flesh" (Subject0) with everything in the world. We are a dance, in this respect, just as our bodies are a biodance and the universe is a cosmic dance. We are not one or the other, ego or other; we are the dance of the two—in the love-making that generated us, in our daily lives, and in our destiny. We are to be fully, consciously, and individually one with the unconscious immensity which generated us for this purpose.

Perception is possible because of our not two/not one nature as Subject3. We are in contact with other objects, animals, and people because we are sprung from the same "flesh" (Subject0). We are one with other people because we have unconsciouses (Subject2s) similar to theirs. In other words, we can know them because we are embodied of the same stuff. On the other hand, I can recognize you as Other than me because my ego and your ego are separate. As Subject3, we are neither unconscious mute blobs nor detached Cartesian egos. Instead, we are what Merleau-Ponty termed "sensible subjects" and "sensing objects." Perception requires the communion of ego and other. It needs our body unconscious to (endo) connect with something or someone. It needs ego, to (ecto/meso) express the hints delivered by the body.

As other (unconscious Subject2), I am in contact with the world, and I am a body. As consciousness, that is to say, as ego, as Subject1, I have a body. As the conjunction of body and consciousness, as Subject3, I perceive. Merleau-Ponty says that at the level of perception, consciousness and the body together constitute "the junction of the for-itself and the in-itself" (1962, p.373). The word that Merleau-Ponty uses in this regard to express the relation between the sentient and the sensible (Subject1 and Subject2) is "chiasm" (an intersection or crossing over).

Madison (1981) circles this same truth when he says,

> The relation between the subject and his body is, so to speak, an inner relationship: at the level of perception the subject is his body. One could say, as does Marcel, that "I am my body," or, as Merleau-Ponty prefers, that "I have a body," that is, qua [as] consciousness, I have a body (p. 24).

So far we have described the kind of world and consciousness that makes perception possible. What remains to be considered are the endo processes that actually produce perception.

*The Processes of Perception*

Perception is not a simple process of transferring what is "out there" to our mind "in here." In even very simple situations, we have to choose what we see. We perceive patterns. Some things we see; some we don't. We are all familiar with the standard gestalt visual tricks; patterns that switch as we first attend to a figure and then to its ground. First we might see, for example, a vase and later, with prompting, we see two faces. We have also probably heard stories of aborigines, who, when they are brought to a big city, do not perceive the traffic and the big buildings and cannot talk about them at all.

One reason that we screen out much of what is physically present to us is our need to avoid sensory overload. It is obvious that we would not survive for five minutes if we perceived everything that science says is going on about us at any moment. There are atoms, quarks, photons, microbes by the trillions in incomprehensible interaction and explosion. We perceive only a limited portion of the visual and auditory spectrum. Our bodies structure our senses so that they are open only to useful, manageable outside influences.

We would also experience overload if we actually perceived every influence that was both present and capable of being registered by our senses. We obviously have a screening mechanism that brings to our attention only those influences that are important for us. It is not clear whether our sense organs selectively block out unimportant signals, or if they, in fact, do respond to them only to have their relayed signals damped out. Either way, the result is the same: only "important" messages get through.

How does the body decide what is important and what is not? For its survival, the body is born preprogrammed to seek certain things as an infant, for example, we instinctively seek our mother's breast, and avoid certain things like extreme heat or cold. Other, more conscious programming of perception is done later in life as we do things like mentally tuning out the TV as we are reading a book. It is the quality of our intention and attention that focuses and modulates the content of our perception. In the terminology of this book: Our Faith in the emotional truth of the moment (F in 0) acts as a strange attractor in the chaos of the sensory input fed to us. It selects out what we have consciously and unconsciously deemed important.

In this connection, Merleau-Ponty seems to have foreseen the importance of consciousness as a strange attractor in the chaos of the world. In the following summary of his thought, even his language resonates with our formulation.

> As it reveals itself in perception, the world is not a chaos wherein everything acts indiscriminately on everything else, but an ensemble of units which manifest a meaning. But this meaning is not something real and does not belong to the world as a natural property. The world is meaningful only for a consciousness which perceives it. (Madison, 1998, p. 19)

In other words, perception is not chaotic, even though the world in its natural state is. Consciousness finds the sense in the chaos in the manner of a strange attractor. Merleau-Ponty died in 1966 long before the advent of chaos theory.

Nietzsche and Heidegger were also on to the scent of chaos. This can be seen in the following quotation:

> The guiding questions for our discussion of Nietzsche's concept of knowledge have been posed: Why does chaos play an essential role in and for knowing? To what extent are practical needs of foremost importance for knowing? Why is knowledge schematizing in general? (Heidegger, 1987, p. 75).

The situation that makes perceiving and knowing possible is described in the following ways:

> Through this body flows a stream of life of which we feel but a small and fleeting portion, in accordance with the receptivity of the momentary state of the body. Our body itself is admitted into this stream of life, floating in it, and is carried off and snatched away by this stream or else pushed to the banks. That chaos of our region of sensibility which we know as the region of the body is only one section of the great chaos that the "world" itself is.
> ...Nietzsche declares...that the body must be made the guideline of observation not only of human beings but of the

world: the projection of world from the perspective of the animal and animality. The fundamental experience of the world as "chaos" has its roots here. But since the body is for Nietzsche a structure of dominance, "chaos" cannot mean a turbulent jumble. Rather, it means the concealment of unmastered richness in the becoming and streaming of the world as a whole (Heidegger, 1987, pp.79-80).

Merleau-Ponty has shown that the body is "the guideline of observation not only of human beings but of the world." Freud, Lacan, and Lyons have shown how our egos and our whole linguistic reality are the projection of the world from the perspective of our animal nature. Chaos theory has shown that chaos is not "a turbulent jumble," but is a "concealment of unmastered richness. The pieces for a "strong pessimistic" (facing unvarnished reality with a will to overcome it) reconstruction of reality are on the table. We need only to fit them together.

**Creativity and Language**

We have been observing how everything proceeds from Being as it chaotically transcends itself. Effusively it projects replicas ("total parts") of itself. By thus scattering itself, Being is able to simultaneously express itself and know itself. The physical world is the body, reflection, and language of Being.

This material language of Being is alive and chaotically purposeful. Its every indeterminate particle co-creates a universal Mandelbrot set. Its every particle is free, creative, and self-transcending.

Although he did not express his ideas in the language of chaos theory, Merleau-Ponty expressed much the same idea: "The essential point is clearly to grasp the project of the world that we are" (1962, p.297). Madison expands on this idea: "At the bottom of his being, in the deepest parts of that involuntary and preconscious region, he [man] is a transforming and creative existence …The ultimate definition of man is thus that he is a "movement of transcendence" (p. 51).

We ourselves are the project of the world, Subject0, which created us and has its plans for us. As such, we are not our own authors. As Madison says, "There is a 'drama' which transpires in the body of which we are not the authors" (p. 51). It is in this drama that the world, Subject0, creates us as egos (Subject1).

We are not thereby passive beings because we, in our totality, as Subject1 (ego), Subject2 (other), and Subject3 (communion), are holographic replicas of Being that can project our own images creatively to further the progress of Being. Our Subjects3s, which straddle the Other-Ego chasm, are our wills to power. They are the creative essence of Being, holographically identical to the universal creative force. They are Being searching for further expression.

Language makes it all possible. The world itself is the languaging of Being—the Word made flesh. The world evolves as a straining towards the consciousness that language makes possible.

With language we created our egos. With it we share life, ideas, and joy with each other. With it we co-create the whole grand living corpus of culture and civilization. Being creates us through language, which language we ourselves as a species have created. Language is the way that we invent Being for itself, or perhaps the way that Being playfully uses us for its own enjoyment and edification.

Language is the means whereby we ground our unconscious endo awareness into our conscious lives. Over the eons, it has provided an ever-growing picture of our personal, social, and cosmic reality. Its operation resembles the pattern slowly appearing on the computer screen as the solution of a fractal equation. It is the second naiveté. It is real. It is material, meaningful like all materiality, but subtle and more meaningful. It exists in words, diagrams, artwork, and the neuropathways of bodies.

It ex-ists. It is outside our bodies. Yet Language is Being in its material, formal, efficient, and final causality (Aristotle); that is, in its stuff, its form, its creation, and its goal. Language is the reality of the universe in the way that the picture on the computer screen is the equation it graphs.

The gingerbread man, for example, is the explicit reproduction of the chaotic brainwork of Mandelbrot, who conceived it. It is also the creation of millennia of mathematicians and their fraternity of language that led up to it. Finally, it is the creation of the chaotically projecting Being who generated it all and who is revealed in it.

As bodies, we are articulations of the seamless web of Being. The uniqueness of our bodies illustrate Being's sense of humor. Our individuality, freedom, and speech are what the world is all about. Our activity in originating speech is Being being Being.

As Subject 3, we seize our destiny to create a human world. Nietzsche expresses this sentiment in the strongest way. His phrase for Subject3 is "the will to power." He says, "This world is will to power—and nothing besides! And you yourselves are this will to power—and nothing besides!" (quoted by Heidegger, 1987, p. 18).

**The Reality of Language**

For many reasons, the basic reality of the universe might be called "Becoming." That reality is a teeming vitality seeking expression that sprouts galaxies and life forms harmonious and holographic to Itself. All of its sprouts, like their source, also teem with vitality and seek expression. They rush on in an indeterminate, chaotic quest for consciousness that climaxes with human beings. Because of their ability of self-expression (language), human beings make evolution (Becoming) conscious. In Nietzsche's words, they "stamp Becoming with the character of Being" (quoted by Heidegger, p. 245). In the terminology we have been using,

Becoming (Subject0) → Beings (Subject1) by way of language.

We could also express this idea using the concept of "dehiscence," which refers to the opening of a seed pod and the discharge of seeds. In this formulation God dehisces seeds that are fractal replicas of Herself. As a result, the created "things" have the nature of Being. The ongoing evolutionary Becoming turns partially into Being for us, however, only after we identify aspects of it with words. Originating language creates history, culture, and Being itself. It fulfills the dreams of Reality and is "Zeus at play."

As we proceed to advance conscious evolution with our philosophy, science, and daily lives, we do not just skim along on the web of signification provided by language. That web does give us a surface on which we skate as we engage in the utilitarian conversations of our days. But that surface web proves to be porous when we try to express how we really feel or face a troublesome situation. At these times we drop through the web into our unconscious teeming depths

(Subject2) where we gropingly formulate (as Subject3) what we want to say or do. These are the times when we make Becoming actual, create new history, and expand the web of signification. Nietzsche called this depth-activity "the supreme will to power." Merleau-Ponty called it "authentic" or "originating" speech. Lacan said it is "a presence made of absence" (1977, p. 65).

Merleau-Ponty stated what we are talking about from a somewhat different perspective. He proceeded from the observation that every idea is a cultural object and rests on a spoken or written tradition. For him, the authentically true idea "calls out to all possible men and all possible times. And it becomes 'eternal' from the moment when it is taken up by other men and enters in this way into the history of culture" (Madison, p. 59).

According to Merleau-Ponty there are two kinds of history: empirical history and true history. Empirical history is the phenomenal order of events which he calls, "the history of death." True history is the "history of advents," the largely unwritten record of those secret, modest, non-deliberative, living expressions of will to power that create "the order of culture and meaning." True history consists of these authentic words and actions that create language and culture.

As science progresses, it is drawn by the oxen of observation and mathematics. Before Pythagoras, the Mayans, the Babylonians, and the early Europeans at Stonehenge, among others, had composed elaborate calendars. The Egyptians had developed a proto-geometry that enabled them to survey their fields and build their pyramids. Thales, the first philosopher, had predicted an eclipse.

Observation is more than just "looking at." Cows look at things. Observation is looking at something with languaged intelligence; that is, looking at something with the desire to express what one is seeing. In looking at a sunset, for example, one would be an observer if he said, "Wow!" Observers take notice. A looker who took no notice by internally, at least, saying something would not be an observer.

As we have noted, perception and language have an oppositional structure based on our subject vs. object perceptual reality. Everything we express, therefore, has a certain oppositional quality. By saying, "It is this way," we have implicitly said, "It is not that way." There would be no language, no diversity, and no articulation without this opposition; there would be just a homogeneous X.

Mathematics is our most sophisticated and elegant language. It proclaims the oppositional nature of Becoming as a harmony. It does so in Cartesian geometry, in topology, and in chaos theory. Its applications in physics, biology, and economics expand our wonder and the scope of our will to power. It both enables and compels us to be conscientious creators of our lived reality; what Nietzsche called *ubermenschen* (supermen).

Mathematicians have long conceded that mathematical systems have no direct relation to physical reality. To a large extent, our number systems and our geometries are arbitrary mental play and delight. What they do for our understanding of physical reality is provide a web of signification in which we can imaginatively locate events. Thus, if we survey a field we use Euclidean geometry as our web of meaning, but if we survey the galaxy we use a non-Euclidean one. If we compute numbers long-hand, we use the decimal system; but if we use the computer, we utilize the binary one. Physical objects never become numbers or any kind of mathematical object; they just receive the meaning that we impose upon them by imaginatively inserting them into the mathematical web. When we assert our will to power in this way, we amuse the universe. We create truth, culture, and history.

Mathematics also recognizes that no mathematical or logical system can be totally self-consistent because every system, of necessity, contains undefined terms. The proof of this theorem was produced by the Czech/American mathematician Kurt Godel who received the Albert Einstein award in 1951. This inherent inconsistency is another evidence of the indeterminate, not two/not one nature of reality. The universe will play and will not be hidebound by anything, even mathematics.

The science of linguistics, following the lead of Ferdinand de Saussure, has come to the same conclusions as mathematics regarding the separateness of the signifier and the signified. As we have noted earlier, his conclusion is most simply stated as,

$$\frac{S}{s.}$$

This means simply that the Signifier (S; a word) never crosses the bar (----) of signification to the signified (s; an object); and vice-versa. Non-mathematical words behave the same as mathematical ones. Things never become words; and a word never directly signifies a thing. What we do with language is give experiences or things meaning by locating them in webs of signification.

George Lakoff and Mark Johnson in their monumental *Philosophy in the Flesh* demonstrate from a linguistic viewpoint many of the points that have been made above. In addition, they demonstrate that nearly all of our concepts derive from common bodily experiences. They do this by specifying the metaphors we use in discussing the nature of time, morality, causation, the mind, and the self.

What then is the reality of Language? It is not a direct signifier of the realities it intends, but it is much more. It is proof that Reality is really Becoming. As Speech, it is the actual will to power, the creator/creation of truth and the stamp that makes Becoming into Being. Language is the cumulative wisdom and culture of the universe. It is the play of the universe. It is our essence. It is the essence of the world we live in.

# CHAPTER FIFTEEN

# Time and Space

**Time**

The nature of Reality as Becoming is the basis of time. The pertinent facts are:

- Reality is self-transcending, is Becoming.
- Reality projects atoms in the manner of the Mandelbrot equation generating fractal replicas of itself.
- Reality's atoms are not two/not one with it.
- Reality's atoms evolve.
- Men and women evolve.
- Men and women are not two/not one with their anonymous unconscious selves as a result of the split caused by language:

$$\text{Subject0} \rightarrow \text{Subject1} + \text{Subject2},$$
or
$$\text{Becoming} \rightarrow \text{Ego} + \text{Other}.$$

Because of this split, they sometimes identify with Ego and sometimes with their bodies.
- Language (purposive, oppositional/integrative action) is the will to power, the instrument of evolution.
- The will to power (Subject3) stamps Becoming with the character of Being (Nietzsche).
- Subject3 is the instrument and goal envisioned by Freud in his dictum: *Wo Es war, soll Ich werde* (where it was, there I will be) which in our terminology is expressed as:

$$\text{Subject1} + \text{Subject2} \rightarrow \text{Subject3},$$
or
$$\text{Ego} + \text{Other} \rightarrow \text{Communion}.$$

- Subject3 creates true history (Merleau-Ponty).
- Subject3 (in the universal sense of Reality3) is the instrument and history instigated by Reality

    Reality0 → Reality1 + Reality2 → Reality3.

- The universe has more and more, and better and better toys to play with.
- There is an arrow to evolution.
- We experience ourselves as becoming; that is, we are not two/not one with ourselves from moment to moment.
- We stamp this becoming with the nature of being by exercising our will to power.
- Our acts instill multiplicity and sequence into becoming.
- We organize our experiences of multiplicity by imposing order on them and create what can be called, natural time.
- We are also constrained by the law of language which decrees opposition.
- In choosing any one system we reject another one.
- We have many systems to choose from.
- Our choices make the universe very happy

*Time and Timelessness*

We can conceive of an absence of time in a world where everything is eternally fixed and unchanging. This kind of world does not fit our experience, but philosophers have argued that the world of change is the world of illusion and that Reality is timeless. Parmenides held this position; he said that everything was One and not Many. Therefore, nothing ever really changes. St. Augustine adopted this idea of static unity as being the essence of eternity. He defined eternity as the contradiction of time, as a kind of time without time. He held that in heaven (eternity) there is no time, space, or motion but only unity with God in the rapture of (the beatific) vision. In other words, in eternity there is just undifferentiated unity with Reality. Scholastic and official church philosophy has never abandoned this position, but has striven valiantly to modify it.

The position diametrically opposed to timelessness holds that there is no now. Because now is just an infinitesimal border between past and future, it is squeezed out of existence. Heraclitus approached this view in stating that change is the only constant reality. Some of his more ardent followers claimed that, "You cannot step into the same river once." Parmenides and Heraclitus represent the extremes of eternity and evanescence in the discussion of time.

We experience time in our hearts at the confluence of the eternal and evanescent. If we attend to our experience during calm, mindless meditation we may notice a kind of alternating current in us that takes the form of tingling, ringing, flashing, or all three at once. The experience may be just the detached observation of everyday experiences. These feeling states catch the tone of our heart and clue us in to the nature of time. Shumryu Suzuki (1970) reflecting on this experience says,

> Movement is nothing but the quality of our being. When we do *zazen* [Zen meditation], the quality of our calm, steady, serene sitting is the quality of the immense activity of being itself. Everything is just a flashing in the vast phenomenal world (p. 105). Everyone comes out from nothingness moment after moment (p. 109).

Each moment we go out of phenomenal existence and each moment we re-create ourselves. This is the cosmic dance. This primal experience can be called the eternal now—understood as the enduring unconscious vitality that undergirds us. The Hindu word for this primal sound current of time is *akasa*. The Sufis name it *Hu* and the Sikhs call it *Ek*. John, the Evangelist called it *Logos*. It is as close as we get to a direct experience of the Other.

Experiences that are not so deeply endo reveal this same eternal now to us. Every time we engage in authentic speech or action we stamp the eternal with the character of now. In the exercise of our will to power we make the endless play of the universe present; at the same time we make it eternal in the concrete sense employed by Merleau-Ponty. Nietzsche called this process, "the eternal return of the same."

There is a jumbled kind of time that we experience in dreams, hallucinations, music videos, and wool-gathering speculation. In this time, stable sequences are disrupted, abandoned, and subject to kaleidoscopic reversals. In the accelerating rapidity of modern life we have become adept at living in a maelstrom. "Juggling our time" is no longer an adequate description of our activity. Rather, we process information and responsibilities in random sequence. Our chaotic control resembles our attention in a situation where we simultaneously watch TV, read a book, and carry on a conversation. This chaotic time exists in primary process thought.

As we order events in terms of before and after, we create natural time which can be ordered in either a circular, cyclical, or linear manner.

Circular time arises from a view that sees one event following another in a sequence that eventually leads back to the original event. Thereupon, the sequence commences again and again and again. The agricultural myths express this kind of time. Astronomical and astrological tables express it as do our clocks and watches.

Cyclic time is a modification of circular time that accounts for the changes in the circles as they periodically occur. Cyclic time is often represented as a spiral. Historians and economists specialize in cyclic changes. Merleau-Ponty related this cyclic time to the dialectic (the dynamic process of growth through opposition) that expresses human evolution as is seen in this statement:

> The dialectic which constitutes human behavior is a dialectic of transcendence and...the structure is a vertical circularity [a spiral]. ...While remaining faithful to its past existence [it] is something dynamic. Its nature, according to an expression of Hegel that Merleau-Ponty takes over himself, is to preserve while overcoming (Madison, p. 13).

Linear time results from the mapping of a spiral into a line. In performing this mapping we ignore the recurring elements of our experience and pay attention only to its non-repetitive elements.

Our usual way of keeping time is cyclic: circular in the way we break down days and years, but linear in the way that we consider each year as different from the one that preceded it. Evolution presupposes linear time.

*Objective and Phenomenological Time*

Objective time is developed by us as we interface natural time and chaotic time. Our Faith (**F**), acting as a strange attractor, juxtaposes perceptions, tests possibilities, and constructs sequences that eventually become codified as circular, cyclic, and linear. With objective time, we make judgments about the real world which we hold to be true. Those judgments then become part of objective reality.

All the kinds of time we have so far considered are varieties of sequential time which enable us to order our experiences according to before and after. There is also cumulative time, which provides us with our sense of continuity in past, present, and future. In our experience, our past is present to us as the accumulation of those innumerable times when we stamped Becoming with the character of Being by exercising our will to power. Our cumulative past then acts as a co-creator with our freedom as Subject3 in exercising our present will to power. Our future is present to us as the limited range of possibilities opened up to us by our cumulative past.

The past that is present to us now is not every decision that we have ever made and certainly not everything that has ever happened to us. The past that is present now consists of our past wills to power that are influencing us now. The future that is meeting us now both shapes the content of our presently experienced past and conforms to the possibilities presented by it.

Van den Berg (1972) gives context to these ideas and expresses them beautifully:

> Past and future are not two distinctive spheres touching one another in a zero point called "present." Indeed, past and present differ: the past is there, behind us; the future yonder, before us. Yet both have an actual value; future and past are embodied in a present. The present has dimensions; at times it contains a whole life—as an exception, it may even contain a period longer than an individual existence. The past is within this present; what was is the way it is appearing now. The future: what comes, the way it is meeting us now.
> 
> This appearing and meeting are closely connected. The past appears in what is coming to meet us; if it does not appear, it is absent. So that, indeed, the past is that which lies there behind us, but only because a future permits it to lie there. And the future is indeed yonder, before us, but only because it is fed by a past. The present is an invitation from out of the future to gain mastery over bygone times. Now it becomes clear why

> the neurotic (and often the psychotic) worries about his past, the past that seems chaos to him. The future became inaccessible, for an accessible future means a well-ordered past (pp. 91-92).

This kind of phenomenological time is our truly human lived time.

Merleau-Ponty says that mute Being manifests its own meaning through symbolic expression. In the summary of Madison:

> Man's cultural history is the history of Being itself, and the becoming of history is the very becoming of Being. ...If bodily subjectivity is Being occurring in the form of time, symbolic expression is Being occurring in the form of history (Madison, p.258-261).
>
> There is a logic in history since history is the "inscription of Being," but this logic does not override man and does not do away with contingency and human freedom. It is man in his freedom and creativity who makes history and is responsible for it by letting Being be; but since in the last analysis the "vague thrust" which man transforms into history does not have its origin in him but comes from Being and is Being expressing itself in him. Human actions always have a richer meaning than that one which each "consciousness" thinks it puts or discerns in it (Madison, p.264).

The "vague thrust" is the grand Mandelbrot equation of Being itself, in which we as free consciousnesses make Being be. Still our consciousnesses are not completely aware of what they are doing because of the unconscious component in our every decision and action.

## Space

"My body teaches me what space is, because it is itself the author of space. It is the body which makes it be that there is for me a far and a near, a low and a high. The world is spatial for me because I inhabit it by means of my body" (Madison, p. 24).

As bodies, we see things and move among them naturally, absorbed in endo awareness of our surroundings, yet with a certain independence of viewpoint. Merleau-Ponty said it this way,

> Visible and mobile, my body is a thing among things; it is caught in the fabric of the world and its cohesion is that of a thing. But because it moves itself and sees, it holds things in a circle around itself. Things are an annex or prolongation of itself; they are incrusted into its flesh, they are part of its full definition; the world is made of the same stuff as the body (1964a, p.162-163).

Our oneness with the world provides our ground of truth. The not quite character of that oneness provides the separation required for movement and vision. As bodies we escape total immersion because of our movement and vision. To move is to have a certain independence and "to see is to have at a distance" (1964a, p. 166).

The human body is a complex, not two/not one kind of self. As Merleau-Ponty put it:

> It sees itself seeing; it touches itself touching; it is visible and sensitive for itself. ...It is a self through confusion, narcissism, through inherence of the one who sees in that which he sees, and through inherence of sensing in the sensed—a self, therefore, that is caught up in things, that has a front and a back, a past and a future (1964a, p. 162).

In their thickness our bodies experience front and back; they double back on themselves using that thickness to establish distances between them and the objects in their environment. Quoting Merleau-Ponty again: "We see things in their places, where they are. ...At the same time we are separated from them by all the thickness of the look and of the body; ...this distance is not the contrary of this proximity, it is deeply consonant with it, it is synonymous with it" (1968, p. 135).

In their awareness of front and back, nearness and distance our bodies locate themselves in their surroundings by means of visual and tactile maps. "There is a double and crossing situation of the visible in the tangible and of the tangible in the visible; the two maps are complete, and yet they do not merge into one. The two parts are total parts and yet are not superposable" (Merleau-Ponty, 1968, p. 134-135).

These maps, like all the creations of bodily perception, are not solitary creations. Rather they are co-creations with the reality they organize. Reality is a Becoming in the direction of articulated consciousness. The objects in the circle around the body exhibit an articulation, a proto-organization that the body makes real in perception. Thus the co-creation. "The thickness of the body, far from rivaling that of the world, is on the contrary the sole means I have to go unto the heart of the things, by making myself a world and by making them flesh" (Merleau-Ponty, 1968, p. 135).

The body is a visible object that turns on itself and becomes a seeing subject; it experiences its flesh touching the flesh of the world; it finds itself surrounded by the objects of that flesh. It still is that flesh, but it has become more; it is flesh that is conscious. Reality has evolved to Subject1 consciousness and can now see itself through the body. The body finds itself being a Reality that wants to look at itself. For this reason Merleau-Ponty says that vision is fundamentally narcissistic.

In the creation of art the narcissism and co-creation of reality is sometimes brought to consciousness. Painters sometimes say, "I feel myself looked at by the things, my activity is equally passivity" (1968, p. 140). Barry Manilow explained that his song, "I Am Music," does not imply that he is the "I" in the title; rather, Music is personified as it plays itself to his inner ear. In a similar way, novelists and actors are sometimes taken over by their characters that take on lives of their own.

The bodily activities of seeing and touching transcend biological boundaries. There is an emergence of the seer from the seen and the toucher from the touched. We experience a circle of touching when my hand touching the keyboard is touched by my other hand. We experience a circle of seeing and touching when we examine the same object with our eyes and our hands. We experience circles of interchange with other bodies. There is a reversibility of the visible and the tangible. There is an immersion of the seer and toucher in the flesh of the seen and touched. Body has evolved into something that is not just corporeal. "This environment of brute existence and essence is not something mysterious: we never quit it, we have no other environment" (1968, p 117).

We sometimes forget our roots. Our bodily awareness lies at the root of our abstract ideas of time and space as the ground that guarantees their meaningfulness. Endo awareness is the "presence and latency" behind our later ideas.

When the body identifies other objects and locates them in space it gives them a proto-objective reality. At the same time, the other objects have made it possible for the body to realize its potential as a feeling, seeing subject. This co-creation is even more pronounced when the seeing subject body that I am sees an object that is also a seeing subject body. In realizing another seeing subject, I realize myself.

> In being realized, they [the others] therefore bring out the limits of our factual vision, they betray the solipsist illusion that consists in thinking that every going beyond is a surpassing accomplished by oneself. For the first time, the seeing that I am is for me really visible; for the first time, I appear to myself completely turned inside out under my own eyes ...For the first time, through the other body, I see that, in its coupling with the flesh of the world, the body contributes more than it receives, adding to the world that I see the treasure necessary for what the other body sees (1968, pp. 143- 144).

In seeing and touching the other body and in being seen and touched by it, my body realizes that it is something special in the world. At the same time it realizes it is especially alike to that other body. Thus begins the drama of mutual exploration and attempts at expression.

> For the first time, the body no longer couples itself up with the world, it clasps another body, applying [itself to it] carefully with its whole extension, forming tirelessly with its hands the strange statue which in its turn gives everything it receives; the body is lost outside of the world and its goals, fascinated by the unique occupation of the floating in Being with another life, of making itself the outside of its inside and the inside of its outside. And henceforth movement, touch, vision applying themselves to the other and to themselves, return toward their source and, in the patient and silent labor of desire, begin the paradox of expression (1968, p. 144).

In this encounter, the body vastly increases its perceptual relationships with reality. Simultaneously, it grasps itself as separate and as yearning to communicate with the other. Reality is moving toward another leap in consciousness. We have reached a frontier.

> At the frontier of the mute or solipsist world where, in the presence of other seers, my visible is confirmed as an exemplar of a universal visibility, we reach a second or figurative meaning of vision which will be the *intuitus mentis* or idea, a sublimation of the flesh, which will be mind or thought. But the factual presence of other bodies could not produce thought or the idea if its seed were not in my own body. Thought is a relationship with oneself and with the world as well as a relationship with the other; hence it is established in the three dimensions at the same time. And it must be brought to appear directly in the infrastructure of vision (1968, p. 145).

This same bodily creation of mind, thought, and ego can be described in the tradition of Nietzsche, Freud, and Lacan.

We are enabled by our new separateness to name things as front or back, as near or far. We make our tactile and visual maps conscious. We expand the area of the visible to include things like the unseen side of a cube resting on the table in front of us. We build our ideal construct of what space is. We become so enamored of our own cleverness that we forget who we are and where we came from. We think we are some kind of grand intellectual being.

Our ideas of space derive from our bodily evolution. They find their cogency in relation to our primal experiences. They manifest the transcendence of the body.

# CHAPTER SIXTEEN

# The Imaginal Realm

**The Creations of Imagination**

The imaginal realm is located in the chasm between the ego and the other. Its sovereign is Subject3. It is a realm where the chaotic imagery of the other is harnessed through the collaborative effort of Subject3 (communion) and Subject1 (ego) acting as strange attractors.

In this process the ego is the dominant attractor as has already been described. Subject3 is the locus of our freedom, the abode of our F in O, the privileged station for our I-feeling, and the augmenter of Subject1. The Other (Subject2) fills the chasm with a maelstrom of unformulated Reality.

The geography of the chasm is surrealistic. As we know from the content of our dreams, hallucinations, and visions, it varies from strangely familiar to exotic to sinister, from rocky ground to airy mirages, from resistive to plastic. The climate is warm, cold, temperate, chaotic, enjoyable, painful, therapeutic, and psychotic. The terrain and climate of our visions are controlled (but not often consciously) by our conscious concern, attention, and the urgency of our Faith. This Faith programs our imaginal productions in the manner of non-linear equations producing fractals. The production is chaotic but purposeful, addressing our conscious concerns in its patented symbolic manner.

The culture of any particular region of the imaginal realm mirrors the culture of its people in the waking realm. Hunting tribes visualize animals, hunting parties, and male chiefs. Old farming villages visualize stability, vegetative deities, and a matrifocal society. Monarchies picture kings and nobility. Modern pluralist societies, with their focus dispersed, represent any and every social organization and expectancy.

The advantage to modern society from this diversity is an immense richness and freedom of cultural expression. The downside is a lack of focus and common purpose in our society because we no longer live in a coherent imaginal world. We yearn for that coherence. In the aftershock of September 11, 2001, we experienced a taste of cultural coherence. We are most of the time frenetically looking for a coherent self and world.

The erosion of myth cohesion can be observed in 20th century United States history. Decades ago, our country was propelled by a common ideology (an uneasy confluence of old time religious values, scientific progress, and manifest destiny). We look back upon that time as our Golden Age, "the good old days." That ideology has broken down. The Vietnam war, assassinations, and our economic concerns have undermined our feeling of moral and pragmatic superiority. Wars and ecological destruction have eroded our adoration of science and technology. The complexity of modern living has rendered obsolete much of the old time religion. We find ourselves out of focus, out of synch, bewildered, and vulnerable.

Other cultures that dabble in Western pluralism experience a similar fragmentation. Some of them, like the fundamentalist Islamic cultures, retreat into safer archaic world views.

Mythic cohesion is important because our dreams and visions interpret our hidden dynamic realities to our conscious minds in terms that are familiar to both of them. Because of our mythic disintegration, we no longer speak the same language of the heart. Bringing to fruition the American dream demands intelligent coordinated effort of a character capable of re-constructing the tower of Babel.

The population of the imaginal realm is as bizarre as the bar scene in the film "Star Wars." There are monsters, body parts, devils, deities, heroes, dwarfs, elves, fairies, angels, oracles, totem animals, and other culturally specific entities. There are historical figures like Jesus, Buddha, Krishna, the Virgin Mary, Napoleon, Marilyn Monroe, gurus, and masters. In addition there are persons known to us in waking life.

Such variety is to be expected in the creation of individuals, cultures, and races that operate with the utmost freedom. We all translate our subterranean rumblings into symbols that are meaningful to us. We thus create our own personal/universal reality.

The imaginal realm is created and populated by our F in 0 working individually, culturally, and racially. This realm and its population are not imaginary in the sense that implies unreality. They are real, distinctly human realities. They feel real (endo test) in our pre-reflective experience; they have influence (meso test) on our personal and societal health, culture, and technology; they are coherent (ecto test) in a thought structure that recognizes the rift in our personal constitution.

Our F in 0 creates the imaginal realm as a complex communications center between the conscious and unconscious poles of our being. If we were totally unconscious Subject2, we would be not two and would have no consciousness to communicate with. If we were a totally rational Cartesian ego, Subject1, we would be isolated islands without the ability to communicate or transcend. As fully alive Subject3s, we are not two/not one and broker communication between our conscious and unconscious dimensions. Our myths are our records of communications past.

The people in this realm have their own brand of reality that is neither historically real nor unreal and unimportant. Of considerable interest is the Christ-figure of Christianity. This figure is immensely more powerful and real than the historical Jesus. The Christ figure holds the devotion of millions of people worldwide, inspiring good works and brotherly love, giving assurance of salvation, creating a trillion dollar religious industry and a dominant worldview. The historical Jesus was a provincial preacher of expanded consciousness ("Seek first the kingdom within and all these things will be added to you") who gathered several hundred followers and was killed at an early age by the civil and religious establishment.

Other less sublime figures are more powerful in their imaginal reality than they were historically. Davy Crockett and the Alamo, for instance, influence Texas history and race relations more as myth than they ever did as historical reality.

Watkins (1976) describes the imaginal realm from the perspective of the waking dream. She says,

> The waking dream, the conscious experiencing of images, has been discovered and lost, refound and shared, countless times. …The attempt to dream while awake, itself paradoxical, involves one in a number of paradoxical states, actions, and attitudes: the half-dream state, action through non-action, controlled abandon, uncontrolling control, disciplined dreaming. The paradoxes point to an effort and a discipline which reverse the natural flow of events. [This effort creates a realm] between sleeping and waking.

> The intermediary nature of metaphor is mirrored by the state of consciousness most often used to strengthen man's connection to the imaginal. The metaphor uses matter in order to convey the immaterial. In doing so, it creates a third realm which lies between the other two. The state of consciousness being described uses the ego to record and to observe the non-ego. The body is relaxed until it nears sleep, and yet awareness is sustained. As the world of images appears, as if from dreams, they are recorded and remembered, and at times interacted with. This state of consciousness has been described as an intermediary state, that of the half-dream. It creates an intersection between two worlds—as the symbol itself does (p. 14).

As Watkins indicates with her final words above, the whole of symbolic reality is located in the imaginal realm. Lacan would point out that all of language, the entire web of signification, is imaginal reality and operates through metaphor and metonymy. He would also point out that our very egos are imaginal creations of our bodies. We need to resist our inclination to relegate the imaginal to an esoteric dustbin. We need to grasp it as central to our lives, as the place where we make Becoming into Being through the exercise of our will to power.

The imaginal realm is the distinctively human realm. In it, we exercise our creativity, power, and freedom. From it, we extract our language, our myths, our knowledge, and our culture. Because of it, we come to love (and hate) one another.

We have already seen how our egos are created and how they in turn create our lives by acting as our principal strange attractors. By actively placing our selves over the conscious-unconscious chasm at the point called Subject3, we assume some control over both ego and unconscious. We exercise this control by tending our strange attractors with our F in 0.

As we do this, we promote two-way communication between ego and other. We tune in (as Subject3) to our unconscious signals, the imagery, feelings, and hunches that are emitted by our other (Subject2). Then we (Subject3) pass our presentiments on to our egos (Subject1) as practical advice or as insights into intellectual concerns. We also vocalize our conscious concerns to create the strange attractors that bring unconscious vitality into our lives. Our freedom consists of the way we listen to the other and in the active way that we program our strange attractors. The role of language (of whatever sort) is crucial. Language gives form.

Over millennia, all primates have learned to sign. Human primates took signing one step further and created language, an oppositional form of signing. In creating language, they created themselves as human, rational beings. This languaging activity was spread among the human primates by endo processes similar to those described in the famous story of the hundredth monkey as told by Japanese biologists.

In this story, the researchers observed a peculiar learning experience among monkeys on a Japanese island. The monkeys usually ate sweet potatoes that they dug out of the ground. They would eat the potatoes and spit out the dirt and sand that clung to them. One younger monkey, however, decided to wash her potato in the ocean before she ate it. Her young friends observed his behavior and began to wash their potatoes before eating them. Then, some of the older monkeys did the same. Eventually all the monkeys on the island were washing their potatoes before they ate them. Then a peculiar thing happened. Monkeys on another island changed their eating behavior, too. They began washing their sweet potatoes. The moral of the tale is: when one hundred monkeys change their behavior the rest of the monkeys will follow suit. Human primates learned language in the way the Japanese monkeys learned to wash sweet potatoes. [This tale is factual up to the point where another island is involved. The rest of the tale is fiction.]

As we grew up, the persons we related to and strove to communicate with were our mothers. Because our families already had language we had merely to absorb it with endo processes and make it our own. When we did, we became egos, individual human beings. Language was the strange attractor that formed the ego from its unconscious potential. Language continues to provide the focus that actualizes the productions of our unconscious.

From our "catbird seats" (as Subject3s) over our personal chasms we coordinate our contact with each other and with outside reality. Over the ages, we have developed languages that help us in that coordination. We developed progressively names, sentences, paragraphs, stories, myths, and myth systems in a system parallel to and co-creative of our system of norms, roles, groups, organizations, institutions, and societies. As we mastered language, we explained reality to ourselves, found our place in it, and created culture. Our understanding of all of that is called knowledge.

We also build a collective mythical storehouse of imagery, stories, and morals with language. This mythical trove tends to have common elements from culture to culture as shown by the archetypes proclaimed by Jung and demonstrated by numerous of his followers such as Joseph Campbell. The archetypes reveal the inchoate structures of unconscious life. In this they resemble language, natural procreation rules, and the strange attractor of chaos.

We all have access to our personal unconscious and personal mythology at any moment by the act of centering ourselves in the catbird seat. In the same way, we have access to our cultural myths in our pluralistic society as do other people in their traditional ones, but with a difference. Our myths are fragmented; theirs are not.

In traditional societies the myths are shared cultural treasures which give meaning to every part of a person's life. People live their myths in their everyday lives and routinely invoke them in mundane and mystical endeavors. In addition, the shamans, wise men, crones, or priests are the appointed custodians of tribal lore who remember it, research it by personal experience, totally immerse themselves in it, and interpret it for the community. In this way, the cohesiveness and survival of the group consciousness (and group) is assured.

In our pluralistic society this ancestral unity is fragmented. In some fundamentals, we share common myth systems like traditional societies. Our myths surround the Constitution, Bill of Rights, cultural Calvinism, manifest destiny, and the progress of science. They manifest in strong individualism, capitalism, free enterprise, resilient optimism, and trust in our own ingenuity. These myths nourish us. We live by them. Our leaders constantly invoke them for us when our faith in them begins to flag.

In the transcendent areas of our lives, however, we lack a coherent religious myth. We lack this coherence on purpose because we value freedom more than we value conformity. This is our strength as a people, but it is also a source of great social strain. It causes strain not only on the fabric of society, but within us.

These strains were not so obvious when America was a country of stout believers. Methodists, Baptists, Lutherans, Catholics, Jews, and other believers were proud to be citizens of the melting pot, but they knew they were right and their neighbors were mistaken. Today's more educated citizens are not sure if anyone is right. They doubt not only their religious myths, but the pragmatic values on which this country was built. We are the nihilists and pessimists that Nietzsche foresaw. Fortunately, we seem to have grit. We are resilient. As the prime minister of Japan said on a Cable News Network interview, "America's strength is its willingness to confront its difficulties openly and do something about them."

We have a daunting task, to forge a consensus reality as an ethnically and religiously divergent people, "*e pluribus unum.*" Our old national myth system served us well, but it has broken down. We need to recapture its values and create a new model. The "Model T" just doesn't work anymore. The old gray mare ain't what she used to be many long years ago.

A pluralistic myth system is more secular than religious, but it is just as compelling. A good myth system creates a good people. Secular values of self-reliance, intellectual rigor, equality, mutual respect, social justice, the rule of law, democracy, and freedom of inquiry, speech, press, religion, and personal orientation admirably reflect the nature of Reality. Combined in a compelling myth they would serve us well.

To work, these values must be believed and not just mouthed. If we are hard-working and enterprising, we can create ourselves as living myths of American industry at its best. If we are rigorous in our honesty and commitment to truth, we create living myths of courage and responsibility. If we do, in fact, respect orientations and choices divergent from our own, we are living heroes of freedom. In short, if we stand by our ideals and our commitments to our families and our world, we are *ubermenschen.*

Religious mythic reality will be examined later.

**Objective Reality**

Objective reality is not the "real world." It is a web of statements about reality as we see it. What we see and what we say depends on what we are looking for and where we are looking from. If we are a Newtonian scientist, we are looking for cause-effect (meso) relations from an objective (ecto) viewpoint and we use our (endo) bodies to provide verification. This viewpoint and method is the scientific method, the paradigm of the natural sciences. It presents us with one kind of objective reality.

The paradigm of Nietzsche, Freud, and Merleau-Ponty provides a different vision of objective reality. With them one adopts the (endo) viewpoint of the body and tries to encompass reality from that perspective. This holistic method later leads to (ecto) rationalization of cause-effect or linear progression in a (meso) effort to make sense of the human situation. Chaos theory adds a further endo touch to this effort by showing the all-at-once, non-linear nature of human development. The objective reality revealed by this (human science) method is different from and complementary to the objective reality of Newtonian science.

The world's mythologies present a somewhat different paradigm of objective reality. With them, the viewpoint is the (endo) dreamscape and visionscape. They elaborate that viewpoint with minimal (ecto) rationalization in terms of story amplification and application for the (meso) purpose of finding direction for one's life and one's society. The reality of mythology exists side by side with scientific and psychological reality. In real strength these primal myths are the most pervasive of objective realities because they are the most unconscious.

None of these objective realities tell us what nature actually is. These objective realities are systems of statements more or less coherent of things we can truthfully say about our world. Every one of these statements is above the bar of signification that divides signifier and signified. At best, these statements fit into a coherent web of language which situates them and explicates their meaning. They rely on a cultural history that extends back to the prehistoric creation of speech.

What then are objective reality, objective knowledge, and truth? The debate in western philosophy about such things goes back 2500 years to the time of Socrates. Plato postulated a world of ideas. Aristotle posited essences in things. The Scholastics labored mightily and futilely with these ideas until William of Occam and other nominalists said "enough already," and declared that concepts were arbitrarily applied to things in order to facilitate communication. The American pragmatists provided the next big advance when they declared that statements were true if they worked. The linguists led by Saussure made the final advance (so far) when they showed that statements found their truth when they worked within a web of signification. In other words, a statement is objectively so if we can fit into our universal language web and successfully use actions based on those statements in our lives.

Niels Bohr reflected this relativistic understanding with his principle of complementarity, of which he said, "It is wrong to think that the task of physics is to find out how nature is. Physics concerns what we can say about nature" (quoted from Rhodes, 1992, p. 3). He declared that we need to build up a composite picture of the real richness of the world by entertaining multiple and mutually limiting points of view.

The slipperiness of the debate over objective knowledge is what turned off young Descartes and led him to publish his *Discourse on Method*. He sought to bring order into our knowledge-seeking, not by solving the theoretical problem, but by prescribing a meso method to avoid the problem. He dreamed that his method would lead to universal knowledge. Bohr was saying, in effect, that a narrowly conceived ideal of the natural sciences cannot achieve Descartes' goal.

Rhodes (1992) relates an interchange in which Bohr used his principle of complementarity to scold Einstein. When Einstein resisted Heisenberg's uncertainty principle by arguing that "God does not throw dice," Bohr responded, "Nor is it our business to prescribe to God how He should run the world" (p. 3). Ian Stewart entitled his book on chaos, *Does God Play Dice?* to emphasize the fact that God does. He runs the world very well that way, too.

The glory of the scientific method is that it has brought order into our (ecto) understanding of the dynamics of our physical world, especially through the language of mathematics. We have been able using these dynamics to (meso) master our physical environment. The more science works the more we believe in it. Scientists have articulated a very impressive web of mostly mathematical signification which we confidently believe is an accurate sketch of the seamless web of physical reality that surrounds us. We have done good.

The scientific method consists of those principles and processes deemed necessary for scientific investigation. They include rules for concept formation, conduct of observations and experiments, and validation of hypotheses by observation and experiment. This method, aided by mainly unrecognized intuitions and endo processes, produced a glorious history of success in the field of Newtonian physics.

In post-quanta theoretical physics and in psychology, intuitive processes have come to the fore. Investigators on the edge in these fields rely firmly on their intuition and sense of esthetics in trying to provide elegantly simple explanations for the realities that they encounter. They strive to construct elegant mathematical webs representing a postulated structure that can account for the physical world. As psychology becomes more humanistic, it adopts more methods from human science. It is important to remember that Newtonian physics is just one viewpoint on the objective things that we can say about our world.

In the science of linguistics, statements specify objective reality if they fit or can be fitted into an accepted web of signification. The universal web of signification is incredibly complex and dynamic. It extends back into prehistory and encompasses everything of present relevance in our culture. It contains sub-webs that are sometimes in conflict with each other and so exhibits an inherent principle of complementarity. The contradictions in the web are inherent in the oppositional nature of language. The contradictions provide the fuel for further exploration.

The reality that is located in one area of the web can grow to the point that it forces a revision of the total web. Descartes, Copernicus, Galileo, and Newton all forced such a revolution. Einstein, Bohr, and Heisenberg forced another. Nietzsche, Freud, Merleau-Ponty, and chaos theory are in the process of forcing a third. Because the web incorporates revolutionary change it provides the bases of objective reality for the past, present, and future.

Given all these qualifications, the concept of objective reality is a strong and necessary one. Every culture needs an objective sense of what it believes. Every individual needs a strong culture to identify with so that he or she can develop a strong sense of self. Because of the nature of language, every worldview is partial, but this partiality is a glory because it culminates in unique, free, holographic replicas of Being.

All objective reality is basically symbolic, dependent upon words developed at some time by human beings in an effort to communicate.

This effort was done at an endo level that involves chaotic imagery which grasps aspects of the unbroken web of unconscious being. This imagery and its resulting understanding were expressed as metaphor and metonymy and created the imaginal realm. Over time a web of signification was developed. The articulated web of signification makes the unconscious to be conscious, provides a mirror for Being, and is the delight of the universe.

The sociological difference between delusion and fact is decided by consensus. If Johnny's perceptions are out of step with everyone else's perceptions, then he is deemed to be delusional. In the linguistic understanding, statements of "fact" are objective if they find sufficient resonance in the web of signification. If they do, they find their niche in the web and become part of general knowledge. If they don't, they die out or become mere idiosyncrasies. When statements deal with personal reality, they sometimes draw on the resources of the web, but create a little niche of their own with a kind of personal mythology. In these cases, the resonance that matters is the felt harmony with one's unconscious reality web. With personal myths we return again to originating force that created language in the first place.

Objective reality, then, is what we say about our world that makes sense to us and to some of our society. It is located in our language. It is caught in our accepted web of signification, somewhere in its scientific, humanistic, or mythical sectors. It changes as the web changes. Its direction of change is toward communion (Subject3) for both individuals and cultures.

**Religious Myths**

Myths are objective in the sense that they interpret what is known but ill-defined in racial, cultural, and personal experience. They symbolically represent unconscious structures of experience and enable us to ritually act out our relationship to them. In a broad sense, scientific reality is a mighty myth system because it represents the unconscious web of physical reality with language and mathematics and helps us negotiate our destiny in the world. Personal myths work on the individual level to bring sense and control into a person's life. Myths are always more or less religious because they express a sense of the meaning of life.

This section focuses on the origin of myths in visions and the dynamics that produce major myths. Visions, including lucid and waking dreams, take place in the hypnagogic state which can be induced in a number of ways (cf. Chapter 13). They are routinely experienced between sleeping and waking. Visions introduce imaginal realities into our conscious awareness. When they are expressed with signing, acting, drawing, or words they become mythic material. In favorable conditions, a culturally relevant vision can become religious myth.

*Religions as Myth Systems*

Religions, of course, exist in all societies. They present to their believers broad cultural myths that provide contexts for living. They present landmarks for life's journeys, heroes for emulation, reasons for personal quests, solace in sorrow, and hope for the future. They provide a consensual language for communication of one's existential concerns and innermost thoughts. They provide the basis for community organization. They make possible advances in humanistic and scientific discovery.

They also, unfortunately, constrain the personal use of our imaginal faculties. The Catholic tradition, for example, does this by its insistence that revelations stopped with the death of the last apostle, an insistence prompted by its need to maintain doctrinal uniformity and political control. Science does this, too, with its exclusive reliance on a narrowly conceived scientific method, which ignores the creative working methods of Descartes, Kekulé, and even Einstein, methods of vision and endo intelligence.

William Blake had a quarrel with Isaac Newton on this matter. Blake, of course, was very much the visionary and he gathered much of his inspiration from the heavens and its denizens. He opposed Newton's new science because it stripped the universe of mystery and transcendence, rationalizing and mechanizing it. He foresaw the atrophy of the imaginal faculty because of the new science's disdain for it and humankind's eventual loss of wonder. He foresaw us today as we continue to uphold the banner of scientific thought and ridicule other thought forms. Ironically, we do this in spite of the fact that our physicists have completed a grand cycle and look again in awe at the oneness and chaos of the universe recognizing the arbitrary nature of both their observations and their mathematics.

Because of our dreams, we do not dwell in complete imaginal atrophy. In our dreams, we are beyond rationalistic constraint. All the same, we generally disregard dreams except in certain psychological or metaphysical circles, and we seldom benefit from their instruction and guidance. We no longer value the role of the visionary in our society. To observe seers in action we need to look to other societies.

Shamans are visionaries who are highly valued by their tribes because of their ability to travel to the other side and report back what they see. Many of them are afflicted with epilepsy, which gives them relatively easy access to visions because their brain chemistry inclines them toward the hypnagogic state. They are protected by the tribe as they are often fragile, possessed with unknown powers and afflicted by them. They are trained from youth to develop and control their visionary power. In their travels to the other side, they often observe totem animals and their symbolic activity. On their return, they interpret their visions to illuminate the tribe's present predicament, its future, and the direction it is to take.

The role of the shaman in various cultures is played by seers, oracles, medicine men, mediums, saints, and prophets. In every case, the visionary moves into a mythic reality which is the common heritage of his/her people, and sees, hears, feels, or channels those parts of it that are important in a life situation. Many visionary experiences meet the three tests of objective validity: (1) they influence people and events (meso test), (2) they feel right to the visionary and his/her culture (endo test), and (3) they fit into the worldview of the people to whom they are addressed (ecto test).

*The Virgin of Medjugorje*

On June 24, 1981, the Blessed Virgin Mary appeared to some Catholic teenagers in Medjugorje, Yugoslavia. She has been appearing weekly since that time. She identifies herself as the Queen of Peace and proclaims a message of kindness and reconciliation, stressing that all peacemakers are blessed of God and not just the Catholic ones.

Medjugorje is located in the embattled new country of Bosnia-Herzogovina that was once a province of Yugoslavia. It is an area that has a violent present and past. In 1914 the Archduke Ferdinand (a Serb) was assassinated there starting World War I. In World War II many of the Catholic Croats were active collaborators with the Nazis even to the killing of thousands of Gypsies, Muslims, and Orthodox Serbs. A recent book, *The Unholy Trinity*, has documented this tortuous history and the postwar involvement of England, the United States, and the Vatican. In the 1990's, Yugoslavia disintegrated. Once again there is racial and religious war and atrocity between the Croats, the Muslims, and the Serbs. The situation in Bosnia has stabilized now thanks to NATO involvement.

Medjugorje's people are fervent Catholics who believe deeply in the Virgin and in the supernatural. The young men and women who have seen the Virgin have a mind-set that allows for the possibility of visions. They seem to be reporting what they see and hear. In spite of government opposition and official Church skepticism, the cult of the Virgin has grown and its fame is worldwide. It draws thousands of pilgrims from all over the world. It is credited with numerous healings of body and mind. It is a growing cult that may someday rival that of Our Lady of Fatima.

The pertinent points for understanding these visions are that: (1) the culture in which they occur is deeply religious without a rationalistic or secular bias; (2) the visionaries are ordinary people; and (3) the visions occur in a strife-torn area and counsel peace. A simple description of what occurs is that the visionaries report what they see: the Queen of Peace counseling kindness, brotherhood, and universal salvation. The facts indicate that the people of this village and its pilgrims are culturally one in ways we barely realize, sharing common images and creating special images together for their own instruction. The visions of Medjugorje are creations of innate divine imagination expressing intense concern and guidance through the strong united religious culture and personality of a particular group of Croatian people. These visions:

- are real experiences for the visionaries;
- are accepted as real by their listeners;
- are of practical importance to the visionaries and their people;
- possess a universal relevance;

- are an effort to communicate the real universal/individual nature of a situation.

These visions, however, do not yet constitute a full-blown myth. They will have to grow in significance and importance to reach that status.

At the beginning of myth is the bard who memorializes the visionary experience, putting it into verse perhaps and singing it to the tribe, elaborating its stories and coordinating them with other tribal lore. Because of his or her efforts, the vision becomes widely known and is passed on from generation to generation, shaping the nature of a people, giving meaning to natural, historic, and personal events, invigorating life.

*The Virgin of Guadalupe*

Will the Virgin of Medjugorje achieve the status of myth? She could, within the confines of that region, much as the Virgin of Guadalupe did in Mexico. In the sixteenth century, the Spanish were destroying the shrines and records of the native religions, including the Aztec, which they considered diabolical. They even debated seriously the proposition that the Indians were not human beings. Dominican theologians argued that Indians were subhuman and, therefore, did not have human rights and, therefore, the killing, raping, and pillaging of them by the conquistadores was not reprehensible. Franciscan theologians argued that Indians were human, just like Europeans and Moors, and that they would become children of God if they became Christians.

In either case, the Indians faced a difficult time. They were drawn to the new Christian religion because of its power and ferocity, but they found it utterly strange. They drew their strength and identity from their native gods and myths, which were now in full-scale retreat. They needed to salvage their identity and their pride in order to maintain some equality of footing with the overbearing Spaniards. Above all, they needed to stop the slaughter and abuse of their people.

In this context (c. 1531), the Virgin appeared to the Indian Juan Diego at Guadalupe just outside of Mexico City. She appeared as radiant Indian young woman clothed and arrayed in a manner that was both Indian and European. She instructed him to tell the bishop of his vision and to tell him that she wanted a house built for her on the spot where they stood. Juan visited the bishop and was politely ignored. After several visits and difficulties the Franciscan bishop, Zumarraga, requested a sign that would prove his story. In response, the Virgin provided a field full of out-of-season Castillian roses, which Juan put in his *ayate* and with the Virgin's blessing, took to the bishop as his proof. At the bishop's palace, Juan emptied his *ayate* of the roses and revealed the famous picture of the Virgin of Guadalupe.

Zumarraga was impressed. He saw the importance and value of this event. He ordered an account to be written, which is preserved in the National Basilica of Guadalupe. Through this story, his official memoirs and correspondence, Zumarraga became the bard of the vision. The rest is history. Race relations improved immensely. Indians embraced a faith that was now humanized by the motherly presence of the native Virgin who became the patron saint of Mexico.

In Medjugorje, in a similar crisis, the Virgin, as Queen of Peace, may be instrumental in resolving the deadly ethnic and religious strife in Bosnia (Croatian Catholic, Bosnian Muslim, and Serbian Orthodox). If she does, she will become Bosnia's patron saint.

If the Virgin has her way, the Croats will become more pluralistic and liberal as they embrace their Serbian Orthodox and Muslim neighbors. They will create a larger family of peace-loving and God-blessed people. In so doing, they will weaken the traditional piety that made vision of the Virgin possible. Will she be disappointed with that result?

*Prayer to God*

In the high philosophical tradition of both East and West, God is discussed under a dual aspect: as both unknowable and known. Shankara in the Hindu Vedantic tradition, for example, states that God is both *Nirguna* and *Saguna*. As *Nirguna,* He/She/It is beyond any human conception, picture, or feeling. As *Saguna,* He/She/It is known in the attributes of experienced reality as Light/Dark, Etheric/Material, Caring/Fierce, Powerful/Yielding, Masculine/Feminine, Wisdom/Dullness, and so on. All of these attributes are *Saguna*, known aspects of God.

A similar ambivalence holds for us in our not two/not one reality. Insofar as we are Subject0, not two, Reality (God) is indescribable because there is no separateness, no distinction, and no possibility of language. As not two, we are Reality. Our amorphous awareness just is. It is not describable.

In our not two/not one imaginal world, God is knowable. God is a creation of our divine imagination, just as is every other imaginal reality in our world. God's describable reality is a product of our ineffable divinity. Our creation of God is inevitable and desirable because we require characters to dialogue with. We impose order and coherence on our world in our dialogues. In other words, the ineffable Word that we are becomes flesh in the characters we create with our divine imagination. In this way, all of creation is opened to us by the mythic and scientific elaborations of our divinely inspired characters.

In simple language, we are divine, aware of our divinity but unable to express it without creating a god character that is separate from other parts (characters) of us. We live, grow, discover our world, and come to grips with it through the interplay of our characters suffused with our divine imagination. We are, as Subject3, God creating a world impregnated with our divine individuality. Each of us creates our own worlds inside webs of great mythic and scientific systems. We create our microcosms that are fractally similar to the universal macrocosm.

Prayer can be understood as an exemplification of how Faith works in our lives. In traditional religious terms, this attentiveness is prayer to God. My mother, for example, exercised her F in 0 at times by praying to St. Anthony. It was uncanny how she found lost things after seeking his help.

The way that prayer works can be explained as follows. When we are anxiously seeking something we are obsessively meso and ecto (Subject1). In this state, we lose our flexibility and our access to endo (Subject3) awareness. We can calm our obsession and re-access our unconscious by prayer. In the clearing this calming provides, our F in 0 is free to locate what we are seeking (Subject3 delivers it out of Subject2).

The drawback to prayer in a religious setting is the coercive power of organized religion. We are led to believe that, because prayer works, the religious system is responsible for its success while, in reality, the reason for prayer's success is our own innate divinity (Subject0). In accepting organized religion, we hand over our innate power to creeds, codes, and their promoters that then prescribe our lives and remove us from further use of our revolutionary potential.

It is useful in a pluralistic society to demythologize visions, images of God, and the uses of prayer. Then we can re-mythologize them with awareness. In doing so, we (as Subject3) will make our relationship with our unconscious (Subject2) relationship with God (Subject0) conscious.

Myths are vital. They are the vibrant hearts of a thriving people and societies. We seem to be suffering an anomie in our globalizing world that can be cured by a healthy incorporation of living myths. Such sharing of updated, genuinely shared myths would go a long way towards solving our practical and existential dilemmas. Is it possible that we can posit a strange attractor that might generate such myths?

## CHAPTER SEVENTEEN

**Death**

Death is a mystery. We want to believe that we live on in some way. As far back as we are able to extend history by means of archeology, we find burial remains that indicate a belief in survival after death in another realm of consciousness. How can we conceptualize how we as subjects might survive death? To answer that question we first have to address the following questions: What is my reality as a subject? Am I Subject0 (unarticulated potentiality)? Subject1 (ego)? Subject2 (other)? Subject3 (communion of ego and other)?

I began life as Subject0, an unarticulated project fractally identical to the universal Creative Project (which Nietzsche called "Becoming"). I now exhibit a dual aspect of that project: ego (Subject1) and other (Subject2), which was created by my use of language. In my life, I have progressively facilitated communication between my unconscious (Subject2) and my ego (Subject1) by exercising my expressive power (Subject3).

In cosmic terms, I began as a human, animal body that manifested Universal Becoming. With language, I came to manifest dual bodily aspects of that Becoming: ego and unconscious other. As Subject3 (communion), I re-unite those dual aspects at the level of consciousness.

So who or what am I as Subject? I am articulated Subject0, a partial expression wrought by my personal creativity (Subject3) of the Divine Becoming. As such, I am part of the universal hologram, a microcosm of the macrocosm, a total part of the universe, a whole fractally similar to, and creative of, the Whole.

I am certainly my ego (Subject1). I have boundaries and make my way in the world. I am also my unconscious other (Subject2). I am pre-eminently Subject3, the dialogue between ego and body-other—one could say that I am the consolidation of authentic imaging and language. As Subject3, I am already the goal of self-transcendence for Subject0. As I progress, I am stamping Becoming with the character of Being, making the Word flesh, and fulfilling a cycle of the eternal return of the same. In a metaphor drawn from fractal geometry, I am becoming an individual gingerbread man in the universal Mandelbrot set.

Death is important in this process of giving Being to the grand Becoming as Heidegger pointed out when he called us beings-unto-death. Death puts a temporal limit on our possibilities and forces life-choices. This limit necessitates the concrete particularity that characterizes authentic gingerbread men—the goal of evolution. What happens to our gingerbread men at death?

As projects of the universal Becoming, our gingerbread men must have some permanence in its ever-evolving web. What future after death can we hypothesize for our gingerbread man? The gingerbread man is a web of signification in a mythic realm that we have created. Is this what goes on? Does Nature still have chaotic intentions to fulfill with our gingerbread men in its ongoing, self- transcending quest? Our gingerbread men may endure as fractal members of an active universal database and chat room.

Near-death experiences give us some indication of what life after death might be. The following description is taken from Raymond Moody (1975).

A man is dying and, as he reaches the point of greatest physical distress, he hears himself pronounced dead by his doctor. He begins to hear an uncomfortable noise, a loud ringing or buzzing, and at the same time feels himself moving very rapidly through a long dark tunnel. After this, he suddenly finds himself outside of his own physical body, but still in the immediate physical environment, and he sees his own body from a distance, as though he is a spectator. He watches the resuscitation attempt from this unusual vantage point and is in a state of emotional upheaval.

After a while, he collects himself and becomes more accustomed to his odd condition. He notices that he still has a "body," but one of a very different nature and with very different powers from the physical body he has left behind. Soon other things begin to happen. Others come to meet and to help him. He glimpses the spirits of relatives and friends who have already died, and a loving, warm spirit of a kind he has never encountered before—a being of light—appears before him. This being asks him a question, nonverbally, to make him evaluate his life and helps him along by showing him a panoramic, instantaneous playback of the major events of his life. At some point he finds himself approaching some sort of barrier or border, apparently representing the limit between earthly life and the next life (pp. 21-22).

It would seem that our bodies construct an intelligent endo, meso, and ecto Subject3 self that has the capability to survive the death of the gross body. This Subject3 exists in the imaginal realm which is the realm of our creation. As such, it is real. It is a subtle body that is not two/not one with our physical bodily self during our lifetimes, and endures on its own after death. This subtle body is our self-created essential self, existing in a world of similarly self-created free selves. The joy that is reported by near-death survivors might be a result of a healing of the ego-other chasm.

The imaginal world as a whole is the repository of not only the imaginative wisdom of our race (and others?), but the accumulated individuality of all of our ancestors. We have created our afterworld. What activities we have created for ourselves there are not mere matters of speculation because we are here and now using the imaginations that create them. The imaginal afterlife, then, works on the principle of Faith, F in 0.

The physical world is in some ways richer than the imaginal one because of its density and complexity. It seems to demand more of us, to be harder and testier. It challenges our imagination and demands mastery. It equips us for the next world.

What really happens in the end is unknown to Becoming itself. All of us—living, dead, and yet to be born—have to work that out.

## The Dance of Life

In a world of dying there is becoming. We die and we become. We do not stay the same. The world constantly dies and becomes; it does not remain the same. The world's dying and becoming joins our personal and cultural existence in a dance of life. That dance creates a field on atomic, human, and astronomical dimensions. It co-creates our experience and we co-create the dance.

As the dance evolves, consciousness expands making present and explicit the unconsciousness from which it springs. New cultural worlds are created. Our collective consciousness grows by leaps and bounds, with severe though temporary setbacks. We create personal consciousnesses, within our collective consciousness, that attain a life of their own.

Within our normal experience we lose ourselves in loved ones and get ourselves back. We do the same with engrossing tasks and novels. We share experiences with our friends. In many ways, we go out-of-body. At death, according to the reports of people who have had death experiences, part of the consciousness we have created goes on to further experience.

It is as zygotes, one with our mothers, that we begin our whole journey. The zygote becomes a body. Later, the body, interacting in a physical, mental, and spiritual field, co-creates itself as mind, spirit, and personality. The whole process starts with a body immersed in the fields created by other bodies.

Our creative bodies are obviously not inanimate physical corpses. They are us: living beings that are both subjects (conscious and unconscious) and objects (things sort of like other things). They are, paradoxically, both us and at the same time things that we observe as we might a squirrel in a tree.

Our paradoxical nature as self-conscious bodies is the key to comprehending both our rooted naturalness and our vaulting spirituality. The simple recognition of the creative power of our bodies, with all their materiality and waywardness, rewards us with an understanding of our wondrous co-creative ability. We are the leading edge of free evolution.

Because our bodies are transcendent, they enable us to understand our world from a detached scientific (ecto) viewpoint, and from a bodily transpersonal (endo) one.

The body viewpoint has been emphasized in various ways by some of the seminal thinkers of our age: Nietzsche, Freud, Lacan, and Merleau-Ponty. It has been most precisely delineated by the American Scholar, Joseph Lyons, who expanded the psychological definition of the modes called: ecto, meso, and endo. The body viewpoint is the endo one.

The love of fate (*amor fati*) was for Nietzsche the body's delight in the chaos of nature. By emphasizing pre-rational reality, Nietzsche pulled our attention to the vitality and wisdom of the body. He proclaimed the imperative to stamp Becoming with the character of Being by our will to power. By this he meant that we must express in language the otherwise undefined truth of nature.

Freud and Lacan emphasized the centrality of the bodily unconscious mind in our lives; they explained the centrality of imagination and language in the development of our egos; they located the origin of the split in us between our ego and our other in the division caused by our use of language and logic; they found that this split creates desire both as Eros and Thanatos (Love and Power).

Merleau-Ponty showed that the body itself knows—and that is also known. The body is both subject and object. In the painstaking tradition of the phenomenological method, he showed how our primal bodily consciousness developed a relationship to space, to other objects, to other similar bodies, and to itself. He portrayed the groping toward communication that led to language, civilization, and culture. He showed that mind and soul are refinements of our flesh. Finally, he saw that the universe itself, which he called, Being, is a flesh that transcends itself toward greater expression of its nature.

Chaos theory provides us with the "strange attractor" that creates marvelous results by chaotic methods. It portrays a world in which organic harmony is the result of the indeterminate (free) activity of its atoms. Bion provides us with the formula **F in 0** (Faith in the emotional truth of the moment). This formula provides a model for how perception, empathy, intuition, and creative imagination work.

Our attention, **F**, acts as a strange attractor in the chaos, **0**, of the unconscious and produces the appropriate percept, feeling, idea, or result.

When we are comfortably at home in a heart-conscious (endo) universe with sufficient (ecto) understanding of what that implies, then we can experience the variety of life with equanimity. We recognize the fluctuation of our I-feeling and the relativity of our boundaries. We merge confidently with others in intuition, empathy, and love. We appreciate our hallucinations and visions. We see how we are situated in time and space. We take joy in the role that language has in fulfilling our destiny: to be the communion of our ego and other. We appreciate the role of myth and religion.

When we come from the heart, everything falls into place intellectually, practically, and spiritually. With endo vision, meso and ecto realities assume their true importance. The chaotic endo processes of F in O facilitate intellectual and practical discovery, making it efficient and magically uncanny. Centering ourselves in our unconscious, chaotic, creative bodily center, we unite with our other and with the universe. In so doing, we make the universe conscious; we express our transcendent reality; we become the leading edge of the evolution of the flesh of the universe.

In this communion with our uncharted depth we have the ultimate freedom to create, through the magic of language, the myths that make the god within and without us coherent. Our universe becomes ever more conscious

\* \* \*

The Great Mother is silent. She speaks not a word by herself. Her prolific progeny speak for her: her sunsets, her rainstorms, the daffodil, the butterfly, the stallion. They proclaim her majesty and beauty. Her human children are her most free, most conscious proclaimers. They speak for her in language. They proclaim her to be many things, contradictory things—all of which are true. In their chaotic way, all the mother's progeny do and say what they will, displaying the beautiful truth of the Mother.

The Great Mother anticipates the past, present, and future with the one great strange attractor: free universal communion. This attractor gathers life and free expression out of chaos. As a result, everything throughout the spectrum of the universe, from indeterminate atomic particle to free human beings, do exactly what they please—in magnificent chaotic harmony.

We are the progeny of the Great Mother—bodies from her body. We function as she does. Our personal great strange attractor is: to make conscious to our egos and each other the wealth of our unconscious identity with the mother. In this communion, we fulfill our destiny. As a people, our common great attractor is like that of the mother and of ourselves as persons: to make alive and conscious the wealth of our unconscious divinity.

Our myths are essential for this purpose. They focus and give dynamism to our lives and societies. If we lack relevant living myths, we have the duty and the wherewithal to create them.

# The How of Heart Vision

The heart is the traditional seat of unconscious knowledge. The vision from the heart is a symbol of body wisdom. This chapter will make explicit some of the qualities of heart vision: How it is possible, how it works, how heart vision contributes to conscious reflection, how we are to interpret what the heart says, and how we can make conscious use of the feeling communication from the heart.

**How is heart vision possible?**

Heart vision is a natural correlate of our holographic unity with the universe. Our bodies are privy to the universe's unspoken secrets. The universe knows everything in its way. It knows it in a delineated way through our conscious use of language. The universe wants us to express its many facets through language and constructive activity. The many, even contradictory, ways that we express it lead us to greater appreciation and awe of the universe and our own privileged position, our awesome resources and power.

    The universe moves in a generally progressive manner. If we are in tune with its direction and rhythm, we are best positioned to tap profitably into the universal wisdom and make desirable changes in our lives and in our societies. Tapping into this wisdom for individual benefit when it is detrimental to the whole sets up counter currents within the main current. These counter currents are short-lived and, therefore, of limited utility in our lives. Egotistical endeavors are generally brought to naught.

**How does heart vision work?**

Our attention attracts elements of the unspoken heart vision that manifest as feelings, images, verbal slips and annoying recurring experiences that compel us to pay attention to important issues. To attend effectively to these messages, we need to keep our intentions clear and our attention steady. If we fritter away our attention on every little thing, we will likely be drawn to multiple desires for baubles. Such divided intention and lack of focused attention will make it very difficult to tap the divine wisdom within us. We will be drawn in many directions at once, and are likely to be immobilized by our indecision.

If we retain a modicum of discipline in our lives, we will often be able to detect the gentle winds brewing in our subconscious. Such gentle feelings are sometimes presented to us repeatedly in different ways. We may have a dream or recurring dreams that point to something we need to attend to in order to get what we want. The images or narrative of the dream when expressed in language will likely point us in the direction we need to go. Sometimes the tell-tale experience is a waking dream, perhaps a Freudian slip, or something more drastic.

For example, if you express a desire to get along with people in order to advance in your career, you might find yourself having recurring bouts of confrontation with a coworker. At this point, you might decide that he or she is a bad person. You might psychoanalyze him or her as an obsessive compulsive or some such demeaning title. You might just try to steer clear of that person, avoiding their company. All of these responses are likely the result of your closed mind.

As long as you maintain a clear desire to get along with people and persist in such reactions, your unconscious will not let up. It will continue forcing you into contact with that person. Now, if you should wonder why, you might approach these situations with an open mind, and conclude that your irritation reminds you of long past, but unfinished arguments with your mother (or some close associate). You might find that making peace with her removes the irritation with the co-worker, and now you have a clear path to getting along with people and advancing your career.

**How does heart vision contribute to conscious reflection?**

Language brings the meaning of these symbols and experiences into conscious awareness. Once the realization has been vocalized, heart wisdom continues to guide us further on our way. Once we have learned to trust this guidance, we have sure indications for what we should do next.

By trusting heart vision, we find the center of our circle where we can view our situation and all our options clearly. Working out of that center we can make remarkable progress.

**How are we to interpret what the heart says?**

We interpret the messages we get on the basis of their clarity and pertinence to our situation. Heart wisdom will sometimes give us an option that we can immediately pursue in a troubling situation. It will rarely, if ever, give us a full-blown plan for moving ahead. A strategic plan will need to be worked out by our ecto and meso modes in constant consultation with our situations and the universal (endo) wisdom of our bodies.

**How can we make conscious use of the feeling communication from the heart?**

We make conscious use of our heart feelings by acting on them and evaluating the results. This attentiveness to our hearts needs to be nourished for us to reap the rewards that heart wisdom can offer us. We need to still ego's constant chatter. We need to retreat into our silent cores for periods of time so that the whispers of the heart can be attended to.

Once we manage to heed the directions of the heart, the world is open to us. We have awesome resources and can accomplish great things. We need to keep our ego in check in order to continue functioning on such a high plane of existence.

# Have Your Say!

I invite you to discuss topics in this book with me and other interested people at my blog www.bodywisdombook.com. There are three possible categories we can explore together: personal applications, societal applications, and academic discussion.

**Personal Applications**

Below is a list of tips for tapping your body wisdom:

- Simplify your life to mute the static of ego chatter that hinders the reception of body wisdom.
- Free yourself of chains to unimportant things that block body wisdom by tying us up in trivia.
- Formulate a clear question that expresses what you deeply want in life. Write that question down and post it where you will see it often.
- Keep an open mind to the messages that may be coming to you in your sleeping and waking dreams.

How would you add to this list of tips?

Do you see different situations where body wisdom would be effective in your life? How might applied body wisdom affect your decision-making and your life in general?

Here are some additional tips for accessing body wisdom.

- Pause and consult your feelings with an open mind when faced with an important decision.
- Set apart times when you calm your egoistic chatter and attend to your body in silence.
- Periodically check your progress against criteria that your heart has set for you.

I encourage you to add some tips of your own on the blog.

Come to the blog and share experiences of body wisdom in *your life* or ask questions. We would love to hear your experiences. Have you had an experience that was prompted by your unconscious? How did you pursue it? What was the impact on your life? I encourage you to put your comments in the Personal Applications category on the blog.

**Societal Applications**

I am also interested in how we might apply body wisdom to society at-large.

- How could accessing body wisdom make a difference in the world?
- Body wisdom will lead us to pay more attention to the feelings of others. How can we move society to respect the feelings of people who might disagree with us?
- Body wisdom demands that we listen to the voices of others with open minds and hearts. How can we encourage authorities to heed the voices of all people?
- Body wisdom requires that the authentic voices of everyone be accorded a hearing equal to that given to and experts. How can we make that happen?
- Body wisdom teaches us that prescribing thought patterns for others closes down access to our own body wisdom. How can we influence society to honor minority cultures and individual conscience?
- Body wisdom opens up sources of consensus in contentious situations. How can our open minds influence participants in contentious situations toward mutual understanding?
- In what specific ways would the world be better if people respected and learned from the wisdom of their bodies?

**Academic Discourse**

I am also interested in scholarly contributions that might concur with or challenge statements in this book. I welcome quotations from authorities not mentioned in the book. I would love to have spirited conversations with you about the impact body wisdom might have on the established paradigm of academic thought. If we stir up a storm, we might eventually produce momentum towards a more humane world.

In summary, when you go to www.bodywisdombook.com, you will see three major categories of blogs: personal applications, societal applications, and academic discourse. You are free to comment on any of the blogs, but I recommend that you click first on the category of greatest interest to you.

I'd love to have your help in spreading the word about body wisdom. I am available for:

- Talks about topics in *Body Wisdom*
- Presentations at conferences
- Web classes
- Entire online for-credit college courses
- Adult education and enrichment courses

If you have any recommendations about colleges or universities that might be interested in courses about body wisdom, please give me the information including the names of the persons who might make the decision about listing the course, and their contact information if you have it.

I really appreciate your help with this. I can be reached at ken@globalagoras.org or 770-473-7336. You can also interact with me on the social media:

Facebook as kencbausch,
Twitter as @kennethbausch, and
LinkedIn as Kenneth Bausch.

Ken Bausch
8213 Hwy 85 #901
Riverdale, GA 30274

# BIBLIOGRAPHY

Aanstoos, Christopher ed. (1991). *Studies in humanistic psychology.* Carrollton: West Georgia College.

Aarons, Mark and Loftus, John. *Unholy Trinity : The Vatican, The Nazis, & Soviet Intelligence*

Acredolo, Linda P., & Goodwyn, Susan W. (1996). *Baby Signs: How to Talk with Your Baby Before Your Baby Can Talk.* Chicago: Contemporary Books, Inc.

Barral, Mary Rose (1984). *The body in interpersonal relations/Merleau-Ponty.* Lanham: University Press of America.

Bion, W.R. (1983). *Attention and interpretation.* New York: Aronson (originally published 1970).

Bly, Robert (1988). *A little book on the human shadow* (William Booth, ed.). San Francisco: Harper.

Bly, Robert (1990). *Iron John.* New York: Addison Wesley.

Briggs, John & Peat, F.David. (1989). *Turbulent mirror: An illustrated guide to chaos theory and the science of wholeness.* New York: Harper & Row.

Campbell, Joseph. (1988). *The power of myth.* New York: Doubleday

Descartes, Rene (1952). *Discourse on Method.* Chicago: Brittanica/Great Books. Haldane and Ross (trans.) Originally published 1637.

Eigen, Michael (1986). *The psychotic core.* Northvale, New Jersey: Jason Aronson.

Eisler, Riane. (1987). *The Chalice and the Blade.* San Francisco: Harper and Row.

Fischer, Alden L. (1969). *The essential writings of Merleau-Ponty.* New York: Harcourt, Brace & World.

Jung, Carl (ed.) (1964). *Man and his symbols.* London: Aldus Books.

Hadamard Jacques. (1945). *An Essay on the Psychology of Invention in the Mathematical Field.* Princeton NJ: Princeton University Press.

Harman, Willis and Rheingold, Howard (1984). *Higher creativity: Liberating the unconscious for breakthrough insights.* New York, St. Martin's Press.

Heidegger, Martin (1973), *The end of philosophy*, (trans. Stambaugh). New York, Harper &Row.

Heidegger, Martin (1987). *Nietzsche, vol.3,The will to power as knowledge and as metaphysics*(trans. Stambaugh, Krell, Capuzzi). San Francisco: Harper and Row.

Levin, Dennis Michael. (1985). *The body's recollection of being.* London: Routledge & Kegan Paul.

Levin, Dennis Michael. (1988). "Transpersonal Phenomenology: The Corporeal Schema" in *The Humanist Psychologist*, 16, pp.282-313.

Keen, Ernest (1975). *A primer in phenomenological psychology.* New York: Holt, Rinehart, and Winston.

Kohut, Heinz (1977). *The restoration of the self.* New York: International Universities Press.

Kohut, Heinz (1985). *Self psychology and the humanities.* New York: Norton.

Lacan, Jacques (1977). *Ecrits* (trans. Alan Sheridan). New York: Norton.

Lakoff, George and Johnson, Mark. (1999). *Philosophy in the Flesh: The Embodied Mind and Its Challenge to Western Thought.* New York: Basic Books.

Loye, David (1983). *The sphinx and the rainbow.* Boulder: Shambhala.

Lyons, Joseph (1987). *Ecology of the body.* Durham: Duke University Press.

MacGregor, John M. (1989). *The Discovery of the Art of the Insane.* Princeton University Press.

Madison, Gary Brent (1981). *The phenomenology of Merleau-Ponty.* (Originally published, 1973, as *La phenomenology de Merleau-Ponty: un recherché des limites de la* conscience.) Athens: Ohio University Press.

Masek, Robert J. (1991). "Knowing the Other in Self Psychology: A Comparative Dialogue between Heinz Kohut and Maurice Merleau-Ponty." In Aanstoos, 1991.

McAuliffe, Kathleen (1990). Getting smart: controlling chaos. *Omni*, 12(5) pp.43-92.

Merleau-Ponty, Maurice, (1962), *The phenomenology of perception.* (Colin Smith, trans.) London: Routledge and Kegan Paul.
Merleau-Ponty, Maurice (1963). The structure of behavior. (Alden L. Fisher, trans.) Boston: Beacon Press.
Merleau-Ponty, Maurice (1964a), *The primacy of perception.* (James M. Edie, ed.). Evanston, IL; Northwestern University Press.
Merleau-Ponty, Maurice. (1964b). *Signs.* (Richard C. McCleary, trans.) Evanston, IL; Northwestern University Press.
Merleau-Ponty, Maurice (1968). *The visible and the invisible.* (trans. Alphonso Lingis). Evanston: Northwestern University Press.
Moody, Raymond (1975). *Life after life.* New York: Bantam.
Muller, John. & Richardson, W. (1982). *Lacan and language.* New York: International Universities Press.
Nehamas, Alexander (1985). *Nietzsche: Life as literature.* Cambridge: Harvard University Press.
Nietzsche, Friedrich (1962), *Philosophy in the tragic age of the Greeks.* (Marianne Cowan,trans.). Chicago, Henry Regnery.
Person, Ethel (1988). *Dreams of love and fateful encounters.* New York: Penguin.
Pfeffer, Rose (1972). *Nietzsche, disciple of Dionysus.* Lewisburg: Bucknell University Press.
Reese, William L. (1991). *Dictionary of Philosophy and Religion.* New Jersey: Humanities Press.
Rice, Edward (1980). *Eastern definitions.* Garden City: Anchor Books.
Ricouer, Paul (1970). *Freud and philosophy.* (Denis Savage, trans.). New Haven, Yale University Press.
Rhodes, Richard (1992). The Philosopher Physicist (book review). *New York Times.* 1/26/92. 3&18.
Root-Bernstein, Michele and Root-Bernstein, Robert. (2008). Ap9ing Einstein. Retrieved April 2010 www.psychologytoday.com/blog/imagine/200808/aping-einstein
Sartre, Jean Paul. (1955). *Literary and Philosophical Essays.*
Schilpp Paul, ed. (1949). *Albert Einstein: Philosopher-Scientist.* Evanston IL: Library of Living Philosophers.
Schurman, Reiner (1987). *Heidegger on being and action.* (trans. Gros) Bloomington: Indiana University Press.

Shankara (788-820 AD). Cf. Reese, W.L. (1991). *Dictionary of Philosophy and Religion.* New Jersey: Humanities Press.

Schneiderman, Stuart (1983). *Jacques Lacan: Death of an intellectual hero.* Cambridge: Harvard University Press.

Stewart, Ian (1989). *Does God play dice? The mathematics of chaos.* New York: Basil Blackwell Inc.

Suzuki, Shunryu (1970) *Zen mind, beginner's mind.* New York, Weatherhill.

Van den Berg, J.H.(1972). *A different existence.* Pittsburgh, Duquesne University Press.

Vernant, Jean Pierre. (1982). *The Origins of Greek Thought.* (Originally published in 1962 as *Les origenes de la pensée grecque*). Ithaca, NY: Cornell University Press.

Watkins, Mary (1976). *Waking dreams.* New York, Gordon and Breach.

Watkins, Mary (1986). *Invisible guests.* Hillsdale, N.J., The Analytic Press.

*Webster's Ninth Collegiate Dictionary.* (1986). Merriam-Webster.

Welwood, John (1988) Psychotherapy as a practice of love. *Pilgrimage.* 14(3) 2-12.

Wertheimer M. (1945) *Productive Thinking.* New York: Harper.

Winnicott, Donald W. (1974*). The maturational process and the facilitating enviroment.* New York: International Universities Press.

# Index

active nihilism, 36
*agora*, 121
Alapack, 92
*amor fati*, 105, 225
Arcredolo, 109
Aristotle, 21, 23, 48, 65, 113, 122, 189, 211
Arons, 92
*asklepia*, 121
bar (----) of signification, 193
Barrell, 92, 93
beginner's mind, 9, 232
Being-in-the-world, 9
beings-unto-death, 9, 52, 149, 222
Bell, 25, 32
Bergson, 1
bifurcation diagram, 58
bifurcation points, 34
big mind, 9, 65, 67, 80, 138, 151
Binswanger, 86, 87
biodance, 68, 70, 184
Bion, 2, 65, 68, 133, 134, 151, 154, 225, 229
Blake, 25, 215
blooming, buzzing confusion, 50, 53
Bly, 18, 19, 20, 229
body-mind-spirit wedding cake, 17
Bohm, 29, 57
Bohr, 211, 212, 213
boundaries, 11, 12, 23, 40, 52, 54, 82, 83, 85, 90, 98, 99, 103, 104, 108, 103, 123, 128, 130, 146, 147, 148, 152, 151, 160, 161, 162, 163, 166, 168, 175, 176, 177, 201, 221, 235

Briggs and Peat, 140, 141, 142
Buddha, 204
Buddhism, 9, 65
Campbell, 92, 208, 229
Cartesian, 1, 15, 24, 26, 28, 65, 79, 80, 96, 101, 147, 170, 184, 192, 205
chaos, 7, 9, 10, 32, 34, 51, 56, 58, 59, 60, 61, 62, 64, 65, 70, 71, 65, 94, 95, 103, 134, 135, 137, 140, 141, 143, 145, 151, 154, 151, 161, 171, 172, 177, 181, 186, 187, 188, 192, 198, 208, 212, 213, 216, 225, 235, 236, 229, 231, 232
Chaos theory, 9, 58, 64, 187, 210, 225
chaotic, 10, 17, 19, 33, 36, 47, 56, 58, 59, 61, 62, 63, 69, 70, 65, 102, 134, 135, 141, 142, 159, 186, 189, 190, 196, 197, 203, 214, 222, 225, 236
Christ, 20, 205
Circular time, 196
*Cogito ergo sum*, 24
collective unconscious, 50, 92, 170
Communion, 126, 128, 129, 130, 132, 151, 154, 167, 183, 184, 194
complementarity, 211, 212, 213
contradiction, 10, 37, 38, 43, 48, 57, 70, 71, 65, 195
Copernican revolution, 11, 17, 28, 149
Copernican universe, 27
Copernicus, 26, 150, 213
Crete, 120
Cyclic time, 196
Da Vinci, 129
Darwin, 29
Daydreams, 174
death, 2, 7, 8, 10, 11, 15, 51, 52, 91, 131, 144, 149, 151, 175, 191, 215, 221, 222, 223, 224
dehiscence, 29, 190
Dilthey, 86
Dionysus, 7, 17, 20, 105, 121, 232
dissipative structures, 34

dreams, 11, 22, 33, 45, 49, 79, 106, 112, 126, 128, 135, 151, 160, 169, 173, 174, 175, 176, 177, 190, 196, 203, 204, 206, 215, 216, 232
ecto, 6, 10, 12, 24, 29, 30, 79, 80, 81, 85, 89, 92, 93, 94, 95, 96, 97, 100, 101, 102, 103, 104, 105, 107, 109, 110, 111, 112, 113, 114, 116, 119, 122, 123, 128, 138, 142, 143, 147, 148, 152, 153, 160, 162, 165, 170, 173, 178, 179, 180, 181, 184, 205, 210, 211, 212, 216, 221, 223, 225, 235, 236
Ego, 1, 5, 6, 116, 126, 128, 130, 132, 133, 137, 141, 151, 154, 167, 188, 193, 194
Eigen, 2, 5, 6, 17, 33, 47, 54, 82, 83, 84, 95, 152, 229
Einstein, 25, 32, 102, 107, 192, 212, 213, 215
Eisler, 20, 119, 121, 229
Eleusis, 121
Empathy, 5, 161, 162, 163, 167, 168
endo, 6, 10, 11, 12, 30, 53, 68, 79, 80, 81, 85, 89, 90, 91, 92, 93, 94, 95, 96, 99, 100, 101, 102, 103, 104, 105, 106, 107, 108, 109, 110, 111, 112, 113, 114, 115, 116, 119, 120, 121, 122, 123, 128, 135, 137, 139, 140, 142, 143, 147, 148, 152, 153, 151, 160, 161, 162, 165, 167, 168, 169, 170, 171, 175, 176, 178, 179, 180, 182, 184, 185, 189, 196, 199, 205, 207, 208, 210, 211, 212, 214, 215, 216, 221, 223, 225, 235, 236
Eris, 121
Eros, 7, 9, 10, 50, 51, 52, 138, 141, 150, 180, 225
Ethel S. Person, 169
Existentialism, 86
experience is unitary, 123
F in 0, 12
F in 0., 68, 133, 173, 176, 207, 223
Faith, 5, 68, 133, 134, 139, 140, 141, 148, 151, 154, 159, 161, 166, 171, 175, 176, 177, 186, 197, 203, 220, 223, 225
far-from-equilibrium, 34
Federn, 5
Feigenbaum, 58, 59
fig tree, 59, 60

flesh, 38, 41, 42, 46, 47, 48, 57, 71, 72, 80, 84, 92, 96, 168, 184, 189, 199, 200, 201, 202, 220, 222, 225, 236
Fort/Da, 55, 131, 138, 143, 144, 182
Fort" and "Da, 55
fractal geometry., 56, 159
Freud, 2, 4, 5, 6, 7, 8, 9, 10, 11, 17, 16, 17, 20, 26, 28, 30, 33, 45, 49, 50, 51, 54, 55, 65, 66, 68, 71, 84, 95, 106, 123, 125, 127, 129, 131, 132, 134, 136, 138, 143, 144, 149, 150, 151, 154, 166, 170, 171, 178, 181, 182, 187, 193, 203, 210, 213, 225, 232
Freudian unconscious, 50
gingerbread man, 62, 63, 70, 159, 189, 222
gingerbread men, 222
God, 4, 6, 7, 11, 16, 27, 31, 32, 34, 36, 58, 61, 64, 65, 91, 137, 149, 151, 190, 195, 212, 217, 219, 220, 221, 232
God is dead, 7, 31, 36, 149
Godel, 25, 192
Goodwyn, 109, 229
Great Mother, 20, 119, 120, 121, 236
Guadalupe, 218, 219
*habrosyne*, 121
hallucinations, 11, 83, 112, 151, 169, 171, 172, 173, 174, 176, 196, 203, 235
Harman, 21, 22, 23, 230
heart, 11, 12, 17, 24, 27, 28, 36, 38, 40, 42, 46, 65, 66, 68, 70, 72, 81, 90, 93, 94, 95, 123, 127, 141, 148, 149, 152, 151, 159, 160, 161, 165, 169, 171, 173, 177, 178, 180, 195, 200, 204, 235, 236
Heart vision, 177
heaven above and earth below, 18
Hegel, 1, 6, 25, 28, 113, 196
Heidegger, 2, 8, 9, 10, 13, 16, 28, 35, 36, 37, 44, 52, 85, 86, 93, 95, 105, 106, 123, 149, 187, 190, 222, 230, 232
Heisenberg, 25, 28, 69, 212, 213
Heraclitus, 1, 7, 8, 28, 31, 64, 68, 149, 195
Hermes Trismagistrus, 122

hierarchical universe, 18
Hindu, 1, 29, 195, 220
hologram, 17, 32, 48, 56, 57, 62, 64, 65, 69, 65, 94, 151, 180, 221
holographic, 10, 57, 181, 188, 190, 213
holoverse, 56, 57
Homer, 120, 122
human lived time, 198
hundredth monkey, 207
Husserl, 25, 37, 85, 86, 89
I think, therefore, I am, 24
I-feeling, 5, 6, 9, 12, 44, 81, 82, 83, 84, 139, 147, 148, 152, 203, 235
imaginal dialogues, 170, 171, 173, 175
imaginal realities, 171, 174, 215
imaginal realm, 6, 54, 65, 151, 174, 181, 203, 204, 205, 206, 214, 223
imagination, 6, 10, 11, 12, 32, 65, 112, 123, 128, 135, 136, 174, 218, 220, 223, 225, 235
imago, 50, 54
implicate order, 29
*intuitus mentis*, 41, 202
Jaspers, 86
Jesus, 64, 91, 204, 205
John the Baptist, 20
Johnson, 193, 230
Juan Diego, 219
Jung, 2, 17, 20, 33, 65, 91, 95, 107, 128, 135, 136, 166, 170, 171, 178, 208, 230
Kant, 6
Keen, 88, 179, 230
Kohut, 2, 9, 24, 33, 82, 91, 95, 135, 139, 162, 165, 166, 167, 182, 230, 231
Krishna, 204
Kurgans, 119, 121
Lacan, 2, 6, 8, 9, 10, 16, 28, 29, 37, 54, 55, 57, 68, 71, 81, 92, 95, 106, 116, 123, 125, 126, 127, 130, 131, 134, 139, 143, 144,

145, 146, 149, 150, 152, 154, 164, 165, 170, 171, 177, 179, 181, 182, 187, 191, 203, 206, 225, 230, 231, 232
Lakoff, 2, 193, 230
Learning, 4, 101, 107, 108, 111
Lennon, 64
Levantine, 120, 121
Levin, 40, 53, 230
Levi-Strauss, 49, 134, 136, 154
Linear time, 197
linguistics, 10, 57, 127, 192, 213
little mind,, 9
Lyons, 2, 11, 33, 79, 89, 92, 93, 95, 96, 97, 98, 108, 109, 110, 111, 113, 114, 115, 116, 120, 123, 153, 168, 181, 187, 225, 230
Madison, 42, 44, 45, 46, 55, 57, 71, 72, 80, 90, 107, 185, 186, 188, 191, 197, 198, 199, 230
Mandlebrot set., 17, 94, 180, 188
Manilow, 201
Mary Magdalen, 20
Masek, 92, 165, 231
Medjugorje, 217, 218, 219
Merleau-Ponty,, 2, 10, 15, 30, 71, 72, 80, 84, 86, 89, 95, 123, 200, 213, 231
meso, 6, 10, 12, 29, 30, 79, 80, 81, 85, 89, 90, 92, 93, 94, 95, 96, 98, 100, 101, 102, 103, 104, 105, 107, 108, 109, 110, 111, 112, 113, 114, 116, 119, 121, 122, 123, 128, 138, 143, 147, 148, 152, 153, 160, 170, 173, 178, 179, 180, 181, 184, 205, 210, 211, 212, 216, 220, 223, 225, 236
metaphor, 17, 57, 62, 64, 127, 140, 177, 206, 214, 222
metaphor of upright posture, 17
metonymy, 51, 127, 177, 206, 214
mindfulness, 66
Monroe, 204
Moody, 92, 222, 231
Mother Earth, 3, 4
Mother Goddess, 4, 120

mother-centered culture, 20
Muller, 28, 49, 136, 144, 145, 182, 231
Mycenaean, 120, 121
Mythic cohesion, 204
Napoleon, 127, 204
natural time, 194, 196, 197
Newton, 25, 213, 215
Nietzsche, 4, 1, 6, 7, 8, 9, 10, 11, 17, 16, 19, 20, 25, 28, 30, 31, 32, 34, 35, 36, 42, 43, 44, 64, 70, 95, 105, 107, 116, 149, 166, 187, 189, 190, 191, 192, 193, 194, 196, 203, 209, 210, 213, 221, 225, 230, 231, 232
not one/not two, 17, 30, 94
objective reality, 11, 85, 197, 201, 210, 211, 213, 214
Objective reality, 210, 214
Objective time, 197
Occam, 1, 211
Original Subjects, 125
Our bodies are our minds, 45
Parmenides, 194, 195
perception, 11, 15, 39, 62, 67, 80, 87, 89, 103, 110, 112, 143, 162, 170, 174, 175, 181, 185, 186, 191, 200, 225, 231
Pert, 34
Pfeffer, 7, 31, 36, 105, 232
Phenomenological reduction, 178
phenomenological time, 151, 198
phenomenology, 8, 11, 12, 37, 42, 69, 85, 86, 87, 88, 89, 90, 110, 150, 151, 170, 181, 230, 231
Phenomenology, 4, 40, 79, 85, 86, 87, 230
Plato, 16, 122, 149, 211
Platonic, 16, 25, 31, 34, 85
*polis*, 121
Pre-reflective thought, 170
pre-Socratic, 8
Pribram, 57
Ptolemy, 26, 27
real world., 210

rebus, 126, 170
religion, 11, 12, 13, 17, 122, 204, 210, 219, 221, 236
Religions, 215
remembering, 11, 69, 93, 96, 101, 112, 113, 114, 115, 153
*res cogitans*, 15
*res extensa*, 15
Rhodes, 212, 232
Richardson, 28, 49, 136, 144, 145, 182, 231
Ricouer, 51, 129, 131, 232
romantic love, 169
Sartre, 37, 69, 86, 232
Saussure, 25, 146, 192, 211
Schrödinger, 69
Schultz, 17
Schumrun, 92
Scripture, 23
Socrates, 19, 211
solitons, 34
Solon, 121
Sophia, 20
*sophrosyne*, 121
Spinoza, 1
St. Augustine, 17
Stewart, 58, 60, 62, 212, 232
strange attractor, 58, 65, 102, 134, 135, 137, 139, 140, 143, 145, 154, 171, 172, 175, 176, 177, 186, 187, 197, 208, 221, 225, 236
**Strange Attractor**, 5, 134, 137
strange attractors, 10, 11, 17, 58, 64, 65, 136, 175, 203, 207
*strong pessimism*, 35
Subject0, 125, 132, 137, 138, 139, 141, 143, 144, 145, 146, 151, 152, 167, 183, 184, 188, 190, 193, 220, 221, 222
Subject1, 125, 126, 128, 129, 130, 132, 138, 139, 141, 143, 146, 147, 148, 151, 152, 160, 161, 163, 164, 165, 166, 168, 183, 184, 185, 188, 190, 193, 194, 200, 203, 205, 207, 221

Subject2, 125, 126, 128, 129, 130, 132, 138, 139, 141, 143, 147, 148, 151, 152, 162, 163, 164, 165, 168, 183, 184, 188, 191, 193, 194, 203, 205, 207, 221, 222
Subject3, 125, 126, 128, 129, 130, 131, 132, 134, 139, 141, 143, 145, 147, 148, 151, 152, 154, 159, 160, 161, 163, 164, 165, 166, 168, 169, 173, 174, 177, 180, 184, 185, 188, 189, 191, 193, 194, 197, 203, 207, 214, 220, 221, 222, 223
subtle body, 223
Suzuki, 70, 195, 232
symbiotic union, 50
Teilhard de Chardin, 1
Thanatos, 7, 9, 10, 50, 51, 52, 127, 138, 141, 150, 180, 225
The body is the soul, 46, 47
the Church, 6
the ego, 5, 6, 7, 8, 9, 10, 39, 50, 68, 81, 94, 105, 125, 126, 138, 139, 140, 141, 143, 146, 148, 149, 150, 167, 174, 183, 203, 206, 208, 223
The lived body, 46
the One and the Many, 10, 64, 71, 128
the Other, 6, 68, 90, 92, 96, 106, 141, 150, 160, 166, 168, 170, 179, 183, 188, 195, 231
the real world, 11, 101, 111, 197
**The Reality of Language**, 5, 190
the Shadow, 17, 18, 19, 20
the Subject, 6, 57, 125, 139, 152
the unconscious, 4, 5, 6, 7, 8, 9, 10, 11, 15, 16, 17, 19, 26, 28, 36, 49, 65, 81, 91, 95, 126, 127, 128, 129, 132, 134, 135, 138, 139, 146, 149, 150, 159, 160, 162, 166, 170, 171, 177, 181, 184, 199, 214, 215, 235, 230
The unconscious, 5, 6, 28, 29, 45, 49, 126, 129, 150, 151, 159
the Wild Man, 20
the world that we are, 42, 188
thickness, 39, 200
thinking, 11, 13, 17, 15, 16, 20, 21, 24, 25, 27, 29, 30, 31, 33, 34, 35, 36, 42, 45, 57, 65, 67, 69, 85, 89, 96, 101, 102, 103, 104,

105, 106, 107, 108, 111, 113, 136, 142, 143, 144, 148, 153, 151, 170, 171, 201
Thoreau, 25
Thou art that, 29
toffee., 61, 64
Uncertainty Principle, 25
upright position, 115
upright posture., 18
urge to love, 51
urge to power, 51
van den Berg, 86, 87
Van Gogh, 107
Vedanta, 1, 95
Vernant, 121, 232
Virgin Mary, 151, 204, 217
visions, 11, 79, 91, 92, 112, 121, 151, 171, 172, 175, 176, 203, 204, 215, 216, 217, 218, 221, 235
Watkins, 2, 65, 170, 171, 172, 173, 174, 206, 232
We are our bodies, 45
*Wei wu wei*, 137
Welwood, 65, 66, 67, 68, 80, 233
West Georgia College, 92, 229
Wheelwright, 28
will to power, 32, 35, 105, 116, 189, 191, 192, 193, 194, 196, 197, 206, 225, 230
Will to Power, 9, 34
William James, 53
William Roll, 92
Winnicott, 53, 233
Xenophanes, 28
Yeats, 107
Zen, 9, 28, 47, 53, 65, 70, 80, 84, 88, 91, 92, 95, 150, 151, 195, 232
Zeus, 64, 190, 192, 193, 194, 196, 214
Zoroaster, 16
Zumurraga, 219

www.ingramcontent.com/pod-product-compliance
Lightning Source LLC
Chambersburg PA
CBHW071704160426
43195CB00012B/1566